The Great Justices   1941–54

The Great Justices   1941–54

Black, Douglas, Frankfurter & Jackson in Chambers

William Domnarski

The University of Michigan Press   *Ann Arbor*

Copyright © by the University of Michigan 2006
All rights reserved
Published in the United States of America by
The University of Michigan Press
Manufactured in the United States of America
⊗ Printed on acid-free paper

2009   2008   2007   2006   4   3   2   1

A CIP catalog record for this book is available from the British Library.

Library of Congress Cataloging-in-Publication Data

Domnarski, William, 1953–
    The great justices, 1941–54 : Black, Douglas, Frankfurter, and Jackson
in chambers / William Domnarski.
        p.   cm.
    Includes bibliographical references and index.
    ISBN-13: 978-0-472-11536-5 (cloth : alk. paper)
    ISBN-10: 0-472-11536-7 (cloth : alk. paper)
        1. United States. Supreme Court—Biography.   2. United States.
Supreme Court— History—20th century.   3. Judges—United States—
Biography.   I. Title.

    KF8744.D66   2006
    347.73'14'0922—dc22   2005016625

For Kathleen, my wife,
and for Colleen & Erin, our daughters,
the three pivots of my life.

The true face even of a public man is his private face.
—Felix Frankfurter

⤳

CONTENTS

~⟩

PREFACE

In 1937 Franklin Roosevelt was finally able to make his own appointments to the Court. He eventually appointed eight new justices to what he expected would be a Court sympathetic to his values and ambitions. Hugo Black (1937), Felix Frankfurter (1939), William O. Douglas (1939), and Robert Jackson (1941) were among the first group of appointees, and with the exception of Black, all were Roosevelt intimates and administration insiders. Under three different chief justices and amid several other personnel changes, they served together and formed the core of the Court from Jackson's appointment in 1941 until his death in 1954, the period principally under discussion here.

Black, the first to be picked, was appointed for his liberal record and as a statement to the Court that the sort of change Roosevelt wanted was on its way. Frankfurter, Douglas, and Jackson were also appointed for their liberal, progressive views. Liberalism was the theme of Roosevelt's program, and these four justices were expected to be its principal exponents. Black, Frankfurter, and Douglas more than fulfilled their expectations in the years before Jackson's appointment in 1941. These four justices then, for a brief time, proceeded to vote and write in ways consistent with a simultaneous commitment to reviewing civil rights legislation expansively and economic legislation narrowly, thereby freeing themselves from the misdirections of their predecessors.

But within a few terms, the once solid group of four justices fractured. First Frankfurter, in contrast to earlier statements and votes, began to oppose the preferred position doctrine, which provided for closer scrutiny of legislation involving individual rights found to be fundamental. This in turn led him to pursue a narrow jurisprudence and to refuse to follow positions that he had embraced prior to his transformation.

Jackson for a few terms brilliantly argued and described the liberal positions he had urged before his appointment, but then he began to follow Frankfurter's move to the right. His embrace of conservative positions deepened when he returned from Nuremberg in 1946 following his stint as America's lead prosecutor in the war crimes trials. He now markedly disavowed earlier positions, such as his belief in the preferred position doctrine, and exchanged his liberalism for a conservatism that, with rare exceptions, followed Frankfurter's. The fractured group of four justices now had Jackson and Frankfurter on the right and Black and Douglas on the left.

The liberalism of the latter pair was both constant and consistent, though it did not control the Court throughout the 1941–54 period as it had in the beginning. Black, with Douglas at his side, staked out the centerpiece of this liberalism: the argument for the total incorporation doctrine. This doctrine held that the due process clause of the Fourteenth Amendment made all of the provisions of the Bill of Rights applicable to the states. The appointments of conservatives Harold Burton and Fred Vinson meant the rejection of the total incorporation doctrine, and with the subsequent appointment of additional conservatives Tom Clark and Sherman Minton the liberals were further outstripped by the conservatives, with Frankfurter now shaping the broad outlines of judicial restraint that the Court followed.

By the end of the 1950s, however, with the appointment of liberals Earl Warren and William Brennan, to be coupled with the later appointment of additional liberals, Frankfurter's argument for judicial restraint was overwhelmed and rejected. All that he opposed was adopted. Douglas grew to accept the selective incorporation doctrine that implemented under a different name that which the total incorporation doctrine had tried to achieve.[1] He maintained his absolutist First Amendment vigilance following the 1941–54 period and continued with an interpretation of constitutional rights that went beyond the explicit language of the Constitution and considered its penumbras. Black, while implicitly accepting the selective incorporation doctrine, never retreated from his advocacy for its total incorporation counterpart and the argument that the basis for selective incorporation was jurisprudentially illegitimate. He insisted that constitutional rights had a textual pedigree and that he could not follow Douglas and the Court in looking to the implications of fundamental rights first and to the text of the Constitution only second.

The problem that these events sketch as it relates both to the justices and to the Supreme Court as an institution can be distilled into this question, important in itself and its implications: How could it happen that these justices, sharing core jurisprudential beliefs and ambitions before appointment, divided as they did into competing liberal and conservative factions? Put differently, Why did three of the four justices dramatically change jurisprudential course during their careers, with Frankfurter and Jackson changing early on and Black waiting until the last decade of a thirty-four-year career on the Court?

In trying to fashion an answer we need to acknowledge as a threshold matter that, when it comes to the way we understand the Supreme Court and its justices, there needs to be a middle ground between the approaches of judicial biography and constitutional history that have dominated the literature. To be sure, these approaches come freighted with difficulties for both writer and reader. Constitutional history presumes too much knowledge on the general reader's part and provides too close a reading of the Court's work in emphasizing, as it does, doctrinal analysis (the way jurisprudential doctrines are formulated and then applied and modified over time). In this approach the justices themselves are mentioned, but only incidentally. Instead, it is the reasoning of the opinions that compels the writer's attention.

That law clerks rather than the justices do much of the actual opinion writing is by itself a problem for analyses of the Court, one that constitutional history, however, eagerly avoids. To confront it is to add an additional layer to the difficulty that the dual nature of the Court already presents to the writer. This dual nature has the Court speaking with an institutional voice in a majority opinion, but at the same time speaking with the voice of the individual justice authoring that opinion.

Judicial biographers certainly have not helped much in understanding this duality. To read a judicial biography is to think that the biographical subject was the fount from which judicial wisdom flowed and that both the Court and its remaining members existed peripherally. It is the justice-as-lawgiver syndrome. Judicial biographers resort to this approach, of course, because the cloistered judicial life rarely lends itself to the satisfying stuff of biography. A justice's life in getting to the Court can sometimes provide enough interesting material, such as with Holmes's life, but generally the life alone will not satisfy readers. The project suffers from the flaw that it exists only because the person under review happened to become a justice and, as a result, wielded a good deal of power. It is not even as though a justice's life before an appointment to the Court has much to do with what happens once there, though in some instances, such as in the case of justices coming of age in the self-reliant American West of generations past, the sensibility that marks the pre-judicial life can influence the judicial life.

Assessment-seeking judicial profiles of the sort that follow suggest that less of what the legal scholars and biographers offer can yield more insight into both the individual justices and the nature of the Court itself. The pivot of the profiles is personality, that personal side of a justice that informs a justice's interactions with the other justices on the Court and helps to shape the arc of a justice's career. Personality is the active biographical ingredient that justices take to the Court.[2]

It was Felix Frankfurter who pointed to the personal when he once noted that, to understand the history of the Supreme Court, the lives of the justices must be understood.[3] Frankfurter's directive was to understand the part of a justice that was not publicly displayed. "The true face even of a public man," he wrote in a review of a biography of Chief Justice Charles Evans Hughes, "is his private face."[4] The private face that Frankfurter points to is the functional equivalent of personality when we define it in part as the way we act and the way we are behind the scenes as people. We certainly need to consider some of the more apparent aspects of life and work of the justices. These would include their backgrounds and the paths to the Court that they followed, their voting patterns, their jurisprudential philosophies, the shaping of their critical reputations, the extent of their jurisprudential influence, and their prose styles.

On the more personal side, we can look at their approaches to judging, their work habits, their friendships on and off the Court, their reading habits, the nature of their correspondence, the ways in which they tried to shape their public images, their political and judicial ambitions, and the ways in which they grappled with their human frailties of jealousy and ambition. But with Justices Jackson, Frankfurter, Black, and Douglas, personality is also expressed in what they wrote, as each was a gifted writer. What Justice Potter Stewart once noted about Jackson in this regard applies to all four justices. He wrote of him that "[b]ecause of [Jackson's] extraordinary gift to express what he had to say with such singular clarity and force, there shines through the pages of his writing not just his intellect, but the whole force of his personality."[5]

I thank Richard Posner, Mark Tushnet, Laura Kalman, and David Currie for reading parts or all of the manuscript and helping with their comments to improve it. Its flaws are my own.

∽

CHAPTER 1

Introduction

W hen the characters are large and the jurisprudential stakes high, an approach favoring personal profile over full-blown biography or constitutional history does its best work. This is true on both fronts here. The period principally under review, the 1941–54 Supreme Court terms, charts the time Frankfurter, Black, Douglas, and Jackson served together. This period ranged from Jackson's appointment to his death, but it also has its own jurisprudential definition. Not by coincidence, Jackson's appointment also marked the new critical mass that the Roosevelt appointments achieved in their liberal response to what can be called the Old Court of the 1930s and its refusal to find all sorts of economic legislation constitutional under the banner of judicial restraint. It includes the jurisprudential responses to the issues that the Second World War and the Cold War raised, and has as a backdrop the debate over individual rights under the heading of the preferred position doctrine and the doctrines of selective and total incorporation. The period ends with the triumph of civil rights jurisprudence in the form of the desegregation case of *Brown v. Board of Education.*[1]

Put differently, the jurisprudential stakes of the period were as high as they could be, since the result of what was then debated led the Court in our time to knock down the levees to federalism and flood the states with constitutional interpretations applicable to them and their citizens. The great Henry Friendly thought that what the Court did went "to the very nature of our Constitution" and had "profound effects for all of us."[2] Observations from such a preeminent source aside, even a casual look at our contemporary culture reveals the handiwork either directly or indirectly of the 1941–54 period in such areas as voting rights, criminal procedure, reproductive rights, welfare rights, and school desegregation. This meant that the stakes for American democracy were also high. The work of the Court from the 1940s and 1950s continuing on into the 1970s has marked a great judicial age.

This is in contrast to our own age, which more surely is a legislative age. Changes in the way we live today come more from Congress than from the courts. The Constitution, to be sure, explicitly provides for the legislature to affect the way we live. But what the Court did during its heyday affected the nation in ways perhaps more profound—consider desegregation, for example—than what the legislature has done before or since, leaving for us the question of how well democracy is served by such an assertion of authority. The answer must lie in part in both what the judicial age accomplished and in the nature of the methods it employed, which is but another way of looking into the nature of judging and, in our case, the relationship between judging and personality.

The contrast on this Court was between judicial activism and judicial conservatism, though the activism label misleads in the sense that judicial conservatism can be seen as activism by another name. Frankfurter, with Jackson joining him after an initial association with the opposing camp, agreed not just that the Court should decide constitutional issues only when forced to but also that the Court should defer to state legislatures and find their legislation unconstitutional in only the most compelling circumstances. In contrast, Black and Douglas, the judicial activists, were eager for the Court to use its power to temper the power of the states and the federal government against the individual. Held in the balance in the fight between the two factions and their philosophies was the jurisprudential course the Court would follow in the war years of the 1940s, the Cold War years of the early 1950s, and the years beyond into the contemporary era.

The Players

But just who were these judicial giants and where did they come from? We can start with thumbnail sketches. Black, the first of the group to be appointed, took his seat in 1937. He would be the only one of the four to come to the Court with judicial experience, albeit as a police court judge in

Birmingham, Alabama. Raised in rural Alabama and marginally educated, Black was a remarkably successful lawyer, handling personal injury and labor law matters, and eventually parlayed his success with juries into success with the electorate, winning a seat in the U.S. Senate in 1927. There he succeeded as well, through shrewd choices, a gift for persuasion, and the commitment of a firebrand liberal. He was a self-made man, and with his appointment his ascendency was complete, though not the rigors of his self-education, which continued throughout his more than three decades of service.

Frankfurter, appointed in 1938, was the intellectual's liberal, a Harvard Law School professor and frequent contributor to the *New Republic*. He had been marginalized as an immigrant Jew in New York, but in Cambridge and then in Washington as a member of Roosevelt's brain trust Frankfurter moved elegantly and pugnaciously in the highest governmental and social circles. He was as academically and professionally polished as Black was self-made.

Douglas was from Yakima, Washington. Like Frankfurter, he had been a star academic and law professor (precociously so), but he had tempered his academic experiences with high-level government service. As the head of the Securities and Exchange Commission, he set out to enforce the Securities Exchange Act of 1934, which Frankfurter had largely drafted. Again like Frankfurter, Douglas was both an outspoken liberal and a member of Roosevelt's inner circle. Here he went beyond Frankfurter and was also one of Roosevelt's weekly poker buddies. He was named to the Court in 1939 at the age of forty.

Jackson played poker with the president also and was, in 1941, the last of the four appointed. Like Black, he had little professional education and was a dazzling courtroom advocate. He made his way from western New York state to take a series of positions in Roosevelt's administrations, rising to attorney general and then to the Supreme Court. He frequently took to the stump during election years on Roosevelt's behalf and was a stand-in for the president with his approved liberalism and political-judicial views, such as his endorsement of Roosevelt's Court-packing plan.

There was much that linked and distinguished the four justices. They certainly had Roosevelt in common, though Black was not as close to Roosevelt as the others. They were all outstanding liberals, though, which mostly explained their appointments. This liberalism transcended their respective backgrounds. Once on the bench and serving together, they were, to be sure, the leading influences on their Court and exerted an unprecedented lasting influence. They expounded the clashing liberal and conservative jurisprudential philosophies on the Court. Black and Frankfurter, in particular, articulated the dispute over whether the Fourteenth Amendment incorporated fully the Bill of Rights and made these rights applicable to the states or whether the rights made applicable to the states were only those selective rights found to be fundamental by the Court.

But beyond this, the four justices had intensely personal clashes that were a function of both their membership in the two competing factions and their personalities. Their political ambitions clashed, as did their gifts as great writers. Partly in response to their rivalries, they attempted in various ways to shape their own images and legacies, and as part of this effort they propelled the academic debate between the theorists of the Legal Realism and Legal Process schools. Most of all, they provided an unparalleled look into the inner workings of the Court, with their accounts and with their personalities that figured prominently in their tragic failings on the Court.[3]

One way to appreciate the careers of Jackson, Frankfurter, Black, and Douglas is to consider by way of contrast the career of Stanley Reed. He, like the others, was appointed by Roosevelt, and he served with the four throughout. Indeed, his service with Frankfurter, Black, and Douglas stretched from Douglas's appointment in 1939 to Reed's retirement in 1957. Reed, however, was never central to the Court during the time of Jackson, Frankfurter, Black, and Douglas or beyond. He often held a swing vote, but this vote held influence of a sort different from the influence of the other four. They were leaders while he was a follower. It is not a coincidence that Reed has attracted so little scholarly attention and Jackson, Frankfurter, Black, and Douglas so much. To understand these four is to understand the Court.

By far the most talented group of writers ever to sit simultaneously on the Court, these four justices used that talent as a weapon in their individual campaigns. Every one was a gifted writer. Jackson was the best writer of the group and was, after Holmes, perhaps the finest writer ever to sit on the Court. They could and often did write their own opinions, a fact essential to the force of their jurisprudential positions. With the exception of Frankfurter, who thought that the justices should be writing only for lawyers and other judges, the members of the group recognized that opinions were a form of communication with the public at large and used them toward three purposes: to advance themselves individually, to advance the positions they were staking out on the Court, and to advance the Court itself as a platform for political advancement.

As a group, the justices were intent on making sure that the ground others gained did not come at their expense. They consistently wrote dissenting and concurring opinions to find fault with a majority decision and to suggest that true judicial wisdom lay instead with their opinions. The result was more than just fractured voting patterns; it was a proliferation of concurring and dissenting opinions with messages rooted in the personal and the ideological that were ammunition in the ongoing war between what developed into the liberal and conservative factions on the Court.

They were the most controversial justices, the most famous, and the most important of their time. They were also the most talented. Only Chief Justice Stone, who served part of the 1941–54 period with them, rivals the four for either talent or significance. Beyond being the most important justices of their particular Court, they became the justices who exerted the most enduring influence on both the Court's jurisprudence and the jurisprudence of the U.S. Court of Appeals. We know this in two ways. The first is that the jurisprudence that Black and Douglas set into motion—a jurisprudence that clashed directly with that of Frankfurter and Jackson—became the jurisprudence that shaped the work of our current Court. Douglas is primarily responsible for this, since Black, who had charged ahead with his liberalism in the 1940s and 1950s, shrank from that liberalism's implication and could not embrace the unenumerated rights jurisprudence articulated most fully by Douglas in the 1960s.

The second mark of the enduring influence of Frankfurter, Jackson, Black, and Douglas is that other judges and justices have elevated them to the pantheon of great justices. Even a casual reader of the opinions from the U.S. Supreme Court and from the U.S. Court of Appeals recognizes that Jackson, Frankfurter, Black, and Douglas are cited in a tip-of-the-hat fashion as often as any other judge or justice, save perhaps Holmes and Hand. The tip of the hat comes when an admiring judge or justice puts the justice's name in parentheses following the citation being used as way to acknowledge the work of one of these four and to mark that justice's voice as one to remember, as in, for example, (Jackson, J.) following a citation to a Jackson opinion. There is no greater honor in the language of the law, and these four continue, decades after their service, to receive it.

The four justices had national political ambitions that mixed with their judicial ones. It is perhaps hard for us to recognize the significance of this fact, given that today Supreme Court justices invariably come from the U.S. Court of Appeals and have no distinguishable political ambitions. Not true with these four. It is a striking fact that of these four justices, only Frankfurter did not think seriously about running for president. He wanted the same power but in a different way. He preferred the presidential adviser role. In contrast, Jackson, Black, and Douglas had each caught the presidential bug, moving in the highest political circles and believing that they could in fact be elected president. Against this backdrop, the justices wanted to use their public visibility on the Supreme Court as a way of enhancing their political possibilities. There had been the example of Charles Evans Hughes, who had resigned from the Court to run for president in 1916, only to be reappointed as chief justice fourteen years later. These political ambitions made the judicial stakes even higher and prompted some of the group to extend their influence within the Court itself as far as they could.

Black, more than the others, kept his attempt at influence within the corridors of the Court. He roamed there looking for votes in cases in which he was advancing his particular ideology. He was equaled, if not surpassed, at this by Frankfurter, whom Douglas considered the most vigilant proselytizer of all. Black's and Frankfurter's methods were strikingly different. Black relied only on his passion, conviction, and skills of persuasion to convince his brethren to follow him. Frankfurter, in contrast, engaged in calculated flattery as his chief tool, and if that did not work, he excoriated his foes with gossip in attempts to divide and conquer the Court. Frankfurter took his influence beyond the Court itself, however, and enlisted the help of his former law clerks, many of whom had gone on to academic careers, to push his judicial philosophy in their books, articles, and teaching and to attack the philosophies of the brethren with whom he was at war. Douglas and Jackson, on the other hand, worked mostly outside the Court. Douglas wrote extensively off the Court to advance his individual concept of liberty, while Jackson gave countless speeches to bar associations and civic groups to define his core beliefs, which favored individual liberties and federalism and disfavored big business.

Their individual stories take us into their chambers and into the conference room of the Court and allow us to see and assess the forces at work. The Court during the 1941–54 period knew a level of animosity unequaled in Court history, with the feuding factions providing the most volatile fuel. Frankfurter hated Black and Douglas most but also Frank Murphy and Fred Vinson, and he did not think highly of several other justices. Jackson hated Douglas and Black. Douglas saw Frankfurter as a mischievous force determined to divide the Court as part of his plan to conquer it. Only Black did not let on, either in public or in conference at least, as to any dislike of his brethren he might have had. For the others, especially Frankfurter and Jackson, their dislike of other justices was all too obvious.

The personal conflicts between the justices led to occasional fireworks at the weekly conference run by the chief justice when the Court was in session to discuss the way the justices were voting on particular cases. Douglas's accounts of these conferences in the 1940s and 1950s, given in a series of revealing interviews from the early 1960s, sketch a picture of the Court at work that is strikingly at odds with the way we typically think the justices deliberate. Douglas describes conferences in which the justices pound on the tables, threaten fisticuffs, and berate each other with insults aimed at their intelligence and integrity. Frankfurter perhaps understated the problem when he complained to Rutledge following the 1944 term that the justices resembled schoolboys throwing spitballs at each other.[4]

Jackson, Frankfurter, Black, and Douglas dominated in part because of their talent and ambition and in part because of circumstances. With the exception of their last year or so together, when they fell under the leadership of Chief Justice Earl Warren, the four justices worked together on the Court under the ineffectual personal leadership of Chief Justices Stone and then Vinson. The combination of their individual strengths and the weaknesses of the chief justices helped make the group of Jackson, Frankfurter, Black, and Douglas the dominant force on the Court for a dozen years. Truman's appointments of Vinson, Harold Burton, Tom Clark, and Sherman Minton had been the weakest group of appointments in the Court's history, which made the contrast between Jackson, Frankfurter, Black, and Douglas on the one hand and their brethren on the other even more striking.

Individually and collectively, Black, Douglas, Frankfurter, and Jackson are four of the most vivid, complex, and tragic personalities ever to sit on the Court. Frankfurter and Jackson were at war with themselves, Black was trying to shed his past and to refashion himself on the Court, and Douglas was working his way toward the liberalism that later distinguished him, some say against the backdrop of his political aspirations, which he finally abandoned in 1952. If personality is my subject, failings and flaws are my themes. Frankfurter and Jackson were great minds and talents who lessened themselves through the weaknesses of their personalities. Jackson's ambition to be chief justice compromised his great talent and led to some of the most startling interpersonal behavior the Court has ever seen. Ambition—propelled by his egotism, elitism, and arrogance—was surely the demon for Frankfurter as well. Pointing to a pedigree that made him think that he was the heir to Holmes and Brandeis, his expectation was to lead the Court. When it did not happen, the fuel of his ambition ignited and doomed him to ultimate underachievement on the Court.

Black's flaw was that he took fidelity to jurisprudential principles too far and ended up with an approach to some matters, such as the dimensions of constitutional rights as defined by the Bill of Rights, that was sufficiently idiosyncratic and rigid that it kept him from growing and evolving as a thinker. Frankfurter, who so often was perceptive about the weaknesses of others—though, ironically, without much in the way of self-reflection—pointed this way when he sniped that Black, the great reader, read only to confirm his beliefs.[5]

Acting as something of a surprising counterpoint, Douglas worked hard in his role of justice and, through an approach to judging that emphasized getting his own work done and recognizing the sovereignty of his brethren, brought a different, admirable standard to judging. Douglas, however, has been caught in the whipsaw of Legal Process critical commentary that stressed craftsmanship and an exalted view of the Court as a neutral decision maker. When he challenged this view he paid a heavy price for committing a sin equivalent to saying the emperor had no clothes. His work as a dedicated jurist growing in his job and making the most of his immense ability has been lost sight of. Toward the end of his career, however, he was also diminished by a flaw in his personality that at times kept him too aloof from the Court. But unlike Black's, his personality flaw—of succumbing to the image he had created of himself—did not interfere with the evolution of his jurisprudence.

Frankfurter, Jackson, Douglas, and Black did their own part to shape their respective legacies. To varying degrees, they all sought to refashion their images to suit their ambitions. On this last front, Douglas, Frankfurter, and Jackson wrote or spoke extensively about themselves to shape the images they sought. Douglas, as commentators have noted, sought to fashion in his volumes of autobiography an image as a rugged individualist and liberal, an image that was often at odds with historic reality.[6] Frankfurter intermittently kept a self-serving diary while on the Court and sat for an extensive oral history that shapes history in his own image. He went further and sought to shape the history of the Court by actively involving himself in shaping the histories that others were writing of Court members. Jackson gave a favorable spin to every career event in an extensive oral history interview he gave not long before his death, and he also helped his biographer by writing out extensive defenses or explanations of certain events, most likely knowing that the biographer would incorporate those defenses into the biography virtually unchanged.

Black followed the others and provided an autobiographical version of his life, but it was only a sketch, which ended before taking his seat on the Court. Of the group, he is the only one who directed that his personal papers be destroyed upon his death. Frankfurter's papers at the Library of Congress and at the Harvard Law School Library are a rich cache of documents that reveal much about him. Douglas's papers at the Library of Congress, especially his comprehensive conference notes, are extensive and useful, though Douglas did not reveal himself greatly on the page. Far more can be gleaned from his correspondence with Fred Rodell (found at Haverford College) and a series of interviews he gave with Princeton University's Professor Walter Murphy during the early 1960s. Jackson's papers are relatively thin in revealing material, but because he was such a fine writer, he betrays himself in his prose. Only Black's Court papers are not particularly revealing.

The Critical Context

In looking at these four justices we also get a chance to understand a recent phenomenon of critical commentary on the Court that illustrates the battles that partisans wage to project the image of the Court and its work that best advances their ideological interests. The justices were the central players—with Jackson less so—in a campaign for the hearts and minds of the nation that went beyond either the corridors of the Court or the pages of the *U.S. Reports*. Frankfurter in particular was responsible for attempting to influence the way the Court was written about in both academic and popular journals. His method was to encourage former clerks and academics friendly to his cause of judicial restraint both to make the argument for judicial restraint and also to disparage the work and approaches of Black and Douglas. Douglas and Black knew full well that Frankfurter was trying to shape public opinion and history, and while they had their own supporters advancing their side of the ideological argument, they did not pursue the public relations angle as aggressively as Frankfurter.

The Legal Process school of thought that originated from the Harvard Law School can be understood as Frankfurter's way of bringing legitimacy to his philosophy of judicial restraint. The Legal Process theorists advocated a jurisprudential approach of what they termed "neutrality" and recoiled at the Legal Realism school, which recognized the subjective element in judging and encouraged judges as fact finders to be more knowledgeable of the actual workings of society. The Legal Process theorists decried what they considered to be the results-oriented jurisprudence of the Legal Realists and pointed to Black and Douglas as the two greatest offenders. The irony of the Legal Process theorists, and a reason they need to be discussed in the context of a personality-based study of Frankfurter, Jackson, Black, and Douglas, is that someone new to the scene would think that the Frankfurter and Jackson faction had won the war of ideologies. If the winning side is supposed to write the history of the conflict and time, then a revision is in order. Frankfurter's and Jackson's philosophy of judicial restraint—and the Legal Process school of thought that articulated that philosophy—did not prevail on the Court.

Paradoxically, while the Legal Process theorists thought the result was reached by the wrong route, they agreed that the Court reached the right result in its landmark cases such as *Brown v. Board of Education* and *Griswold v. Connecticut*.[7] It was of course Douglas who wrote for the Court in *Griswold*, relying on his earlier landmark opinion in *Skinner*, the punitive sterilization case that redefined fundamental rights on its way to holding the right to procreate to be a fundamental right.[8] And because the Legal Process theorists did not think that the process had been the pure one they advocated, Douglas did not get the credit he deserved. This study in part seeks to outline the history of the time by drawing attention both to the forces that prompted the justices to define themselves as they did and to reveal the forces of constitutional history writing themselves at work. Personality is involved on both sides.

The chapter profiles that follow are meant in large part to be self-contained, but to accommodate two subtopics that extend beyond the principal 1941–54 period the profiles are slightly cumulative. One subtopic is jurisprudential trends, which I follow into the 1960s and 1970s, first in the Black profile and even more so in the concluding Douglas profile. The second subtopic is the way Court commentators have tried to shape how the Court and its justices are understood. This subtopic also finds its culmination in the Douglas profile. As a general matter, the progress of the profiles is toward Douglas. His profile, as a result, more than any other, goes beyond its specific subject and makes an attempt at bringing the Court in general into focus.

Some Key Cases

With these organizational observations made, I next set out the context of constitutional history to give these cases from the 1941–54 period and beyond meaning to the reader. There are two sets of cases that appear throughout the profiles, though frequently the sets overlap. One set of cases reflects the jurisprudence of a particular justice, so that a case might be important to the career of a particular justice but not to the Court as a whole. The other set of cases provides the picture of an evolving Court on the key issues of the time. To identify these key issues of course leaves a great quantity of the Court's work unmentioned, but inasmuch as my principal interest is with the work that affects us still today, we can, with some plausibility, say that the key issues of the period centered on civil liberties issues that grew out of both the Second World War and the cold war, with civil liberties including here both the constitutional rights of the criminally accused and civil rights as we ordinarily think of them (as involving voting rights, racial equality, First Amendment rights, and reproductive rights).

This study makes no claim to being a constitutional history of the 1941–54 period and beyond, though the Court's jurisprudential trends over this nearly sixty-year period are important to the profiles I sketch. Cases are invoked for different reasons. The cases of today's Court, of course, are the ones that determine what the law is, making preceding cases obsolete almost by definition. Seminal cases, that is, cases in which the Court first marks the development of an important doctrine, will always have historical significance. In that sense a case such as *Skinner* remains important because of the way in which the doctrines of fundamental rights and strict scrutiny are shaped if not developed anew. A successor case such as *Griswold* will also continue to have significance because of the new and perhaps novel way in which the Court, in looking at fundamental rights again (this time the fundamental right of a married couple to contraceptive privacy), adjusted or expanded upon what had been said before. I make more than passing mention of these cases, not only because they relate so directly to both the Court's evolving jurisprudence of individual rights but also because both majority opinions were written by Douglas and figure prominently in his individual career.

Other cases are important historically because they indicate shifts in the voting patterns of individual justices, because they reflect turmoil on the Court, or because they mark key points of consensus in the development of the Court's jurisprudence. The 1943 *West Virginia State Board of Education v. Barnette,* known as the Second Flag Salute case,[9] is a case that reveals a Court in turmoil. It is a case rarely cited today, in large part because the preferred position doctrine that the case employs no longer has any particular currency, having long faded from the Court's contemporary jurisprudence. To be sure, the doctrine was important in its time and has historical significance because of its predecessor role to the Court's current individual rights jurisprudence. It was of course Harlan Fiske Stone, as an associate justice in 1938, in perhaps the most famous footnote in Supreme Court history, who started the Court down this jurisprudential path when he distinguished between economic rights and individual liberties and argued that the Court should look more searchingly at legislation that fell "within a specific prohibition . . . such as those of the first ten amendments," or that "restrict[ed] those political processes which can ordinarily be expected to bring about repeal of undesirable legislation" or directed against "discrete and insular minorities."[10]

But apart from its historical and doctrinal significance, *Barnette* is important because the decision marked a turning point in the personnel alignment on the Court. Felix Frankfurter's career cannot be understood without appreciating the full dimensions of *Barnette. Barnette* was the Court's second look at the issue of whether public school students could be compelled to salute the flag, and it is in the changes between these first and second cases that we find significance. In the first, *Minersville School District v. Gobitis* three years earlier in 1940,[11] the Court, speaking through Justice Frankfurter, upheld a state statute compelling public school students to salute the flag. His argument stressed the civic participation that the salute emphasized and emphasized the virtues of this participation. The costs in the loss of individual liberties were negligible in light of the overwhelming benefit that could be defined as national unity. When the issue of whether a state could discipline dissenting students came to the Court the second time, Jackson was now sitting, and Justices Murphy, Black, and Douglas changed their votes for a new majority that reversed the prior decision. Jackson spoke for the Court, with perhaps his most memorable opinion, in the face of Frankfurter's strenuous and articulate dissent, as the Court charted a new direction in civil liberties.

Frankfurter's vehement rejection of the preferred position doctrine in his dissent in the Second Flag Salute case marked the beginning of the end of his leadership on the Court. Douglas thought that with the case an irreparable cleavage developed between Frankfurter and his group of Murphy, Black, and Rutledge.[12] He explained in his Princeton interviews that he and his cohorts had been repelled by what they considered to be Frankfurter's machinations and general deceitfulness in his relations with them.[13] Frankfurter was not privy to the foundations of their resentment. What he knew instead was that Murphy, Black, and Douglas had voted with him in the First Flag Salute case, that they had lavished praise on his opinion, and that they were now changing their votes in the Second Flag Salute case. Their defection seemed to shake Frankfurter to his roots.

The construction and tone of his dissent in this Second Flag Salute case suggests that it was no ordinary dissent. It was also more than the credo he claimed it was. It was an articulation of his views on the preferred position doctrine and judicial restraint to be sure, but it was also Frankfurter's dressing down of his colleagues. He had been personally affronted by their disavowal of him and the First Flag Salute case and did his best to shame them.

His first move was to open the dissent with a startling, gripping personal commentary to clear Jackson's dazzling rhetorical soldiers from the field and to take the high ground. "One who belongs to the most vilified and persecuted minority in history is not likely to be insensible to the freedoms guaranteed by our Constitution," he writes. "As judges we are neither Jew nor Gentile, neither Catholic nor agnostic . . . as a member of this Court I am not justified in writing my private notions into the Constitution, no matter how deeply I may cherish them or how mischievous I may deem their disregard . . . I cannot bring my mind to believe that the 'liberty' secured by the Due Process Clause gives this Court authority to deny to the State of West Virginia the attainment of that which we all recognize as a legitimate legislative end, namely, the promotion of good citizenship by employment of the means here chosen."[14]

After rejecting the preferred position doctrine, he trotted out a list of luminaries who had agreed in earlier cases with the principles he was reaffirming in the case, and he noted the number of times in prior cases the Court had followed his position and had rejected that of the majority.[15] He even listed the number of judges who had at various times agreed with the principles he was articulating.[16] While at times eloquent, Frankfurter's dissent is most notable for its sustained petulance. Frankfurter the professor would not let his students desert him before challenging their very cheek in doing so.

The consequences for Frankfurter and the Court were profound. Frankfurter's dissent was an open declaration of war and divided the Court into two groups—those with Frankfurter and those against him. For Frankfurter at least, the dynamics among the brethren centered on Frankfurter's attempts to undermine the Black and Douglas group both in strength and in numbers. Equally significant, Frankfurter, in insisting on positions that were strained to meet unnatural objectives, painted himself into a jurisprudential corner and stunted if not killed his chances of evolving with the Court. As Joseph Lash, his sympathetic biographer, felt compelled to acknowledge, Frankfurter, with his dissent in the Second Flag Salute case, "uncoupled himself from the locomotive of history."[17] The Frankfurter of the Flag Salute cases was not the Frankfurter that Court observers expected. If Frankfurter had caused many of his supporters to wonder how their voice of liberalism could write the opinion he did in the First Flag Salute case, his dissent in the Second Flag Salute case came as a deeper disappointment. Frankfurter, for his part, was proud of the opinion and encouraged Roosevelt to hang a copy of the decision in the Hyde Park Library. Frankfurter defended every part of the opinion, even the opening, which some of his brethren had pleaded with him to delete. There was clearly no way back for Frankfurter.

Another case important to the Court's story as I tell it and to my profiles is the 1947 case of *California v. Adamson.*[18] Here the issue was the doctrine of selective incorporation and the Court's emphatic reaffirmation of this doctrine and its rejection of its competing doctrine of total incorporation.

With this latter doctrine, the due process clause of the Fourteenth Amendment was seen as incorporating as a group the rights set out in the Bill of Rights. Here more than personalities were involved. Here the battle lines were drawn that defined the liberal and conservative camps headed by my profiled justices, with Frankfurter and Black taking their respective points. This was the central jurisprudential argument of the period and in large measure ultimately shaped Black's career.

At issue was the constitutionality of a California statute that allowed the prosecution in criminal cases to comment upon a defendant's silence in not refuting evidence offered against him. The theory of the statute was that at a certain level every innocent person would protest against evidence of his guilt, so much so that the failure to protest the evidence by way of refutation was tantamount to evidence of guilt. Adamson had not testified, and the prosecution had taken advantage of the rule and commented upon his silence, and on appeal Adamson had argued that his Fifth Amendment right against self-incrimination had been violated. Finding no relief with the California courts, Adamson appealed to the Supreme Court. They all agreed, at least arguendo, that the prosecution would not have been able to comment upon his silence had he been tried in a federal court, either in California or anywhere else, making the issue whether, as Adamson claimed, his Fifth Amendment right against self-incrimination extended to state court proceedings by way of the Fourteenth Amendment. Justice Reed for the majority cited to *Twining v. New Jersey*[19] and quickly dispatched Adamson's claim, pointing further to unshaken precedent rejecting the argument that the Fourteenth Amendment incorporated the Bill of Rights and made it applicable to the states.

Frankfurter may have been right in his concurring opinion in arguing that history did not support the proposition that the drafters of the Fourteenth Amendment thought that they were incorporating into it the first eight amendments of the Bill of Rights,[20] but that was not what was important about his opposition to the total incorporation doctrine. Rather, it was the way in which his arguments against the doctrine articulated his view of the constitution, judiciary, and federalism. Frankfurter rejected the total incorporation doctrine in large part because splicing the Bill of Rights onto the Fourteenth Amendment would destroy the distinction between the federal and state governments. States must be allowed to experiment as they saw fit, he argued, within the broad dictates of the Fourteenth Amendment.

Imposing the dimensions of the federal provisions of specific rights would, moreover, limit the extent to which the states could provide protections to their citizens if they so chose.[21]

Frankfurter also thought the total incorporation theory unworkable because it relied on subjective interpretations.[22] The specific provisions of the first eight amendments of the Bill of Rights could hardly be interpreted uniformly because what would offend one judge when it came to the Fourth Amendment's prohibition against unreasonable searches and seizures, to use an example cited by Frankfurter, might not offend another judge. Selective incorporation, for Frankfurter, did not solve the problem of subjectivity, as choosing the provisions to be incorporated would be subjectively based and therefore unacceptable.

For Frankfurter, the question was not whether specific provisions of the Bill of Rights had been violated. It was whether the criminal proceedings deprived the defendant of due process of law as set out in the Fourteenth Amendment. Here the question was whether the proceedings "offended those canons of decency and fairness which express the notions of justice of English-speaking peoples even toward those charged with the most heinous crimes."[23] Frankfurter believed that judges must "divine the deep, if inarticulate" feelings of society as best they could.[24] The fact that judges could differ on what is an acceptable notion of justice in a particular case does not, Frankfurter added, disprove the premise of the standard he wanted to apply, that interpreting the due process clause in his way was not based on "the idiosyncrasies of a merely personal judgment."[25]

The argument Black made in his dissent for the total incorporation was straightforward and in many ways blunt, leaving the reader not with questions about its refinement but with the simpler question of whether Black was right or wrong. Black turned to precedent and began with the premise that the Court in interpreting the Fourteenth Amendment needed to look to the intention of its framers.[26] He then produced copious excerpts from debates and commentaries from the framers of the amendment to show that they intended it to incorporate and make applicable to the states the entire Bill of Rights. The matter in some ways was quite simple for Black. To deal with the majority's argument, also rooted in precedent, that the Court had rejected the total incorporation argument each of the several times it considered it, Black, paradoxically, given his own reliance on precedent, dismissed the majority's list of cases on the grounds that these cases had not considered the legislative history he had set forth and that the precedent was not entitled to deferential obedience.

But Black went further and tried to use the Court's Fourteenth Amendment jurisprudence against the majority. He argued that the fact that the Court over time had selectively incorporated various provisions of the Bill of Rights using Cardozo's articulated "essence of ordered liberty" principle and analysis meant that there was no obstacle to the recognition of the total incorporation theory. The argument ran that, if the Court was willing to incorporate a certain provision of an amendment, such as the Fifth Amendment, then surely all provisions of that amendment must be subject to incorporation because it would be anomalous to view some aspects of the amendment as fundamental, to use Cardozo's language, and not others.

That there could be anomalies in the interpretation of the Bill of Rights disturbed Black and animated the core of his jurisprudence. He concluded that the problem was the exercise of discretion under the Cardozo formulation and analysis. His solution in the total incorporation theory eliminated the ability of judges to determine what was fundamentally important to civil liberties and what was not and compelled them instead to look to the Bill of Rights and its judicial glosses. Discretion for Black was an evil even when it held out the possibility of protections that went beyond the Bill of Rights. Black could not accept the anomaly that whether fundamental constitutional rights attached was determined by whether a defendant was being tried in a state or federal court. Frankfurter, in contrast, considered it to be an anomaly but a harmless one; the great believer in judicial discretion and in the rights of self-determination for the respective states believed that rights were granted by the judiciary and were not endemic to the citizenry.

However, to set out the background of these doctrines is to miss the significant role that personality had in why the justices believed as they did and why, in some instances, they changed their minds about the doctrines. The cases and the doctrines form the backdrop against which the drama of these judicial giants lived their lives and moved through their careers. Their responses to doctrines tell us a good deal, but it is with their full-bodied lives and personalities that we learn more about them and the Court. It is to those lives and personalities that we now turn.

CHAPTER 2

The Tragic Figure of Robert Jackson

The distinguishing aspect of Robert Jackson's career is not that he went from a small, solo law practice in western New York state to become the solicitor general of the United States, the attorney general of the United States, a U.S. Supreme Court justice, and the nation's lead prosecutor at the Nuremberg war crimes trials following the Second World War. Others reaching the Supreme Court have had equally humble beginnings. No, Jackson is most remembered for ruining his reputation, in one bewildering episode of anger and frustration, with a personal attack in 1946 on fellow Supreme Court justice Hugo Black on the grounds that he thought Black had scuttled his chance at the chief justiceship that he thought was his due. Sadly, Jackson's experience with Black and the chief justiceship only reflected Jackson's fundamental inability to keep in check his ambition, which revealed itself most tellingly in his fight to keep the personal element out of his judging as he struggled with the demons of his ambition, jealousy, and resentment.

Jackson's beginnings were modest at best.[1] He was born on February 13, 1892, at Spring Creek in western Pennsylvania. When he was five years old, the family moved across the state line to Frewsburg, New York, a small town five miles south of Jamestown. Jackson graduated from Frewsburg High School in 1919 and then spent a postgraduate year at Jamestown High

School. He wanted to study law, but his father, who worked as a lumberman, stockbreeder, and farmer, was adamant that he should pursue medicine and refused to help him financially. Jackson's solution was to borrow enough for one year at the Albany Law School, which he left without taking a degree. He immediately returned to Jamestown and began as a solo practitioner sharing space in the law office of his mother's cousin, Frank Mott, who schooled him in the practice of law and in politics and who was also, as Jackson noted to an inquiring correspondent, "a brilliant speaker, deeply interested in English literature."[2]

Jackson's was on-the-job training. As he much later put it in a speech at the Stanford Law School, he was a "vestigial remnant of the system which permitted one to come to the bar by way of apprenticeship in a law office."[3] This was in the nature, he said, of being the country lawyer that he was. He practiced alone for many years in Jamestown and eventually formed successive small partnerships. He sometimes went to the nearest large city, Buffalo, New York, on business, but he remained throughout his career a Jamestown lawyer. As was true of many small city or town practices, his was a general practice with an emphasis on the diversity of clients and work. By the time he left Jamestown for Washington, when he was forty-two years old and had practiced law for half that time, he was earning thirty thousand dollars a year, he proudly noted in the oral history interview he gave for the Columbia University Oral History Project in the last years of his life. He had made enough money to go to Washington, he said, meaning that his wealth would immunize him from the pressure to hold an unwanted job.[4]

Jackson was proud of his professional roots as a county seat lawyer. In an age before the rise of law firms, in a time of either solo practitioners or small partnerships, he admired the members of the local bar both for their camaraderie and for their sense of independence, going so far as to characterize the niche of the country lawyer within the profession in a deeply felt review essay on the subject.[5] He also memorialized this stalwart lawyer's life when he described his own early days among lawyers in his oral history interview, saying that "in those days, before the automobile, lawyers would go to court, stay all day—sometimes go up for the week—and gather at the tavern in the evening with the judge. There was perhaps a big table where everybody would have supper—as we called it there—together. You were always very quickly taken into the fellowship as a young lawyer if they thought you had anything in you at all."[6]

Jackson's own practice intertwined political and bar activities and led him to success on the national stage. He was elected to the Democratic State Committee at the age of twenty-one and was, at various times, the president of both the Jamestown Bar Association and the Federation of Bar Associations of Western New York. On the statewide front, Jackson served on a commission established by then New York governor Franklin Roosevelt to study the fragmented and many-tiered New York state court system.

Jackson was an inveterate public speaker from the beginning of his career, speaking to local and statewide audiences on substantive legal topics and on matters relating to the bar. He came to the attention of Democratic leaders in New York state through his political and bar activities and first met Roosevelt in 1913 when he served on the state Democratic committee, and Roosevelt, then assistant secretary of the Navy, was the committee's contact in Washington for patronage positions.

Their paths crossed again in 1930 when Roosevelt, now governor of New York, appointed Jackson to serve on the commission to look at the organization of the New York courts. He also got to know James Farley, the New York political power broker and chairman of the Democratic National Committee. Farley and Roosevelt both liked what they saw in Jackson, and Roosevelt as president a few years later offered him a job in Washington as general counsel to the Bureau of Internal Revenue in the Treasury Department. He found upon arriving there that he did not much resemble the New Deal lawyers, about whom much has been written for their role in the bureaucratic revolution that was the New Deal.[7] At forty-two, he was not particularly young, nor had he trained at an elite law school under members of a class of law school professors helping to create and develop the bureaucratic, administrative culture of New Deal Washington. He went to Washington, instead, as an immensely talented and experienced lawyer, albeit on the local and state level.

He rose quickly in the Roosevelt administration, spending two years as general counsel to the Internal Revenue Service. He headed a much noticed prosecution against Andrew Mellon for a tax deficiency, which led to meetings with the president and other high cabinet officials. He was made an assistant attorney general, working with administration insiders Benjamin Cohen and Tom Corcoran, which ensured that the president would learn about Jackson's talents from them. He had choicer projects there and argued many cases for the government before the Supreme Court. His work there galvanized opinion as to his talent, and he was moved to the front of the Justice Department as the head of the antitrust division. Vigorous, successful prosecutions in this field in which he had a keen interest led to more success and an eventual promotion, on March 4, 1938, to the post of solicitor general, replacing Stanley Reed. Jackson's star shone brightly as solicitor general, prompting Brandeis's much repeated observation that Jackson should be solicitor general for life.[8] Jackson was solicitor general for only twenty months, or forty-four cases, of which he won thirty-eight, before he was promoted again, this time to attorney general, replacing Frank Murphy, who had moved to the High Court.

Jackson's rise through the Department of Justice had more to do with the quality of his work than with the contacts he made, though he was able to impress on both fronts. He was, ultimately, a man who could get the job done. And in a city in which many officials rose because of the work their underlings did in their name, Jackson did his own work, according to one lawyer who worked with him.[9] This is not to say, though, that Jackson wrote each of the briefs for cases he argued before the High Court as solicitor general. Paul Freund, Jackson's top assistant in the Office of Solicitor General, as he had been for Jackson's predecessor, often wrote the briefs that Jackson argued. If Jackson had any weakness as solicitor general, Freund recalls, it was that he sometimes did not spend enough time with the briefs and did not always master the record. Jackson, he said, spent most of his time polishing his oral arguments, which Freund described as "scintillating."[10] Sadly, Jackson's appearances before the High Court came in a time before arguments were tape-recorded and are not, as a result, available. Fortunately, though, at least one argument made its way into the record to give us a glimpse of Jackson the advocate at work. His argument in the 1937 cases testing the constitutionality of the tax provisions of the Social Security Act was put into the *Congressional Record* and shows Jackson in complete control of both his facts and his arguments.[11] He is not as witty as we might expect, coming across generally instead as an amiable advocate who understands the nature of his function. His lean, cohesive presentation impresses from the beginning.

That Jackson handled his new jobs in the Roosevelt administration so well is especially impressive given Jackson's prior legal work. As a practitioner in upstate New York, he had rarely appeared in federal court and had little familiarity with federal law. Put differently, Jackson had moved from arguing "bull and horse" lawsuits (as he called them) in the justice courts of western New York to arguing cases of unparalleled sophistication before the Supreme Court of the United States. That he might have preferred the former to the latter, as he once wrote a Jamestown lawyer friend, shows only that the city could not take the country lawyer out of Jackson.[12] That he had been able to do both reveals his enormous capacity to assimilate information and adapt to new settings.

Jackson's success in the Roosevelt administration led to a place as one of Roosevelt's intimate advisers. At play, he became a regular member of the president's poker-playing group, which included administration officials such as secretary of the interior Harold Ickes and William Douglas, then chairman of the Securities and Exchange Commission. Jackson saw the president regularly, going with him on fishing expeditions and spending time aboard the presidential yacht. At work, he wrote speeches for Roosevelt, and for the election of 1936 he campaigned vigorously, tirelessly, and successfully for him.

Moving in the highest circles of government, Jackson was considered a political force in his own right. There was much discussion in 1937 as to whether he should run in 1938 for governor of New York. The Democratic incumbent, Herbert Lehman, had expressed reluctance about running again, and Roosevelt tried to persuade Jackson to take a crack at it. Jackson feigned a lack of interest, but in fact he warmed to the idea. Initial steps were taken, but ultimately Lehman decided to seek reelection, scotching Jackson's ambitions. With this initial political ambition came Jackson's first taste of political manipulation and betrayal. Jackson may well have been manipulated by Roosevelt, for example, who was trying to coax Lehman into running again. And in the brief time that his name was being floated as a candidate, Jackson ran into significant opposition from Jim Farley, who opposed Jackson's attempt at political office, believing that Jackson posed a threat to him in New York state. It stayed with him that Farley, who at one time had been an ally, had worked against him.

On the more important national stage, talk of Jackson as a presidential candidate began as early as 1937. Jackson had impressed enough people, most notably Roosevelt himself, that Roosevelt considered him a front-runner to succeed him. Harold Ickes wrote in his diary that it had come straight from the White House that the president's first choice for 1940, given his disinclination to seek a third term, was Bob LaFollette, followed by Henry Wallace and then Robert Jackson.[13] A leading national newsmagazine described Jackson as "the man Franklin Roosevelt thinks will some day be a great liberal U.S. President."[14]

Ickes, for his part, was taken with Jackson. After meeting him for the first time, he wrote in his diary that "Jackson is a quiet person and sometimes his reactions seem slow. But he is thoughtful and well-poised and fundamentally very sound from my point of view. I was very much taken with him. There is no doubt that he is a real liberal."[15] Several months later he notes that "Jackson undoubtedly has great qualities,"[16] that he "is one of the finest and most upright men, as well as one of the ablest, that I have ever known."[17]

Roosevelt, of course, did run for a third term, but thoughts of Jackson as presidential material did not diminish. Some of Roosevelt's closest advisers wanted Jackson to give the keynote address at the 1940 nominating convention, as a way of getting Jackson greater political exposure, but Farley, the head of the Democratic National Committee, blocked that movement, and Jackson lost out on a great opportunity. Toward the end of the campaign, Jackson, impressive speaker that he was, nonetheless was billed for speeches in three small, unimportant upstate New York cities.

Marked as a Roosevelt insider, Jackson advanced the president's causes throughout the nation and in Washington. He and Ickes delivered speeches around the country inveighing against big business and promoting Roosevelt's agenda on the antimonopoly front, earning Jackson a reputation in the process as a radical. He did not play a role in the formation of Roosevelt's 1937 plan to pack the Court, but he defended the plan before the Senate Judiciary Committee.[18] But while Roosevelt promoted his plan by attacking the integrity of the Court, Jackson took a different approach. He argued that the problem with the Court, in invalidating repeated congressional economic legislation, was not that it lacked integrity but that it had assumed a stance of stubborn integrity in refusing to defer to the will of the legislature. The Court-packing plan of course failed, but Jackson succeeded with both the president and the country.

Jackson followed with a book defending the Court-packing plan. *The Struggle for Judicial Supremacy* (1941) was written with the approval and at the suggestion of the president, Jackson later said, because the executive branch's struggle with the Court had been poorly recorded.[19] Some have speculated that the bulk of the book was written by Paul Freund, by then of the Harvard Law School, who had worked with Jackson in the solicitor general's office.[20] The correspondence between the two on the book, however, suggests that Jackson wrote the book, with the assistance of Freund.

In the book Jackson took some of the cases in which the Court had struck down New Deal legislation, put them in a broader historical context, and explained how the Court's response to the issues at hand had been inadequate.[21] The Court's approach, he argued, was anachronistic, applying horse-and-buggy law in the age of the automobile. "The difficulty was that this group of judges," Jackson later said in his oral history, "were applying the standards of their youth to the legislation of an entirely different period. They thought they were applying the Constitution, but they were really misapplying it, in our view, because what is reasonable also has to depend on the environment and the circumstances. They were not open to conviction on the facts. They were not open to the conviction that conditions had changed. They were striking down a good deal of legislation on the basis of what conditions were when they were brought up on the frontier."[22]

Perhaps Jackson's most interesting contribution in *The Struggle for Judicial Supremacy* comes near the end when he sketches his understanding of the preferred position doctrine, which held that the Court, while deferring to the wisdom of the legislature on economic matters, can, without contradicting itself, scrutinize legislation dealing with civil liberties without presuming its validity. "The presumption of validity which attaches in general to legislative acts is frankly reversed in the case of interferences with free speech and free assembly," he wrote, "and for a perfectly cogent reason. Ordinarily, legislation whose basis in economic wisdom is uncertain can be redressed by the processes of the ballot box or the pressures of opinion. But when the channels of opinion and of peaceful persuasion are corrupted or clogged, these political correctives can no longer be relied on, and the democratic system is threatened at its most vital point. In that event the Court, by intervening, restores the processes of democratic government; it does not disrupt them."[23] The Court had, in fact, just begun intervening with the application of this so-called preferred position doctrine, and Jackson supported both the intervention and the application.

Six months after the publication of his book, Jackson was promoted from attorney general to a seat on the Supreme Court. As Frankfurter recounted the event in a memorandum to himself, as a way of refuting what others had speculated, Roosevelt sought Frankfurter's counsel when Chief Justice Hughes in 1941 decided to retire.[24] Roosevelt was torn between putting Jackson on the Court as the new chief justice and elevating Stone from his place as an associate justice to the center seat. Frankfurter, ever the presidential counselor, recognized the benefit that would flow from the appointment of Stone, a Republican, to replace Hughes. As a result, even though he personally wanted Jackson to be named chief justice, he recommended that Roosevelt go with Stone. Frankfurter immediately told Jackson of his conversation and his recommendation. Jackson accepted his fate without anger or grudge and became, Frankfurter said, a closer friend for it all. Roosevelt nominated Stone to be chief justice and Jackson was named to replace Stone as an associate justice. Jackson, Frankfurter speculated, had reason to believe that he would be moved to the center seat upon Stone's retirement or death.

Jackson began his career on the Court with impressive success. He took the opportunity in just his second opinion to give notice that he was both a gifted writer and independent thinker. The case, *Edwards v. California*,[25] also known as the anti-Okie case, was the product of California's Depression-era statute designed to keep indigents from entering the state by making it a crime to assist them in relocating. Justice Byrnes, as new to the Court as Jackson, wrote for the Court and held that the law was an unconstitutional burden on interstate commerce.

Jackson, sensing an opening, stole the day and concurred on the broader, more aggressively liberal basis that the statute violated the privileges and immunities clause of the constitution. Adding flair, he concluded his opinion by invoking the aptest literary allusion possible, Shakespeare in *Macbeth* on paupers and broken promises: "Rich or penniless, [the indigent's] citizenship under the Constitution pledges his strength to the defense of California as part of the United States, and his right to migrate to any part of the land he must defend is something she must respect under the same instrument. Unless this Court is willing to say that citizenship of the United States means at least this much to the citizen, then our heritage of constitutional privileges and immunities is only a promise to the ear to be broken to the hope, a teasing illusion like a munificent bequest in a pauper's will." Jackson was rightfully pleased with himself.²⁶

He then enhanced his reputation as a liberal leader of the Court in the next term with his dazzling opinion in *West Virginia State Board of Education v. Barnette*.²⁷ He then followed with a powerfully articulated liberal sensibility two terms later in the important case of *Korematsu v. U.S.*, which during the fevered first years of the Second World War found as constitutional the military orders allowing for relocation and detention of Japanese-Americans.²⁸ Here Jackson was boldly in dissent, taking on the rest of the Court save Murphy in a majority opinion by Black and a concurring opinion by Frankfurter.

But what had started out so well for Jackson turned sour. Four years into his tenure on the High Court, he took leave of his judicial responsibility and at the request of President Truman served as America's lead prosecutor at the Nuremberg war crimes trial. What was expected to be a relatively brief leave from the Court ultimately lasted more than a year. He was everywhere involved—in determining the crimes with which the Nazi leaders would be charged, establishing the judicial procedures to be used, choosing a site for the trial, working out staggering logistical problems created by the many languages and represented countries, and actually trying the case.²⁹ He gave memorable opening and closing arguments and engaged in vigorous, if not always successful, cross-examination of some of the most important Nazi leaders. The trial, lasting 216 days, was a major production. For his contribution to the effort, Jackson was honored by the governments of several European countries. The University of Brussels conferred on him the degree of Doctor of Laws, and, fitting for the barristers he so closely resembled, he was installed as an Honorary Bencher of the Honorable Society of the Middle Temple of London.

It was while in Germany that Jackson erupted at being passed over for the center seat upon Stone's death and indelibly stained his own reputation by attacking his colleague, Hugo Black. Jackson vainly tried to couch the matter as one of principle as it related to Black's role in a pre-Nuremberg case, *Jewell Ridge Coal v. Local No. 6167* ³⁰ of nearly a year before, but his motivation was transparent.[31] In *Jewell Ridge* the Court had held for the union in its claim that compensable time should be portal to portal, that is, to include travel time to and from the mine itself. The losing mining company then sought reconsideration of the decision, arguing that Black should have recused himself on the grounds that he had once been the law partner of the union's counsel.

Black wanted the denial of this motion to enter without elaboration, but Jackson insisted in filing a memorandum with the order in which he distanced himself from the Court's decision. Black took this as an implicit criticism and an attack on his integrity. What really troubled Jackson, in fact, was Black's attempt to have the opinion deciding the case come down sooner rather than later and give the union some advantage in its ongoing negotiations with the company. Observers, however, have thought there had been nothing particularly wrong either in Black's sitting on the case or in whatever attempts he had made to push the decision along. Nothing else came of the matter at that time, and in the fall Jackson went off to Germany to prosecute Nazi war criminals.

Trouble broke out only when the chief justiceship was put into play. Chief Justice Stone died on April 22, 1946, which promptly triggered press speculation as to whom Truman would name as his successor. Many thought Jackson was the favorite. On May 16, however, Doris Fleeson wrote a *Washington Post* column in which she argued that there had been bitter discord on the Court relating to the *Jewell Ridge* case and that the president had been told by one senator that Black would resign if Jackson were named chief justice. The next day a Jackson ally wrote him that Black himself had told the president that he would resign, which, to Jackson, meant that he needed to act quickly to counteract Black's leverage. Jackson set out to write a letter to the president giving his side of the *Jewell Ridge* affair. But before he had sent this letter, Truman, on June 6, named Fred Vinson to be Chief Justice. Jackson reworked his letter to reflect the latest development and then cabled it to Truman. The cable became a virulent attack on Black, accusing him of extorting the president by threatening to resign if Jackson were appointed to the center seat.

While the contrary was clear to everyone else, Jackson persisted in arguing that his concern was for the principles behind the *Jewell Ridge* case. Committed, he could only press on. He sent a cable to Congress based on his cable to Truman. The cable ostensibly recounts the *Jewell Ridge* events as part of Jackson's argument that Black's actions compelled him to write his dissenting opinion, but Jackson's bruised ego and roiling emotions were all too apparent. He tried to portray himself as the Court's defender, but his transparent petulance and threat of reprisal revealed that his grudge was personal. "There may be those," he wrote, "who think it quite harmless to encourage employment of justices' ex-law partners to argue close cases by smothering objections which the bar makes to this practice. But in my view such an attitude soon would bring the court into disrepute. However an innocent a coincidence these two victories at successive terms by Justice Black's former law partner, I wanted that practice stopped. If it is ever repeated while I am on the bench I will make my *Jewell Ridge* opinion look like a letter of recommendation by comparison."[32] Never had a Supreme Court justice so embarrassed himself; never had a Supreme Court justice so misread what was at stake and the proper response to it.

⁓

Back on the bench, Jackson served seven more years until a heart attack felled him. He voted in more than 1,400 cases and wrote 318 opinions: 149 majority opinions, 36 concurring opinions, and 112 dissenting opinions.[33] But there was more, in the form of both extrajudicial writing and speaking engagements. Columbia University Press in 1945 published a Jackson lecture on the full faith and credit clause as a slender book,[34] and Harvard University Press in 1955 posthumously published his Godkin Lecture as *The Supreme Court in the American System of Government,* which was all but completed when Jackson died on October 9, 1954.[35] A second posthumous book is his 2003 *That Man: An Insider's Portrait of Franklin D. Roosevelt,*[36] though the success of this volume lies more with the editor, John Q. Barrett, than with Jackson. Jackson gave thirty-six addresses to a variety of audiences that were later published in legal journals and magazines.[37] He also wrote magazine and law review articles, including a historical tour de force on Falstaff's descendants in the Pennsylvania courts.[38]

His passing was marked in the *Columbia, Stanford,* and *Harvard Law Reviews* with memorial essays by those who knew him well, such as Felix Frankfurter, and with law review articles analyzing his body of judicial work by distinguished scholars such as Paul Freund, Charles Fairman, and Louis Jaffee.[39] Bench and bar leaders came together fifteen years after his passing with a series of lectures in his honor. They were published in book form by the Columbia University Press, with contributions by Charles Desmond, Paul Freund, Potter Stewart, and Lord Shawcross addressing various aspects of Jackson's career and jurisprudential thought.[40] In 1969, Glendon Schubert, the distinguished political scientist and commentator on the judicial mind and behavior, brought out a collection of Jackson's best and representative opinions, helping to extend Jackson's shelf life as a judicial writer.[41]

Jackson developed recognizable patterns in the cases he voted on. He voted with the Court 83.4 percent of the time, more often than any of his brethren.[42] He was above his average in both his first four terms on the Court, 1941–44, and in his first term after returning from Germany, 1946. He fell below his average for the next six terms, 1947–52, dropping in his lowest years to 71.8 and 72.2 percent respectively for the 1947 and 1948 terms. His average then continued to rise. His highest average, 98.3 percent, came in his last term on the Court, 1953. As for individual justices, Jackson had his favorites. Putting aside Justice Byrnes and Chief Justice Warren, with whom Jackson served with for only one year, Jackson, in descending order of frequency, voted most often with the majority opinions of Stone, Roberts, Frankfurter, and Reed.[43] He voted with each justice at a rate greater than the Court rate of 83.4 percent. He voted least often with Rutledge, Douglas, Burton, Clark, Murphy, and Black, with the frequency for each below his Court average. Here Jackson's voting pattern fluctuated as well over his tenure on the Court. He voted against majority opinions written by Black and Douglas far more often following his return from Germany than he did before going, while the rate with which Jackson voted with Frankfurter's majority opinions remained relatively constant throughout his tenure on the Court.[44] Not surprisingly, Jackson voted together with Black and Douglas least often. Turning the table, three Truman appointees—Minton, Vinson, and Clark—voted with Jackson's majority opinions most often, with Frankfurter in fourth place, coming in at a slightly lower rate.[45]

Jackson developed a recognizable judicial philosophy distinguished but not dominated by a belief in judicial restraint. As his voting patterns suggest, Jackson did not vote for restraint at the beginning of his tenure. He had made the case as assistant attorney general in 1937 to the Senate Judiciary Committee on the inadequacy of the Old Court in failing to exercise restraint when it invalidated the legislative efforts of the New Deal, and once given his own chance on the Court he adopted a position of judicial deference to congressional legislation, especially when it was economic legislation. No justice had a wider concept of the commerce clause, for example, which Jackson outlined early on in his tenure in the case of *Wickard v. Filburn,*[46] perhaps the high-water mark of the Court's nearly all embracive interpretation of what constitutes interstate commerce. He also believed in the widest application of the full faith and credit clause, as it, like the commerce clause, was vital to interstate commerce.[47] With this deference he looked first to the Congress for the interpretation of the important labor statutes, such as the National Labor Relations Act. But in related matters, he thought there was no formula for interpreting legislation. The words of statutes, he said, do not have "an automatic significance."[48] He thought a statute should be read "not narrowly as through a keyhole, but in the broad light of the evils it aimed at and the good it hoped for."[49]

How Jackson responded to the preferred position doctrine that was applied in First Amendment cases in the 1940s lies at the core of Jackson's view not only of civil liberties but also of the important subject of federalism. In the beginning, he vigorously supported the doctrine. He also explicitly invoked the preferred position doctrine in the Second Flag Salute case, which involved the First Amendment's free speech clause, to justify the Court's invalidation of a local school board rule that infringed upon the free speech rights of the schoolchildren. "It is important to distinguish," he wrote,

> between the due process clause of the Fourteenth Amendment as an instrument for transmitting the principles of the First Amendment and those cases in which it is applied for its own sake. The test of legislation which collides with the Fourteenth Amendment, because it also collides with the principles of the First, is much more definite than the test when only the Fourteenth is involved. Much of the vagueness of the due process clause disappears when the specific prohibitions of the First become its standard. The right of a state to regulate, for example, a public utility may well include, so far as the due process test is concerned, a power to impose all of the strictions which a legislature may have a "rational basis" for adopting. But freedoms of speech and of press, of assembly, and of worship may not be infringed

on such slender grounds. They are susceptible of restriction only to prevent grave and immediate danger to interests which the state may lawfully protect.[50]

Jackson's view of the preferred position doctrine began to change, however, following the Second Flag Salute case, most notably following his return from Germany in 1946, and he grew to disparage and even ridicule the doctrine.[51] Jackson joined with Frankfurter in advancing the two arguments Frankfurter had been making since he had dissented from the Second Flag Salute case and Jackson's own peroration on the importance of the doctrine. First, to give preferred status to any one of the provisions of the Bill of Rights is to perforce denigrate the others, cheapening the spirit and majesty of the Bill of Rights. Second, the imposition on the states of federal constitutional standards disrupted the delicate balance of federalism to which Jackson deeply adhered.

On the relationship between the Fourteenth Amendment and the Bill of Rights, Jackson also rejected the total incorporation theory advanced most notably by Black but supported by others as well. Federalism here is again the point. Late in his career, Jackson explained how the incorporation doctrine attacked his understanding of federalism. He wrote in a criminal case involving the issue of group libel, in which the constitutionality of a state law was challenged, that the "adoption of the incorporation theory today would lead us to the dilemma of either confining the States as closely as the Congress or giving the Federal Government the latitude appropriate to state governments . . . The inappropriateness of a single standard for restricting State and Nation is indicated by the disparity between their functions and duties in relation to those freedoms. Criminality of defamation is predicated upon power either to protect the private right to enjoy integrity of reputation or the public right to tranquility. Neither of these are objects of federal cognizance."[52]

The selective incorporation theory met the same fate as its more expansive cousin. Jackson expressed the concern that states would lose their chance to experiment in the administration of criminal justice if federal standards for various criminal procedure provisions were imposed on the states by way of the Fourteenth Amendment. In a case involving the way the state of New York selected its juries, Jackson wrote that "beyond requiring conformity to standards of fundamental fairness that have won legal recognition, this Court has been careful not so to interpret [the Fourteenth] Amendment as to impose uniform procedures upon the several states whose legal systems stem from diverse sources of law and reflect different historical influences. We adhere to this policy of self-restraint and will not use this great centralizing Amendment to standardize the administration of justice and stagnate local variations in practice."[53]

Once he had rejected the total and selective incorporation doctrines, Jackson grew increasingly to restrict the application of the Fourteenth Amendment to instances in which the claim was that a fair trial had not been possible for the defendant. The result is that he would let stand egregious invasions of a defendant's rights, such as in cases involving police interrogation, which he would not have tolerated if those same invasions had occurred as part of a federal rather than state prosecution. He grew increasingly entrenched in his view that different standards should be applied to state and federal prosecutions. The rights of the states to pursue what they thought was right in criminal matters should not be trampled upon, he argued. As he said in dissent in a case in which the Court reversed a state conviction on the grounds that the defendant's confession had been coerced, Jackson, taking the line that coerced confessions are not per se objectionable, writes that "the use of the due process clause to disable the States in protection of society from crime is quite as dangerous and delicate a use of federal judicial power as to use it to disable them from social or economic legislation."[54]

In another confession case, Jackson argued that if the Supreme Court insisted on second-guessing state appellate courts as to whether confessions should be invalidated, the states would be at risk in the war on crime.[55] He thought that the restrictions on the Fifth Amendment that the Court wanted to impose on the states went too far. In sounding an alarm that was by itself alarming for its tolerance of questionable police tactics, Jackson invoked the "ends justify the means" argument and wrote, "I doubt very much if [the Bill of Rights restrictions] require us to hold that the State may not take into custody and question one suspected reasonably of an unwitnessed murder. If it does, the people of this country must discipline themselves to seeing their police stand by helplessly while those suspected of murder prowl about unmolested. Is it a necessary price to pay for the fairness which we know as 'due process of law'? And if not a necessary one, should it be demanded by this Court? I do not know the ultimate answer to these questions; but for present, I should not increase the handicap on society."[56]

But at the same time, Jackson was vigilant in applying a higher than usual standard in Fourth Amendment cases. In the wake of his experience at Nuremberg, he wrote that "uncontrolled search and seizure is one of the first and most effective weapons in the arsenal of every arbitrary government. And one need only briefly to have dwelt and worked among a people possessed of many admirable qualities deprived of these [Fourth Amendment] rights to know that the human personality deteriorates and dignity and self-reliance disappear where homes, persons, and possessions are subject at any hour to an unheralded search and seizure by the police."[57]

Cutting against this passion for justice in criminal cases, including federal criminal cases, was Jackson's questionable stance that the extent of a defendant's rights is relative to the seriousness of the alleged crime. He wrote that "if we are to make judicial exceptions to the Fourth Amendment . . . it seems to me that they should depend somewhat upon the gravity of the offense. If we assume, for example, that a child is kidnapped and the officers throw a roadblock about the neighborhood and search every outgoing car, it would be a drastic and undiscriminating use of the search. . . . However, I should candidly strive hard to sustain such an action . . . if it was the only way to save a threatened life and detect a vicious crime. But I should not strain to sustain such a roadblock and universal search to salvage a few bottles of bourbon and catch a bootlegger."[58]

Unfortunately, Jackson has not been well served by his biographer and would-be biographers. Eugene Gerhart's 1958 effort is nothing more than hagiography and has value only because Gerhart recorded information from primary sources no longer available to biographers.[59] His biography exercises no critical judgment of Jackson and goes so far as to incorporate, without a proper disclosure to the reader, memorandums Jackson wrote in defense of his Nuremberg behavior.[60] But beyond an inadequate critical perspective, Gerhart's biography all but ignores Jackson's work on the Court, preferring instead to track Jackson's work in the Roosevelt administration and his service as the nation's chief prosecutor at Nuremberg. Gerhart later supplemented his biography with a slender, obscurely published volume that sought to detail Jackson's contributions to the Court.[61]

Former Frankfurter law clerk Philip Kurland had planned to write a biography that likely would have been commensurate with Jackson's importance to the Court, but Kurland, who took possession of the Jackson papers at the suggestion of Jackson's son, never completed the job, despite the proddings and assistance that Frankfurter himself provided. He collected massive amounts of material for the task, he noted in a symposium on judicial biography, but concluded that "the biographical job was well beyond [him, as it] required imagination and skills not readily available to the workaday law professor."[62] Instead, his biographical contribution has been the thirty-two page entry on Jackson in Friedman and Israel's *Justices of the Supreme Court*.[63] But here, in what could have been an independent biographical essay, Kurland chose instead to let Jackson speak for himself by relying heavily, to the near exclusion of other sources, on Jackson's oral history interview with the Columbia University Oral History Project and its interviewer, Harlan Phillips. Kurland, however, makes no critical assessment of the reliability of Jackson's oral history account of his life. The result is that Kurland presents Jackson as Jackson wanted to be remembered. As to Jackson's papers, they ultimately found their way to the Library of Congress and are awaiting a biographer.

Jackson's work on the Court has attracted limited assessment by scholars and commentators. Compared with Frankfurter, Black, and Douglas, he is by far the least written about. His most favorable notice came recently in David Currie's magisterial two-volume constitutional law history, in which Currie describes Jackson as "one of history's most illustrious Justices."[64] He praises Jackson's opinions in federal criminal law and procedure cases in which he sided with the defendant and his memorable opinion in the Second Flag Salute case. Most recently, Jackson's contribution to the Court's tax jurisprudence has been examined and praised.[65] Jackson's most unfavorable review came from Fred Rodell in his popular and influential 1955 book on the Supreme Court. Rodell wrote that Jackson's ambition and bitterness at not being named to replace Stone in 1946 pushed him further to the right and marked him as the "New Deal Court's most obvious turncoat-to-conservatism."[66] Rodell acknowledged and praised Jackson's gifts with language, only then to use them against him, arguing that without his gifts Jackson's career would have been distinguished by a more obvious interest in political conservatism and the self-serving maintenance of property rights.[67]

Among others assessing Jackson's career, G. Edward White devotes a chapter to him in his influential *The American Judicial Tradition.*[68] He concludes that Jackson did not handle particularly well the tension brought on by the Cold War between national security issues on the one hand and individual rights on the other. His rather damning assessment is that "his solutions were idiosyncratic and not particularly influential."[69] Jackson, for him, mirrored the contradictory jurisprudential impulses of the time. He brought personalized judging to the Court, reflecting the theme of the "legal realists," who believed that a judge's orientation more than any other factor influenced decisions, but who at the same time urged restraint on the Court.

Glendon Schubert, in the introduction to his collection of Jackson opinions, pointed to the major tension in Jackson's career on the bench when he noted that Jackson professed a belief that judges should bring neutrality and dispassion to their judging but that Jackson was, in contrast with his expressed ideal, a very human person on the bench. The result was, in Schubert's language of political science, a "dissonance between the ideal and the actual in adjudicative behavior."[70] As much as Schubert clearly admired Jackson and his opinions, he was, at the same time, willing to point to the demon of Jackson's ambition. "Jackson's judicial career," Schubert writes, providing a theme that Jackson commentators have all but ignored, "is the story of the denouement and dissolution (in no small measure masochistic) of his political ambitions."[71]

For his own part, Jackson was sensitive to others' perception of his work on the Court, as when he bristled at suggestions that his liberalism had been overtaken by his conservatism. When distinguished political scientist C. Herman Pritchett made this argument in his study of the Court, Jackson acknowledged that Pritchett had tried to be fair in the way he determined the justices to be either liberal or conservative on various issues, but he nevertheless makes it clear in a letter to a hometown friend that the matter is not so easily settled. "Then there is a unique way of determining whether a judge is a 'liberal.' If he voted for the defendant in any case in which [the] defendant raised a civil rights question, he is called a liberal; if he voted against the question, he is called a conservative. The assumption that every man who wants to get out of jail is right every time he raises some questions about civil rights, seems a rather naive standard."[72]

His irritation at what he considered false labeling was more apparent in a letter to Wiley Rutledge when Rutledge described restraint exercised by the Court as "a policy of strict conservatism." Jackson wrote Rutledge that the description left him "a bit groggy," as he was unsure whether it was "intended as compliment or an epithet." After all, he wrote, when conservatism during the 1930s was most practiced on the Court, "the self-denying attitude was the 'liberal' attitude. Perhaps," he added, "this is simply a reflection of the confusion of the era."[73]

Jackson was also sensitive to the praise of others, especially when he was found wanting by comparison. He was jealous, for example, of the praise Black received from commentators such as Fred Rodell, the Yale Law School professor who frequently wrote for national magazines on Court-related issues. In 1944 Rodell wrote a piece on Hugo Black for the *American Mercury* that described Black as the nation's most influential legal figure. He compared him favorably to Holmes and concluded that history "may yet record that the quiet country boy from Alabama gave more to the growth of American law than any man since Chief Justice Marshall more than a century ago."[74]

Rodell included a criticism of Jackson on his way to praising Black. "Only three of the other Justices fail to recognize Black as the ablest legal judge and the most brilliant legal mind among them," Rodell wrote.[75] One was Roberts, who was out of place on the Roosevelt Court; another was Frankfurter, who had proved a disappointment to the liberals who advanced him for the Supreme Court. The third was Jackson, who saw Black as standing in his way. With cutting language, Rodell writes that Jackson "plays along with Frankfurter, for his White House influence, in dwindling hope of being named Chief Justice, an honor he once missed by a hair; for he is smart enough to see in Black the biggest threat to his ambition."[76] Rodell then not only skewered Jackson in his Supreme Court study *Nine Men*,[77] he used the contrast between Jackson and Black to support his theme of judicial virtue and vice.

It is unlikely, however, given the book's actual publication in 1955, that Jackson ever saw any part of it before his death in October 1954. What Rodell had said in 1944 was enough, however, to linger in Jackson's mind and to prompt his enduring hatred of him. That he wrote scathing marginal comments on the article is one indication of Jackson's response. Another comes from Jackson's widow, who in 1955 wrote to Frankfurter to thank him for his kind words in his *Columbia* and *Harvard Law Review* tributes.

She makes a point of contrasting Frankfurter's sentiments with uncharitable ones that had been published in Jackson's life, referring specifically to the hated Fred Rodell and the damning attack he had made on her husband.[78]

By all accounts Jackson away from the Court was a man with many friends. This was a principal theme of the proceedings before the Supreme Court in Jackson's honor upon his passing. One speaker noted, for example, that "[f]riendliness was one of his outstanding characteristics. It is safe to say that no member of the Court in our history has had a wider circle of intimate and devoted friends among lawyers and jurists all over the world."[79] The speakers described the frequency with which he gave public addresses to the bar and public alike throughout his career, including his time on the Supreme Court, and the many friends he made. But the frequency of Jackson's speech making only partly explained his extensive web of friendships. There was also his personality. Speakers described his wit, affability, and good humor. Frankfurter identified another element of Jackson's engaging personality when he wrote in a memorial essay for the *Harvard Law Review* that Jackson "was ineluctably charming, but his charm was not a surface glitter."[80]

Jackson preferred the outdoors for his leisure activities. Throughout his adulthood, he found satisfaction and solace in activities of his youth. He liked to hike, to fish, to shoot, and to ride horses. While at the Court, he lived in a county rural enough in nearby Virginia to own several horses. He was fond of boating and camping. Toward the end of his life he frequently spent part of his summer vacation in California, where a camping companion was none other than former president Herbert Hoover.

A lifelong reader, Jackson's reading habits were strained by his judicial work. He reported that on the Court he was able to read widely but not deeply. The most he could do was dip into books, he said. He thought that the reading required of a justice was oppressive, so much so that they should be given sabbaticals occasionally "to be devoted entirely to reading up on the facts of life."[81] In contrast, Jackson said, he had far more time for reading when he practiced law in Jamestown.

As for the quality of his reading, he gives glimpses in his correspondence that he read with sensitivity for tone, irony, and subtle meaning. In a letter to Bernard Baruch, for example, he gives a thoughtful reading to Bacon's *Essays*. In part he writes, "the great Lord Chancellor and Attorney General has always fascinated me, and I hope to get the time to make a detailed study of his philosophy and career. A man who vowed that he was 'fitted for nothing so well as to the study of truth' and who confessed that as Lord Chancellor he took bribes, but never delivered anything for the bribe and often decided cases against the briber, had a most complex personality, to say the least. The most severe condemnation of his conduct came from himself, which at least saves posterity from moralizing about his derelictions, for no one could outdo him. I often think of the opening lines of his first essay, 'Of Truth': 'What is truth' said jesting Pilate; and would not stay for an answer.' I wonder if Pilate could have gotten an answer by staying?"[82] The temptation is to say that Jackson succeeded in applying the truths to his own life that he derived from reading about others, but there is little evidence of that, on at least this issue of self-awareness flagged by Bacon.

Jackson had a biting wit and a ready quip. On one occasion during a Court session, for example, one of the lawyers arguing his case noted that there were two clocks in the chamber, one in the front and one in the rear, and that they did not agree, making it difficult for him to know how much time he had left to him, he said. "Well," Jackson retorted, "possibly that is the influence of the atmosphere of the Court."[83] As an advocate, Jackson was once arguing a tax case in the Supreme Court that turned on whether the taxpayer's gift of money was taxable as a gift in anticipation of death. Crusty Justice McReynolds asked if it were not true that the gift at issue took place when the taxpayer, a Scotsman, was still vigorous. "Exactly so, your Honor," Jackson answered. "And on this point the government bases its case. Being a Scotsman, the respondent would not have given away his money except in anticipation of death." An appreciative Court, including McReynolds, laughed.[84]

On the Court, Jackson was a loner who cultivated that image. Douglas thought that Jackson "was a lone wolf on the court, with no close friend except Frankfurter."[85] In his first years on the Court, Jackson even worked at home, in the tradition of the justices before the new Supreme Court building opened in 1934, a habit only Chief Justice Stone shared.[86] Jackson was fond of quoting his favorite line of poetry, from Kipling, that "he travels farthest who travels alone."[87] He acknowledged in a speech as well that "by temperament he was an individualist."[88] Jackson was certainly not one to seek the counsel of others. Most tellingly, he consulted no one before he acted as he did in the Black affair. As he told Harlan Phillips, "I consulted nobody. Nobody knew that I was issuing [the cable]. If anybody had been consulted, they probably would have urged me not to do it."[89]

Jackson could count only a few of his brethren as friends. Frankfurter reports that he was close to Minton and to Byrnes,[90] though Jackson's correspondence provides little evidence of this. He was close enough to Stanley Reed that on one occasion Jackson and his wife, Irene, spent a week with Reed and his wife at Reed's Long Island property, but, again, his correspondence with Reed reveals little of a personal relationship. By all accounts, there was a genuine friendship between Jackson and Frankfurter, who seems to have been Jackson's closest friend. For his part, Frankfurter considered Jackson to have been "a delectable colleague,"[91] his "oasis in the desert."[92] He conspired with Jackson against Black and Douglas, and at least one commentator has written that Frankfurter considered Jackson his intellectual equal,[93] a position that is difficult to square, however, with Frankfurter's elitism. Jackson revealed his closeness with Frankfurter by on occasion bringing him into an orbit of intimacy not shared by anyone else. When Jackson's world was coming apart in Germany, for example, Jackson wrote to Frankfurter within days of his outburst and provided him with an inside, and most likely true, account of what had happened to him. He may not have consulted Frankfurter as to what he should do—indeed, he consulted no one—but he did confide to Frankfurter that his outburst had been the function of desperation and audacity.[94]

Additional, more important evidence of Jackson's friendship with Frankfurter comes from Harlan Phillips in 1955, who had interviewed Jackson for the Columbia University Oral History Project and who was at the same time also in the process of interviewing Frankfurter for the same project. Phillips knew how Jackson had felt about Frankfurter and thought it important that he write Frankfurter several months after Jackson's death to pass on the information. "He told me once," Phillips writes, "that the only caller—and he had many—whose talk and companionship he 'thoroughly enjoyed' was you. Whatever and however deep the differences mattered not. What was important to him was the clash of minds, the full and free discussion which ensued, which gave him opportunity to hone his ready blade, freshen his insight and bedevil you with 'Jamestown Jurisprudence.' He loved to rassle with your quality, and, I suspect, this was the only kind of love unhappy circumstance permitted him."[95]

Jackson hated Black and Douglas and disparaged both. He saw them as trying to manipulate other justices and to take control of the Court. As early as 1942 Jackson was bitterly complaining to Frankfurter about the efforts of Douglas and Black to have Murphy and then Rutledge join them in cases.[96] He complained as well of the advantage they both took of Roberts, known to all to be naive in his appreciation of the motives of his brethren. Moreover, he went further in conference and acted on his dislike for them. According to Douglas, Jackson spewed venom at Black. Douglas explains that Jackson had the highest praise for Black when Black was appointed to the Court, "but having come on the court and starting working on a team of nine, he developed this very quickly, this animosity to Black. Whether it was a feeling of Jackson that he should be the leader of the liberal block and he finally found himself more and more on the other side, in the minority, or associated with so-called conservative decisions, I just don't know. But it was very evident in almost all our conferences that Bob Jackson thoroughly disliked Hugo Black and was out to destroy him. I mean destroy him in the sense of discrediting him. And his words were very acid, very derogatory. A lot of that carried over to me also but Black, I think, was his primary target."[97]

Jackson had a rare gift with language. Others on the Court have written smoothly, eloquently, and even elegantly. Others, as well, have been able to turn a phrase, to employ a figure of speech effectively. Holmes, who could do all of this and more, is generally considered to be the finest writer ever to sit on the Court, but his prose is a world apart from Jackson's. Holmes had an Olympian view of life and the law, and his prose, with its smoothness, detachment, and elegance, reflected that attitude. Jackson, on the other hand, wanted his reader to know that he was very much of the same world the reader inhabited. Jackson's was a muscular, concrete, tactile prose that in its purest expressions startles the reader with its vigor, edge, and essence. What Holmes once wrote of Kipling applies equally well to Jackson: "[h]e puts his fist into the guts of the dictionary, pulls out the utterly unavailable and makes it a jewel in his forehead or flesh of his flesh with no effort or outlay except of the pepsin that makes it part of him."[98]

Jackson's prose makes the language of the law become something few have associated with it. His prose merges the distance between language and idea and suggests to the reader that the way Jackson has expressed an idea is the only possible expression of it. At its best, Jackson's prose gives life to the language of the law and shows it not as a distinct branch of learning or science but as life in its essence. He achieved an immediacy with the language of his opinions that has not been equaled by anyone sitting on the Court. Consider, for example, this brief snippet from Justice Jackson's most notable majority opinion in the Second Flag Salute case.[99] Wisdom, learning, and style come together for Justice Jackson when he writes that

> struggles to coerce uniformity of sentiment in support of some end thought to be essential to their time and country have been waged by many good men as well as by evil men. Nationalism is a relatively recent phenomenon but at other times and places the ends have been racial or territorial security, support of a dynasty or regime, and particular plans for saving souls. As first moderate methods to attain unity have failed, those bent on its accomplishment must resort to an ever-increasing severity. As governmental pressure toward unity becomes greater, so strife becomes more bitter as to whose unity it shall be. Probably no deeper division of our people could proceed from any provocation than from finding it necessary to choose what doctrine and whose program public educational officials shall compel youth to unite in embracing. Ultimate futility of such attempts to compel coherence is the lesson of every such effort from the Roman drive to stamp out Christianity as a disturber of its pagan unity, the Inquisition, as a means to religious and dynastic unity, the Siberian exiles as a means to Russian unity, down to the fast failing efforts of our present totalitarian enemies. Those who begin coercive elimination of dissent soon find themselves exterminating dissenters. Compulsory unification of opinion achieves only the unanimity of the graveyard.[100]

Part of Jackson's gift for writing was his ability to recognize the dramatic moment and to seize and exploit it. This bespoke his supreme confidence in pairing language with idea and, as a related element, his desire to feature himself. Jackson was a man who wanted to be noticed. He knew he had the gift of language and sought to display it. He exhibited this trait even as a boy. A local lawyer in Jackson's youth describes for us how this desire to shine presented itself. "I recall the first time I ever saw 'Bob' as we, in Chautauqua County, call him," he told Jackson's biographer, Eugene Gerhart. "As a (then) young lawyer, I was called to Frewsburg, his home town, to sit on a board of judges in a high school debate between Frewsburg and Sinclairville. The debate was going very well indeed for Sinclairville until the last speaker for Frewsburg burst into a song. He was a mere stripling of a boy, wore knee pants, as I recall, and was not more than fourteen years old. Holy Moses! You should have heard that boy debate. I was astounded."[101]

Jackson as an adult did not burst into song to carry the day. Instead, he broke into his glorious prose. There is little question but that Jackson took the Nuremberg post because it would give him a world stage, one from which he could advance his judicial, and perhaps even political, ambitions. What better place to display rhetorical flourishes commensurate with the occasion? In his closing argument at the war crimes trial, with the world as his audience, he concluded with a pairing of the acts of the greatest villain of literature, Gloucester in Shakespeare's *Richard III,* with their counterpart in life, the reign of terror of Hitler's Nazism. About the defendants, he said, "they stand before the record of this trial as bloodstained Gloucester stood by the body of his slain King. He begged of the widow, as they beg of you: 'Say I slew them not.' And the Queen replied, 'Then say they are not slain. But dead they are . . .' If you were to say of these men that they are not guilty, it would be as true to say there has been no war, there are no slain, there has been no crime."[102]

But even though he was a fine writer, Jackson's correspondence makes for surprisingly dull reading. His circle of correspondents was not particularly wide—certainly not as wide as Frankfurter's. He wrote most often to a select few lawyers and friends from his Jamestown days. In these letters he stays away from Court topics and restricts himself to fond recollections of his time in Jamestown and the outdoor activities he had shared and continued to share with his friends. His tone is amiable, though slightly stiff. Wit and humor make only rare appearances. He adopts a businesslike tone for most of his other correspondence, showing enthusiasm of any sort only occasionally. In a long letter to the English barrister Norman Birkett, who had been a judge at Nuremberg, for example, Jackson brightens and chatters on about political and personal topics, clearly trying to impress Birkett.[103] His pattern generally is to keep correspondents at a distance by assuming poses, as when he feigns a lack of interest in any job other than the one he has.

One of the few correspondents with whom Jackson seems to be himself was the lawyer and former solicitor general John W. Davis.[104] Jackson's sincerity and personal candor in his letter to Davis describing his feelings about the solicitor general position and about Davis as a lawyer and person might be due to the gap in their ages and Davis's stature. Davis was not a rival, which likely released Jackson to reveal more of himself.

Jackson was an active, though not particularly quick, opinion writer. His average of 12.41 majority opinions per term was slightly below the full Court's average of 13.03 per justice.[105] His averages of 3.0 concurring and 9.33 dissenting opinions per term were above the Court averages of 2.53 and 8.84 respectively. A study of the Vinson Court found that Jackson took an average of fifty-five days to write his majority opinions, while the Court's average was fifty-one days.[106] He ranked as the fifth quickest opinion writer. One law clerk described Jackson's work habits this way.

> He has a natural flair for writing, but the smoothness of his opinions comes as much from working over as from his natural style and ability. We would often go through 4 or 5 typewritten and hand-corrected drafts before sending anything to the printer—and then three or four versions were printed before we circulated anything to the Brethren. Often a draft changes hands twice a day here for several days in a row—he of course writes the draft, gives it to me for suggestions, criticisms, and checking; I have an absolutely free hand to do whatever I will with it, and he buys what he likes, discarding the rest. But he receives all criticism fairly and welcomes all suggestions. Once he has produced a draft of course, I drop everything else and see what I can do with it. So it often happens that he gives it to me at 9 AM; I give it back at 6 PM; and I find it back on my desk the following morning; and another round begins. He is a great worker. And he respects others who work, even if he disagrees with the results they produce.[107]

One of Stanley Reed's law clerks, on the other hand, recalls that Jackson had the ability to write a fifteen- or twenty-page opinion straight through, without any difficulty, and then have that opinion appear in print without much modification.[108]

Jackson, almost from the beginning, was not happy on the Court. There was the happiness and contentment following Jackson's opinion in *Edwards v. California,* but ironically, as Jackson was apparently leading a newly directed Court in the Second Flag Salute, forces were already in play that were deeply dividing Jackson from the duo of Black and Douglas and the group of liberal justices they led. Jackson's life on the Court was never again the same once it was clear to him that Black and Douglas were moving to control the Court.

This is no mere speculation. In a 1942 diary entry Frankfurter quotes Jackson's complaint with Black, Douglas, and their cohort Murphy. Even at this early stage of his Supreme Court career, Jackson is making noise about retiring from the Court. Frankfurter writes that "[i]n the afternoon Jackson, in the course of a talk about the problems before the Court, again reverted to his own very great unhappiness on the Court. He said, 'I have a rather long expectancy of life and I don't know whether I want to spend it in this atmosphere. It is an awful thing at this time of the Court's and country's history, with the very difficult and important questions coming before this Court, to have one man, Black, practically controlling three others, for I am afraid Rutledge will join the Axis. But on the other hand, I say to myself it would be rather cowardly to leave the field to them. But I can tell you that it is very sad business for me and it isn't any fun to be writing opinions to show up some of their performances.'"[109]

Achilles-like in his tent, Jackson again considered retiring from the Court in 1946, in the wake of his fiasco in Germany involving Black and the chief justiceship. In the days after Jackson's cables from Nuremberg, some newspapers argued that both Jackson and Black should resign to relieve the pent-up pressure on the Court. Frankfurter promptly wrote to Jackson in Germany and advised against resignation.[110] With equal promptness, Jackson responded to Frankfurter in a revealing letter. "It is easy to say that I should not resign," Jackson begins. "But the question is whether this is a good use of one's life. I am certain that the position on the Bench would have been intolerable if I had not taken this audacious and desperate step. I am not sure it will be tolerable after it."

Black, in Jackson's mind, was the enemy. "Black," he writes, "is now rid of the Chief, whose reputation as a liberal made his opposition particularly effective and irritating. Black, as you and I know, has driven Roberts off the Bench and pursued him after his retirement. Now if he can have it understood that he has a veto over the promotion of any Associate, he would have things about where he wants them." Jackson was especially bleak about his future on the Court because he sensed that public opinion is both with Black and indifferent to his version of the story.[111] The effect the incident had on Jackson himself was obvious even to those outside the Court. Max Lerner, for example, wrote in 1950 that "the ever more frequent ironic smile that plays about his lips, and has become almost settled there, reveals his role. On a Court full of individualists he is the supreme one . . . [Since his return from Nuremberg] the edge of outrage and contempt has been added to an already sharp style. To read his opinions is to delight in the literary result while mourning the personal bitterness and frustrations that give rise to it."[112]

In Douglas's version of Jackson's career, however, Jackson was unhappy from the beginning due to his bitterness at not being chosen as chief justice. Douglas, pointing to Jackson's behavior in conference not only toward Stone but also to his successor, Chief Justice Vinson, offers a different interpretation of Jackson's reaction at not being named chief justice, not once but twice, and the effect it had on him. In an expanded assessment of Jackson's ambition for the center seat in which he gives new details about Jackson's behavior at conference, Douglas begins with the premise that Jackson had been promised by Roosevelt that he would be appointed chief justice upon Hughes's retirement.[113] When Stone was instead made chief justice and Jackson an associate justice, Jackson, according to Douglas, had been promised the next time around. Douglas recounts that:

> Jackson was satisfied that he had been promised that while he couldn't be Chief Justice after Hughes, he would be Chief Justice after Stone. How good or great a Chief Justice Bob Jackson would have made nobody knows, but it was a force that worked in him to make him extremely disagreeable to the regime of another Chief Justice. It was true under Stone. Jackson was more and more irritated with Stone, more and more curt, more and more disrespectful, and then, of course, Roosevelt died and his promise to make Bob the next Chief Justice was not kept by Truman, who may or may not have known about it. I don't think Truman liked Jackson anyway. And under Vinson, the Chief Justice that Truman named, the relationship between

Bob and Vinson was a very unhappy one. Vinson told me one day that he thought that anyone who sat in the chair of the Chief Justice, as long as Jackson was on the Court, would get about the same kind of treatment that he, Vinson, was receiving from Jackson, which was one of curtness, disrespect, flying up to little inconsequential things, harboring apparently inside him a great resentment that the man who sat in the chair of the Chief Justice was not Bob Jackson. It did, I think, have a side effect on Bob Jackson's whole life. He became morose and bitter. He was not the happy, freewheeling, ebullient, friendly person that we had known as Solicitor General and later as Attorney General.[114]

As staggeringly unprofessional as it was, Jackson's behavior toward his brethren at not being made chief justice in some ways was almost predictable. From the beginning of his professional career Jackson did not take kindly to not getting what he wanted, not getting what he deserved, or, for that matter, being challenged or directly attacked, to say nothing of being singled out for what he considered to be personal attacks. There was, to put the matter differently, a wide prima donna streak in Jackson. That he could in his Jamestown practice lose a trial and be forced to bring an appeal as an appellant could prompt him to pepper his brief with intemperate language.

Richard Posner reports that he encountered such briefs when he researched his book on Cardozo and the appellate court he sat on and to which Jackson would file his appeal.[115] Jackson filed a trial brief on a procedural point filled with intemperate language in his tax prosecution of Andrew Mellon (or at least that was the way Jackson characterized the contents of his opponent's motion and brief).[116] When the court granted Mellon's motion to strike Jackson's brief from the record because it contained the offensive intemperate language—a ruling, of course, suggesting that the language was indeed intemperate—Jackson, in a favorite ploy of his, offered to resign, an offer that the secretary of the treasury turned down.[117] Instead, he gave Jackson what he likely thought Jackson was implicitly asking for, a reaffirmation that the secretary still thought highly of him and that he wanted Jackson to continue with the prosecution in the manner that he, Jackson, saw fit.[118]

He threatened to resign again when, as solicitor general, he was not being promoted through the Department of Justice ranks as quickly as he wanted. He might have recognized that Roosevelt was playing a game of musical chairs in trying to shuffle cabinet positions and Supreme Court appointments, but that did not stop him from complaining to Harold Ickes and getting Ickes to pass along both Jackson's frustration, impatience, and threat to resign if he was not soon satisfied. After all, he argued, the promotion to the Court had been promised to him. Tom Corcoran, one of Roosevelt's fixers, had to come in to calm Jackson down and keep him from going directly to Roosevelt. Luckily for Jackson, a death and a resignation on the Court cleared the way for his appointment.[119]

These two examples portray the adult Jackson responding to disappointment and frustration and are of course instructive. The third and perhaps most telling example comes from Jackson's young adulthood. With this example we can be sure that the other examples are not aberrations and that Jackson indeed counted petulance as one of his closest friends. This third example comes at the very beginning of his professional career and relates to what Jackson perceived to be a political slight. Jackson was all of twenty-one years old when in 1912 he was serving as something of an adjunct to the executive committee of his local Democratic county committee in New York, which had been created primarily to prosecute the 1912 campaign. The committee, following the campaign, adopted procedures that centered the power to appoint Democrats to various positions in its power elite and sent out letters to committee officials such as Jackson advising them of this position. Jackson saw this move as a way of freezing him out of the power structure and sent a blistering letter to the chairman of the committee that is so streaked with the anger, petulance, and indignation that characterized his cable from Nuremberg in 1946 that it needs to be quoted at length.

Jackson opens the letter with a sarcastic tone that continues throughout the letter. He assumes that his position has been filled and notes that, if it has not, the committee should consider his letter to "constitute his resignation as such." Then the accusations begin to fly, with Jackson's emotions getting the best of him. The committee, in arrogating to itself the authority to endorse candidates, has acted impertinently, he claims, a position that is particularly galling since the party and the committee had neglected Jackson's own city of Jamestown during the campaign, ensuring defeat. That the party has seen fit not to endorse him will not silence him, he warns. He will, despite the party, make his own views of candidates known. He cannot be controlled.

He writes, "I am not deceived as to the value of my endorsement [to possible candidates]. I know a more worthless one could scarcely be obtained. But such as it is, it will be given irrespective of the views of this imitation Tammany. The fact that a man has found favor with your committee will not alone win him my humble help, nor that he may be unpopular with you will not cause it to be denied. I shall not be found taking a straw vote of support for party position to determine whether a friend is worthy of my support for party position. If a man be of that type which public life so needs, and so seldom gets, I am willing to enlist in his cause tho he be opposed by all mysterious 'powers' that shape our politics. And if an appointment be pending which seems to be improper, I shall marshall every available resource to defeat the prospective appointee tho he be the momentary idol of the executive committee. If a candidate have your support he will not need mine, yours refused, mine is valueless—but I prefer it to count for nothing than to be given only at the committee's command. In other words, I don't care to play the game according to your rules."

Wanting to be defined by his virtue and belief in principles, Jackson's conclusion blends ridicule with sarcasm as he tries to hide his anger, humiliation, and disappointment. He writes: "I know full well how little my views will influence party conduct. I am, however, confident that the wildest endorsement I might make would compare favorably as to the aspirant's character, qualification and availability with some that have heretofore been made by the members of your eminent erstwhile committee. The distribution of party patronage is something which I do not care to influence further than this: As a party we are not to be criticized because Republicans are displaced by Democrats, it is the kind of Democrats who are appointed that will win or lose the next election. And I do not want the appointments of any organization to discredit the principles of government in which I believe and for the success of which I am willing to make almost any sacrifice. Further than this and the possession of a hearty contempt for office seekers as a class, I have no interest in the general job hunt." It is perhaps with the closing that Jackson most reveals himself. With petulance, he writes, "[t]hanking your committee for its 'advice' and assuring you that it will be most cordially disregarded, I am, Yours truly . . ."[120]

Here, then, at the beginning we find the same Jackson who was unable to control himself thirty-five years later. That the letter is the oldest letter in his general correspondence file in his Library of Congress papers by some ten years suggests that Jackson considered the incident particularly important. We find a power in the prose of this letter that is matched only by the depth of his anger. It shows that when the issue is the denial of career advancement, Jackson's core emotions are revealed. True to the suggestions of his letter, he never sought a political post after that, making it easier for us to understand his performance on the Court once the prize there had been denied him. The letter is a tour de force of anger and denunciation, relying, beyond its sparkling prose, on threats, sarcasm, righteousness, condescension, and derision. He is a wounded, rejected person of worth who finds conspiracies among those excluding him. The approach, if not the language itself, eerily foreshadows the Nuremberg outburst.

Jackson's hatred of Douglas and especially of Black could have been heightened in part by Jackson's resentment that they were able to exert themselves in ways that were apparently beyond him. Jackson, we learn from those around him, lacked the political instincts that defined Black and Douglas. Ickes recognized these political failings and was joined in his assessment by none other than Roosevelt, the consummate politician. In one diary entry, Ickes, after noting that Jackson "undoubtedly has great qualities," gives us Roosevelt's and then his own assessment of Jackson as a politician. "The President says that he does not have political 'it' and probably this is true. Tom Corcoran, who wants him to work into the leadership of the Democratic party, thinks that his one fault is that he is too likely to become discouraged. He has not yet learned to stand up under fire directed at him personally with all the equanimity in the world. But every leader has some faults, and these of Jackson's, even if they be admitted, are trivial as compared with what they might be. My respect and liking for him grow every time I see him."[121] Ickes then contrasts Jackson with Douglas, writing, "Douglas, too, is a fighting liberal. He is quicker on the uptake than Jackson, and I believe that he is thoroughly sound, although I do not know whether he has Jackson's steadfast qualities. Probably he can 'take it' better than J."[122]

Sixteen months later, following the nominating convention in which Farley had kept Jackson off the center stage by blocking plans for Jackson to give the keynote address to the convention, Ickes then cuts closer to Jackson's fundamental weakness—passivity. "I saw a good deal of Bob Jackson in Chicago and in different circumstances than at any other time," Ickes writes. "I discovered that he is far from aggressive, but disposed to accept what comes along without really fighting for a different result even when he finds himself in dissent. I did not really find out just how he regarded Harry Hopkins and his activities. That he was unhappy about the tone and temper of the convention there was no doubt and he was willing to go along with others in an effort to take control of the convention from Jim Farley. But he would never have been active, even though willing to go along. He did give expression to the remark that I have quoted about Harry Hopkins' purloined plan to have Lester Hill nominate the President. And he left for the East without enthusiasm before Henry Wallace was nominated." Ickes concludes, "I have not changed my opinion about Bob's ability or his fundamental liberalism, but I do have a different view as to his qualities of leadership. He is more of a lawyer than an aggressive leader. If he is ever to become President I hope that he will develop a disposition not only to stand for what is right but to fight for it."[123]

Roosevelt agreed with Ickes's assessment of Jackson's deficient political instincts. Following Roosevelt's reelection, Ickes on December 1, 1940, again raises the notion that Jackson is presidential material. He tells Roosevelt that he can see only Douglas or Jackson as possible successors in 1944. In response, Roosevelt identifies what Jackson lacks as a politician, making a favorable assessment of Douglas's political talents in the process, something that would have cut Jackson to the quick. "The President said in effect, this: 'It is a funny thing about Bob Jackson. He can make a perfectly magnificent speech, but he cannot do the sort of thing that you and I can do . . . But Bob Jackson is too much of a gentleman. You and I are not. He seems to lack some fundamental fighting quality.'"[124]

By his own admission, Jackson took the Nuremberg job to relieve his unhappiness at the Court and to give himself fully to his ambition with a larger stage to showcase his talents. Jackson wanted to be where the action was. He told Harlan Phillips, his oral history interviewer, that he "accepted [the Nuremberg job] because in the first place there was relief at the frustration at being in a back eddy with important things going on in the world. I'd be less than candid if I did not admit that influence."[125] Moreover, he told Phillips that "if internal matters at the Court had been pleasant and agreeable, and if I had not already considered leaving the Court, I probably would not have undertaken it. All things considered, I don't know but what it might prove to be a good exit from the Court, and I wasn't all that sure that . . . I would ever return to the Court."[126]

Jackson's frustration with his work at Nuremberg likely spilled over and helped spark his outburst at Black. Jackson disputed this but in the process revealed its likely truth. In his oral history interview, Jackson, in setting out the unfolding events of the feud, notes that Drew Pearson had raised the notion that Jackson was under enormous strain in Nuremberg and that this strain resulted in an irresponsible act—the cable condemning Black—for which there was no rational explanation. "Well," Jackson continued, "I may have been mentally irresponsible." This, at least, was what Jackson said to Harlan Phillips. When Phillips sent the transcribed interview to Jackson for review, Jackson then deleted this revealing, if not incriminating, statement.[127] That Jackson likely had been in the state of mind he described, but later suppressed that fact, is made clear by Jackson's statement to Frankfurter soon after the cable that he had acted desperately and audaciously.

Jackson's disavowal of what he had said about Nuremberg in his oral history interview is perhaps the most dramatic example of his pattern, throughout his interview, to rationalize or to explain self-servingly all that had gone wrong in his career. His approach is to deny interest in events or positions that disappointed. Added to the mix are healthy doses of historical revisionism. He says, for example, that he gave up his job on the Democratic State Committee when he was in his early twenties not because he felt slighted but because the committee job was cutting into his law practice.[128] Rather than admit to the frustration and bitterness he expressed to Ickes and others when various promotions were slow in coming, he says that he was happy with his various posts in the Roosevelt administration and that he had told the president that he was happy to wait his turn for promotion.[129]

As for his appointment to the Supreme Court, he says, first, that he agreed with Roosevelt that he should come on as an associate justice and, second, that Roosevelt never promised him the center seat upon Stone's retirement.[130] Not becoming chief justice did not trouble him, he says. He had never in his life gone seeking a job, and he wasn't going to seek that one out.[131] He argued that he was, in fact, better off as an associate justice, since the associate justices actually have a better time of it when the chief justice's other responsibilities are considered.[132] His account of the Nuremberg incident and his feud with Black was that it had all flowed from an issue of principle and that he had been right in acting as he did. He says that he would probably, if he had it to do again, act the same way.[133]

The extent to which Jackson tried to use his oral history to shape the assessment others made of him appears most markedly in the exaggerated significance he gave to his Nuremberg experience. In his oral history he continued the line he had been advancing in his correspondence and elsewhere upon his return from Germany that his work at Nuremberg was the most important work of his career.[134] Even before going to Germany, Jackson had tried to deflect attention away from his work on the Court by claiming that his work as solicitor general had been the most important work he had done. But with his work at Nuremberg done, he consistently pointed to it as the measure of his legacy.

Given what Jackson had said at various times about the great good that a Supreme Court justice can do in the promotion of a healthy democracy and society, it is difficult to believe what Jackson says about his Nuremberg work. The judgment of many, both at the time and historically, is that Nuremberg was a deeply flawed attempt at justice. It could hardly qualify as justice, critics contended, since the prosecuting authorities after the fact devised the crimes, the procedures, and the punishments. It was little more than the victors exercising their power over the conquered, albeit for a salutary reason. Moreover, it was not as though the results were ever in doubt. Jackson was well aware of these criticisms but brushed them aside.[135] His desire to shine was likely too great to resist the opportunity at the time it was offered, and later he had too much to gain by exaggerating its significance to acknowledge that the idea itself was fundamentally flawed. The result in the oral history was that Jackson argued for the importance of Nuremberg as a way of fashioning an image of himself that would obscure the mess he had made on the Supreme Court.

Contradictions lie at the center of Jackson. A fundamental contradiction undergirding both Jackson the man and the way he has been remembered is that this man with the public touch, this man who was remembered in part for having so many friends, was, by his own admission and by his behavior, a loner who did not form intimate friendships easily, if at all. But there were contradictions in Jackson's life and career that went well beyond the contradiction relating to the theme of friendship.

There was also a fundamental contradiction in Jackson's acceptance of the Nuremberg job. The expectation of the trials, of course, was that the Nazi war criminals would be tried, found guilty of war crimes, and then hanged. Jackson, however, personally opposed the imposition of the death penalty. He made this position clear in *Louisiana ex rel. Francis v. Resweber*,[136] a case in which the issue was whether the due process clause prohibited a state's second attempt at an execution when the first attempt failed. Jackson wrote a concurring opinion that he never published in which he began by proclaiming that "if my will were law, it would never permit execution of any death sentence. . . . I have doubts of the moral right of society to extinguish a human life, and even greater doubts about the wisdom of doing so. . . . A completely civilized society will abandon killing as a treatment for crime."[137] Rutledge, for one, was quick to notice the two sides of Jackson. In a memorandum he wrote, "I consider it to be more than absurd for the prosecutor at Nuremberg to say that he doesn't approve of capital punishment. If he didn't approve, he should never have taken the job."[138]

Even on the disqualification issue, which Jackson claimed lay at the heart of the Black feud, Jackson contradicted himself. Not only did Jackson get some of his facts wrong in alleging that other justices had disqualified themselves in circumstances similar to Black's with his former law partner arguing *Jewell Ridge* for the labor union, Jackson had in 1943 responded to journalist Irving Dilliard's query about disqualification by setting out examples from the Court's history which, if applied to *Jewell Ridge*, would have made clear that Black was acting in the best tradition of the Court in not disqualifying himself merely because a former law partner was handling the case before the Court.[139]

Jackson also contradicted himself in the development of his judicial philosophy. He came to the Court believing in the application of the preferred position doctrine, but he later bitterly denounced it in both his opinions and his Harvard lectures. His growing opposition to Black and Douglas over the years, because they consistently applied, at a minimum, the preferred position, tracks Jackson's own apostasy of the preferred position doctrine. That Jackson would so violently oppose Black, whose positions were consistent with each other not only during his tenure on the Court but also with those he had advanced before going to the Court, reveals this contradiction relating to Jackson and ideology. He had praised Black's appointment to the Court in 1937, for the very reasons he later came to use against

Black. He had written Black upon his appointment to the Court: "[Y]our appointment to the Supreme Court brought great satisfaction to many people who have high confidence in your capacity to translate into law our aspirations for a better social order. A Justice of the Supreme Court has the opportunity to carry on a continuous tradition of liberalism, irrespective of administration, and I look to see your record one in which those connected with this administration will take great pride."[140] The contradiction was with Jackson, not with Black.

As he tried to do with other aspects of his life, Jackson tried to revise history relating to his abandonment of the preferred position doctrine. He strikingly invoked the doctrine in his memorable opinion in the Second Flag Salute case, in 1943, and he rejected the doctrine with equal intensity in *Brinegar v. United States*[141] in 1949. In that case he argued that he had opposed the doctrine from the beginning. Not only does he cite questionable cases to support the point he is making, he altogether neglects his majority opinion in the Second Flag Salute case, which is an explicit invocation and affirmation of the doctrine.[142]

Ironically, as hard as Jackson tried to shape his image by reshaping events in his oral history interviews, and as hard as Frankfurter tried to manage Jackson's legacy by guiding the writing of Jackson's biography by Kurland, it was Harlan Phillips, the man who interviewed Jackson for his oral history, who trumped the efforts of both in etching Jackson's enduring portrait with a penetrating, devastating analysis premised on Jackson's fundamental weaknesses. Jackson, it should be noted, was pleased with the oral history interviews project and thought that it went well. He wrote to the distinguished English barrister Norman Birkett, "I don't have a high opinion of biographies done during one's lifetime in any event. However, Columbia University has an interesting project in which I have participated and it has taken a good deal of time. A trained historian is assigned to go through one's papers and then conduct a quiz which is taken on a recording machine. He probes one's recollections of events, personalities, etc., as refreshed by the documents. He then prepares a narrative, which is submitted for editing and can be sealed indefinitely or made accessible, as one may wish. The purpose is to preserve a detailed account of our times by persons who would never get time to write an autobiography. It is a good idea and seems to be well executed."[143]

Harlan Phillips spent dozens of hours interviewing Jackson. He had been interviewing Frankfurter also for the Columbia University Oral History Project when Jackson died in 1954, and Phillips knew that the two had been close. His letter to Frankfurter in 1955, in which he dissected Jackson's personality, was occasioned by Frankfurter's comment, in a *Harvard Law Review* tribute to Jackson, that Jackson's charm with people was not based on "mere surface glitter." This did not ring true for Phillips, and he felt compelled to write Frankfurter and give his view of Jackson's personal relationships, which in turn related to the whole of Jackson's personality. He suggests no feelings of ill will toward Jackson. His analysis seems rooted in great respect, empathy, and fondness for Jackson. His analysis is at the same time dazzlingly probing and brilliantly written. Nothing ever written about Jackson remotely compares to it.

Phillips begins with the emptiness that had come to define Jackson in his last years. He writes:

> When [Jackson] looked at those lovely, but empty, human vessels immediately around him the sight sickened him, and, during those last few years spent largely in unsettling self-inventory, this piranha-like awareness chewing away at his vitals made him wonder, as I doubt he had ever wondered before, whether his own growth and adventure hadn't been purchased at too great an expense. I don't mean that the passage of time altered him in essentials—I don't believe it did— rather did it present opportunity to develop what he was fully and richly. Fortune that impishly returned his grin offered his immediate circle only a succession of detours away from the quality he was and prized. Keeping our eyes on the "bird on the wing" sometimes encourages such ambition that we devour our young. In the midst of comfort and the acclaim which attended his performances, he was the loneliest figure, but one, I've met, and, with the end in sight and eager reaching for the release it would bring, I believe he considered himself fundamentally a hollow man. 'Tis sad, but I believe it true.[144]

Turning more directly to Jackson's personal relationships, Phillips points to a distinguishing characteristic: Jackson's suspicious nature. The import of Phillips's insight is that it suggests that the deep ties Jackson forged with the profession and the image he pushed of himself describing the profession, as in his description of working and eating with lawyers in his youth, were revealing examples of Jackson's attempt to overcompensate or hide, from himself and from others, a gaping void in his personality. Phillips writes, "Just why he permitted the intrusions on time and energy by the non-descript many—unless it be, in part, a cracker barrel approach to life never quite lost—I can't explain, nor am I aware that he spread them liberally with charm, but the spraying was as misleading as it was unreflective. He was just too suspicious of people to be other than charming with them, and while loneliness drove him to collect them, I think even he would confess that the effort was hardly rewarding."[145] Then, describing Jackson's struggle with himself, Phillips moves even closer to the essence of Jackson, at least as he saw it, giving expression to what Jackson could not. There was for Jackson the great success, but it was not enough. "Essentially," he writes,

I believe him to have been solemn and serious, a man who felt too deeply to easily find words with which to clothe his feelings. Traditionally they weren't anybody's business but his anyway, and the acceptance of this canon removed him the more from other human kind. The emptiness about him drove him to his work and if his work was his life, it was also his prison. To be sure there was satisfaction in accomplishment, but it was not the kind of satisfaction which makes my own echo at its most profound. Perhaps he was so disturbed at his real feelings that he concealed them behind folksy charm for fear of discovery. He hated what he supposed was weakness and hated even more to be ridiculed for it. The turbulence of his nature which was the measure of his unhappiness frightened and saddened him. He sought companions to soothe the ache, to belong, and never quite made it.[146]

Knowing of the contradictions that helped define Jackson, Phillips then tries to explain, by way of closing, some of what at first seemed incongruous. "Even his celebrated wit harbored the deadly stiletto that aching seriousness is," Phillips writes. "Many laughed at what appeared on the surface as joke and overlooked intent. He never did. This is not to say he used wit maliciously, but certainly it was not without its measure of malice. Somehow this doesn't add up to charm for me, except as 'surface glitter.' Perhaps that is why some with whom I've talked who 'knew him well' remember him today chiefly for his charm. What they don't even remotely suspect is that they never really knew the man at all."[147]

Frankfurter never responded in writing to Phillips's assessment of Jackson, an assessment Frankfurter could well have found troubling. He did see Phillips when he taped more of his own oral history interview sessions, and perhaps they discussed the matter then. Frankfurter, however, never sent the Phillips letter along to Kurland when he was pushing and guiding him in Jackson's biography, and Frankfurter apparently never discussed the letter with anyone. There is a complete absence of references to it in his correspondence. The likeliest explanation for Frankfurter's failure to pass Phillips's insights on to Kurland is that Frankfurter did not think Phillips's analysis reflected well on Jackson. And of course he would have been right. What Frankfurter might not have wanted to acknowledge is that Phillips's analysis explains so much of Jackson that has either gone unexplained or at least weakly explained.

Principles for Jackson, in the end, gave way to ambition and personal grudges. The changes in his voting patterns and his judicial philosophy are best understood as a function of Jackson's inability to find a comfortable place on the Court where he could be his own man. Rather, his judicial performance was often linked to the demon of his ambition and the ugliness of his temper. Jackson ultimately sacrificed his judicial self to his personal self and lost the ability to decide cases without regard to baser motives. He let his emotion get the better of him. One of his law clerks, E. Barrett Prettyman Jr., wrote to Frankfurter a year after Jackson's passing with the observation that Jackson's faults "included that the personalities of others affected him strongly, often influenced his thinking. I think how he felt about Justice Douglas had some effect in some of his votes."[148]

He was unable to retreat from his shocking behavior in his feud with Black, never apologizing to Black or ever acknowledging that he was wrong to react as he did, and as a result he ruined his chances to redeem himself. That, after his return from Germany, his voting patterns became more erratic and that he with increasing shrillness rejected the ideological position he had once embraced show that Jackson had backed himself into a corner. It was with sadness that Black said to his law clerks, "if Bob and I could just get together, back to back, we could break down what is happening to the country . . . but Bob can't go with me because of what he said at Nuremberg."[149] Jackson might have closed some of the distance between himself and Black near the end of his life as Black's biographer suggests,[150] but even if it were not just a fraternal gesture, it had come too late.

Ironically, or to his credit, Jackson recognized near the end of his life and judicial career that he had failed to live up to the judicial ideal. He told Harlan Phillips in his oral history interview that "something does happen to a man when he puts on a judicial robe, and I think it ought to. The change is very great and requires psychological change within a man to get into an attitude of deciding other people's controversies, instead of waging them. It really calls for quite a changed attitude. Some never make it—and I am not sure I have."[151] It is perhaps not a coincidence that Jackson, after suffering his first heart attack in 1953, took a different tack on the Court and voted with the majority more than 95 percent of the time in his last year. His physician had told him that a return to work would likely be fatal, but to the Court he returned.

In the most important case of that time and perhaps any other time, *Brown v. Board of Education*,[152] Jackson ultimately, after some resistance, voted with the Court in the unanimous opinion. He had written his own concurring opinion for the case, but decided against filing it to preserve that unanimity.[153] The argument against the plaintiffs in *Brown* was the argument that Jackson and Frankfurter had been making for years in other contexts, that the Fourteenth Amendment and its equal protection clause should not visit upon the states such profound change by creating rights out of whole cloth in the face of controlling precedent to the contrary. Jackson, as the draft of his undelivered concurring opinion makes clear, saw that the argument had to yield in the face of acknowledged injustice.[154] With this act he at least partially redeemed himself.

In looking at Jackson, the long lens of history will not remember the *Brown* vote, however. It will remember the event that so disabled Jackson on the Court—his encounter with Black over the chief justiceship—that it cannot even be mentioned lest the presented image of Jackson change in a flash. Consider that when Justice Sandra Day O'Connor recently dedicated a life-sized statue of Robert Jackson in his hometown memorializing his life and work, she recited all the pertinent facts of that life, replete as it was with honors and successes, save one—Jackson's Nuremberg outburst and his feud with Justice Black.[155] She simply ignored the conflict with Black. She had to, since no amount of historical alchemy could change the sheer and unpleasant fact that Jackson failed in his relationships with his brethren and that these failed relationships steered him to a contrarian jurisprudence.

CHAPTER 3

Felix Frankfurter & Arrogance Rewarded

Felix Frankfurter came to the Court in 1939 at the age of fifty-seven, believing he had been better prepared to do its work than anyone in its history. Twenty-three years later, he left the Court, implicitly hectoring his brethren for their failure to follow the standard he had articulated throughout his career and claimed to have followed.[1] The disappointment and thinly veiled anger in his parting letter was but the final scene in a drama in which the elements for tragedy had been established during the years he served with Jackson, Black, and Douglas. There was a brief honeymoon of leadership when he was new to the Court and then, rejected in the first years of the 1941–54 period, he proceeded to years of bitter carping at the ascendancy of Black and Douglas, enjoying only occasional moments of success for himself. His tragedy was that, as a self-appointed chosen justice who was never able to accept his brethren as equals, he ironically failed to appreciate the essential nature of the Court and the role of the justices.

Frankfurter's was the great story of immigrant success. Born in Vienna, Austria, in 1882, he came with his parents to America when he was twelve years old, not speaking a word of English. Five years later he was graduating from New York's City College's combined high school and college program, having gorged himself on all that he could read. Following an interim year of work, he serendipitously ended up at the Harvard Law School in

1906. He conquered this alien cultural milieu, graduated first in his class, and fell under the influence of Harvard's legendary teachers, though the one who influenced him most, James Bradley Thayer, had died shortly before Frankfurter began his studies in Cambridge. Off to New York City, Frankfurter's stint in private practice lasted only a few months. Next was the U.S. Attorney's office of Henry Stimson in the Southern District of New York. He followed Stimson to Washington in 1910 and served as the chief legal officer of the Department of War's Bureau of Insular Affairs and then as special assistant to Stimson, now secretary of war.

He returned to Harvard in 1914 and stayed there, with occasional absences for government service, for twenty-five years. This government work, mostly between 1916 and 1919, helped shape Frankfurter's liberal inclinations. As a roving presidential investigator, he saw the labor battles of the American West firsthand. He served on the President's Mediation Commission as secretary and counsel, traveling widely and living for many weeks in a railroad car. He defended the rights of labor organizers and wrote an influential and highly critical report on the trial of labor organizer Tom Mooney. The academic life to which he returned did not slow his liberal activism. Involving himself in both individual cases and general causes, he worked strenuously on a defense of Sacco and Vanzetti; he wrote on the *Scottsboro* trial for the *New York Times* and argued that the Court had vindicated constitutional rights when it overturned the convictions; and he worked with the NAACP, the ACLU, and the National Consumer's League. He was a founding member of the *New Republic* and wrote countless articles and editorials for it. He worked on Zionist causes on an international scale, sometimes in the stead of Justice Brandeis, and on the Harvard campus itself he fought for better treatment of Jews in student admission and faculty hiring policies, often to the consternation and irritation of Harvard's president, A. Lawrence Lowell.

Frankfurter's principal interests as a teacher and scholar were in administrative law and the federal courts, especially the Supreme Court. His administrative law seminars were known as the Case-of-the-Month class because of Frankfurter's habit of taking one case at a time and dissecting it from front to end. His articles and books on the business of the Supreme Court brought a new perspective to the study of the Court and influenced generations of scholars. His writings and casebook on the federal courts similarly influenced countless students who went on to academic and judicial careers. Some commentators, in fact, have argued that Frankfurter's contributions from the ivory tower might exceed those from the bench.[2] He spread his influence as well by acting, at various times, as the law clerk placement agent for Holmes, Brandeis, and Hand, providing them with the best Harvard had to offer.

Frankfurter held out for a seat on the High Court. He mentions in his correspondence that he was first offered a seat on the U.S. District Court by President Taft in 1911, when he was but twenty-nine years old, but gives no explanation for refusing it.[3] He was nominated for a seat on the Massachusetts Supreme Court in 1932 but turned it down after making sure that he would have otherwise been confirmed. Roosevelt wanted to make him solicitor general, a frequent stepping-stone for Court appointees, but even this Frankfurter turned down. Finally, as reward for his help with his Court-packing plan, which Frankfurter privately supported but nonetheless said nothing about publicly, Roosevelt nominated him to the High Court in 1939. In this Court era dominated by the Old Guard, which was only reluctantly relinquishing its grip on economic legislation, liberals were delighted with Frankfurter's appointment. The *Nation* wrote that "[f]rom the time he was instrumental in saving Mooney from execution to his defense of Sacco and Vanzetti, Frankfurter has shown his devotion to justice and his courage."[4] Friend Archibald MacLeish looked ahead and said that Frankfurter would want to give "legislatures the widest latitude in framing economic measures altering property relations while sharply rejecting all attempts to curtail or restrict civil liberties."[5] The *New York Times* pointed as well to Frankfurter's "devotion to the integrity of human rights."[6] Frankfurter's own ambitions seemed to match these expectations. Harold Ickes, a Frankfurter insider at the time of his confirmation, reported that Frankfurter "was plainly delighted with his appointment, but I really think that this pleasure was not altogether personal. He feels that he is a symbol and that his appointment means much to the liberal cause."[7]

On his way to the Supreme Court, Frankfurter achieved insider status through good fortune and the assiduous cultivation of others. His acquaintance with Roosevelt in Washington early in the careers of both blossomed into an intimate friendship, as revealed in the volume of their correspondence.[8] He advised Roosevelt somewhat before he was governor of New York, but with Roosevelt's election as president, Frankfurter became one of his closest advisers. He was frequently called on for a variety of tasks. Chief among these was drafting legislation, such as the Securities Act of 1934. He continued to draft legislation and to serve as an adviser even once he was put on the Court, to the surprise and dismay of many because of the conflicts such work involved.

Frankfurter had also achieved insider status with Holmes and Brandeis. Visiting them frequently in Washington or at their summer homes, he sat at their feet and later committed the details of their conversations to writing, drawing upon this store of wisdom and observation throughout his career. He learned all he could from them about both the Court's work and its justices, making no effort to hide his sycophancy. His letters to each embarrassingly and shamelessly flattered.[9] From Holmes Frankfurter would have learned about the strategy of reputation building. He would have recognized that Holmes was using him to write approvingly and flatteringly about him in both his academic work and journalism and that this was one way to use others in shaping one's own legacy.[10] With Brandeis, Frankfurter was, in Brandeis's words, half brother, half son.[11] In an arrangement that later brought both of them a spanking for unethical conduct from the *New York Times,* Brandeis subsidized Frankfurter's work in certain liberal causes while Frankfurter was an academic.[12] Moreover, Frankfurter became Brandeis's only confidant on the workings of the Court and its personalities. In commentary that helped shaped Frankfurter, Brandeis opined on the minor and the major. He delivered his ideas for enhancing the deliberative and writing processes, for example, and he provided evaluations of his brethren, through which he described his overall system of values for life and men. Still fifteen years from the Court and only a man of forty, Frankfurter learned of the justices as the flawed, diminished men that they were in Brandeis's eyes.[13] Only Holmes was exempt.

As a result of all of this, Frankfurter took his seat on the Court with fully worked-out ideas about the judge's and the Court's role. His judicial philosophy was founded on disinterestedness and the application of cool reasoning to the legal problem at hand. This philosophy was inextricably bound to his twenty-five years of teaching and scholarship on the workings of the High Court at the Harvard Law School. "I made a pact with myself when I came on the Court," he writes, "that I would try to my utmost to continue to behave here as I did as an independent scholar at Cambridge, that is, act on the best judgment I am able to summon with reference to a particular case regardless of where it would land me in relation to the votes of other people on the Court and to eschew all combinations or machinations, active or tacit playing of politics on the Court."[14]

Then there was his connection to Holmes and Brandeis in which he basked in a glow of reflected excellence by association. He saw himself in many ways as their successors in interest on the Court and made sure that his brethren knew not only of the closeness of his association with each but also that whatever position he was advancing would have been endorsed by these Court giants. This led him to note in an extraordinary diary entry that "[s]ince the history of this Court was my business for a quarter of a century, I knew all there was to know as far as print could convey it, on what had gone on behind the scenes and beginning with my friendship with Holmes in 1911, greatly reinforced during the course of the years, I learnt a good deal, of course, about the Court's doings since the time Holmes came on in 1902, and after Brandeis came here in 1916 and Cardozo in 1932. I learnt with cumulative intimacy from them about the inner workings of the institution and the behavior of the various personalities."[15]

To enhance his influence on the Court, Frankfurter pursued a variety of strategies relating to the way the Court as an institution operated. For example, he drew upon his own studies of the Court and his discussions with Holmes and Brandeis and made suggestions for improving the Court's efficiency. Frankfurter first made ad hoc suggestions and then, with the appointment of Chief Justice Warren, he settled on an annual memorandum to the Court. He advocated changes in the conferences and in the way opinions were circulated, commented upon, and even published. Not surprisingly, many of the changes would have provided more time and opportunity for him to persuade his brethren to follow him.[16]

He had hardly warmed his seat before he argued in a concurring opinion that the Court should resurrect the practice of its earliest years of seriatim opinions.[17] Frankfurter's position, in just his third opinion as a justice, was that when a Court with new personnel changes announces a major shift in constitutional law, each of the justices should weigh in with his own belief, no doubt because he believed that when judged against the rest, his voice would sound sweetest. In practical terms, Frankfurter was seeking to usurp the chief justice's opinion assignment prerogative and eliminate the vastly inferior precedential value of concurring opinions. The opinion, for Frankfurter, would become the sword in his conquest of the Court's legal landscape.

Ironically, Frankfurter, who wanted to be heard as often as possible, was handicapped by his slowness in writing the majority opinions assigned to him. Following the approach of Chief Justice Hughes, both Chief Justices Stone and Vinson assigned opinions only to those justices who were current with their work. Frequently being behind in his, Frankfurter as a result had fewer opportunities to speak for the Court. During the thirteen-term period of 1941 through 1954, Frankfurter wrote 142 majority opinions.[18] He compensated by throwing his energies into writing concurring and dissenting opinions in record numbers—105 concurring and 190 dissenting opinions. Not only did he write more concurrences than any other justice, he wrote them at a rate nearly twice that of his nearest rival. He also dissented at a rate greater than that of any other justice.

Frankfurter's most aggressive—and grossly improper—approach in increasing his influence on the Court, however, came during the time the Court was considering the desegregation cases in the early 1950s. In one of the most startling revelations of recent memory, Philip Elman, Frankfurter's 1941–42 law clerk, has told of ongoing, detailed ex parte conversations Frankfurter had with him when Elman was in the solicitor general's office and acting as the government's lead counsel in fashioning the government's amicus curie brief. To help him prepare and argue his case, Frankfurter told Elman all that he could about the positions that the various members of the Court had on the desegregation issue. He revealed what his brethren said in conference, and he helped Elman as best he could to bring about the result that he wanted to see in the case. That Elman, who considered himself Frankfurter's law clerk for life, either did not perceive the conflict or did not act upon it of course does not relieve Frankfurter from the responsibility he bears for breaching the Court's rules of secrecy and confidentiality and engaging in such extensive ex parte conversations.[19]

For Frankfurter, the rules simply did not apply to him, no doubt because he felt he was acting in what he knew to be the Court's best interests.

Frankfurter's Supreme Court offices were more a command center than judicial chambers. From them he generated a steady stream of correspondence on a wide variety of subjects and met with the countless diplomats, friends, and government officials he was seeking to influence. This led Douglas, ever the critic, to note in 1962 that "I don't suppose anytime since he's been on the Court did he ever spend more than about four hours a day doing Court work. Most of it, most of his time was spent in getting things done in government, getting judges appointed or other people not appointed in various departments, in getting lawyers or whatnot salted away in government."[20]

Frankfurter's clerks, picked for him by Albert Sacks and Henry Hart of the Harvard Law School, were important to his operation. The law clerks had no set schedule of duties, one of them recalled. It was whatever particular topic Frankfurter was interested in researching. Frankfurter handled the petitions that litigants filed with the Court to have their cases heard, of which only a small fraction were eventually granted by the Court. He read with dazzling speed, one clerk reports, and he usually dictated his opinions.[21]

Later in his career Frankfurter used his law clerks to write not only opinions but even law review articles for him.[22] The issue was not, as it was for a justice such as Frank Murphy, Frankfurter's competence in writing an opinion. It was, as suggested by Douglas's observation, a question of time. During the war years in particular, when his time and talents were being taxed from all quarters, Frankfurter did use his law clerks to help him with his opinions, though the general consistency in Frankfurter's mixed styles—the epigrammatical, the magisterial, and the Germanic—suggest that Frankfurter made his opinions his own.

Frankfurter's jurisprudence during the 1941–54 period is summarized by looking at his voting patterns. The arc of his influence on the Court in part tracked the Court's receptivity to the preferred position and incorporation doctrines. He appeared to be leading the Court in his first two or three years, but with personnel changes in 1941 and the Court's dramatic turn-about in the Second Flag Salute Case, Frankfurter lost whatever hold he had on the Court. He was on the losing side of the preferred position debate in the Second Flag Salute case, and while that position continued to domi-nate in the next few years, Frankfurter was grouped with the dissenting, more generally conservative members of the Court. His conservatism ascended in the late 1940s, though, with the rejection of the incorporation theory, which Frankfurter helped bring about with his concurring opinion in *Adamson*.[23] But then, with the new, more conservative Truman appointees of Clark, Minton, Vinson, and Burton, Frankfurter became by contrast more liberal and dissented in a number of important cases.

The degree with which Frankfurter voted with the majority varied through the 1941–54 period. It peaked in the first year at 90.0 percent and dipped to 65.5 percent in 1949, with an average of 80.3 percent for the thir-teen terms of the period.[24] As to individual brethren writing the Court's majority opinion, Frankfurter preferred some justices to others. Stone, Roberts, and Jackson were his favorites, with his rate of agreement with them much in excess of his Court average.[25] Not surprisingly, he voted with the majority opinions of Douglas and Black at a rate lower than his overall Court rate.[26] More to the point, his rate of disagreement with them increased as the 1941–54 period progressed, and it was greatest in the last years of the period.[27] His rate of agreement with the other brethren was, in contrast, more or less constant. Black and Douglas were Frankfurter's favorite targets for both concurring and dissenting opinions. He needed to have the last word. Black and Douglas by a fair margin agreed less often with Frankfurter's majority opinions than with any of their brethren.[28]

The legacy Frankfurter desired for himself and the one his supporters have advanced is as the voice of judicial restraint. He insisted to the end that this was what his career on the Court had stood for. As it pertained to the jus-tices individually, Frankfurter thought that restraint was found in the disci-plined, disinterested decision-making process. He wrote in his retirement letter to his brethren in 1962 that

[m]y years on the Court have only deepened my conviction that its existence and functioning according to its best historic traditions are indispensable for the well-being of the nation. The nature of the issues which are involved in the legal controversies that are inevitable under our constitutional system does not warrant the nation to expect identity of views among the members of the Court regarding such issues, nor even agreement on the routes of thought by which decisions are reached. The nation is merely warranted in expecting harmony of aims among those who have been called to the Court. This means pertinacious pursuit of the processes of reason in the disposition of the controversies that come before the Court. This presupposes intellectual disinterestedness in the analysis of the factors involved in the issues that call for decision. This in turn requires rigorous self-scrutiny to discover, with a view to curbing, every influence that may deflect from such disinterestedness.[29]

As it applied to the Court as an institution, judicial restraint appeared in two general forms. In the first, the question turned on which cases the Court was to decide. Here Frankfurter's guiding principle was that the Court should strive above all to avoid deciding constitutional issues. "The most fundamental principle of constitutional adjudication," he wrote, "is not to face constitutional questions but to avoid them, if at all possible."[30] Frankfurter was and remains as eloquent as any in articulating the many jurisdictional and procedural doctrines that determine whether the Court should hear a case and decide a constitutional issue, writing on the case or controversy requirement and the standing, mootness, and ripeness doctrines.[31] He contributed to the Court's jurisprudence on abstention, particularly abstention based on the political question doctrine.[32] His opinion in *Colegrove v. Green*[33] set the standard for many years on the thorny issue of reapportionment, but to his dismay the Court a year before he left overruled it with *Baker v. Carr,* no longer believing that state legislatures were to be relied upon to fix electoral problems when it was so easy for legislatures to simply look the other way.[34] In the second form of judicial restraint, the issues turned to how the Court should decide those cases it took. Here Frankfurter wrote on doctrines such as stare decisis, which looked to the relationship between the Court's prior decisions and its present issues.[35]

His most important contribution in the area of federalism, at least as it related to the Court's role in reviewing state court decisions raising constitutional questions, was in a series of cases involving the preferred position and incorporation doctrines, both of which he rejected.[36] In his first extended discussion of the preferred position doctrine, the Second Flag Salute case, he argued that there was no constitutional basis to distinguish between the Court's role in the review of economic as opposed to other types of legislation. The principle that courts should not supplant the work of the legislature, for him, necessarily meant that it did not matter whether the legislation at issue was economic or otherwise. The test was only reasonableness; it was not a more searching scrutiny as Stone had called for in his *Carolene Products*[37] opinion or as Jackson was applying in the majority opinion.

The central feature of Frankfurter's analysis was that he limited himself to interpreting the meaning of the liberty provision of the Fourteenth Amendment's due process clause rather than interpreting the First Amendment right. So long as the legislation was reasonable, for him it was constitutional. Beyond his rejection of the preferred position doctrine, Frankfurter also rejected the idea advanced by Black and Douglas that the Due Process clause of the Fourteenth Amendment incorporated and made applicable to the states, in total, the provisions in the first eight amendments of the Bill of Rights.

Frankfurter did his own part to help shape his legacy on the Court. One of his strategies was to promote his only ally on the Court, Robert Jackson. The better Jackson looked, the better he looked. He encouraged former law clerk Philip Kurland to write Jackson's biography and gave detailed instructions as to what Kurland should explore. More generally, he wanted the Court presented in the most favorable light, which would by extension shine on him. On one occasion he even tried to dissuade Alexander Bickel from spending any time on John H. Clarke, a weak Court member in the Holmes Devise history of the Court he was writing. His distress at the prospect of Clarke weighing down the project was apparently so great that he failed to recognize an unintended pun. "He was an inferior judge before he was promoted," Frankfurter says of Clarke, who served in the lower federal judiciary before being appointed to the Court.[38]

Frankfurter had gone even further in 1955, seeking, in a time when the Court's role was being questioned in the wake of *Brown v. Board of Education,* to reinforce the notion that the Court does not act on political impulses by revising the history of the famous "switch in time" vote of Justice Roberts in 1937, which more than any other had suggested the political nature of the Court. In a memorial tribute to Roberts, Frankfurter argued that Roberts's switch was unrelated to Roosevelt's plan to pack the Court, and as proof of this he described a memorandum Roberts had prepared for him, in 1945, recounting the history of Roberts's thinking so as to corroborate Frankfurter's argument. The problem with the memorandum, some have argued, is that it likely never existed and that Frankfurter merely concocted its description.[39]

To promote himself more directly, he helped former law clerks he had cultivated for this purpose, such as former law clerks Edward Pritchard and Philip Elman, who brought out collections of his extrajudicial writing in 1939 and 1956 respectively.[40] He also sat for a series of oral history interviews of his life up to his Supreme Court appointment for Harlan Phillips and the Columbia University Oral History Project, which was published in 1960.[41] He intermittently kept a diary during his court years, which was published with an extensive and excellent biographical introduction by Joseph P. Lash.[42]

He gave hints as well to those around him as to where they should look to find what was significant about him, ironically telling former law clerk Philip Kurland, for example, that he did not much believe in psychoanalysis and that if he were to be found at all, it would be in his opinions on the Court.[43] Former law clerk Alexander Bickel was to write Frankfurter's biography, but it never came to pass. It fell to Philip Kurland, who had to abort his planned biography of Robert Jackson, to keep death from stilling Frankfurter's voice. Kurland brought out the third volume of Frankfurter's extrajudicial writings in 1965,[44] and in 1970 he published a collection of Frankfurter's opinions interlaced with commentary on Frankfurter's place on the Court.[45]

As Frankfurter would have wanted, his former law clerks have been influential in shaping his critical assessment. Former law clerk Albert Sacks wrote the entry on Frankfurter in the influential multivolume series *The Justices of the United States Supreme Court.*[46] Alexander Bickel frequently mentions Frankfurter in his important study *The Least Dangerous Branch,*[47] and former clerks Kurland, Sacks, Bickel, Wallace Mendelson, and Anthony Amsterdam wrote articles defending Frankfurter or the jurisprudential positions he took.[48] Mendelson in particular pushed for Frankfurter. He championed Frankfurter in his battle with Black even before Frankfurter retired.[49] Then, within two years of his retirement, Mendelson brought out two more volumes, one a collection of tributes by friends and former law clerks, and the other a collection of substantive essays, mostly by former law clerks, on Frankfurter's work on the Court.[50]

The Legal Process school of theorists, of which Frankfurter's star clerks were an integral part in the 1950s and 1960s, however, took the boldest tack in advancing Frankfurter's reputation. These theorists reacted to the Legal Realism advanced by members of the Yale faculty with a theory of the judicial process that located the very exercise of judicial power against the competing interests of the administrative and legislative process. Principal among them were former law clerks Bickel and Sacks along with Harvard professor Henry Hart, his former coauthor of annual articles on the Court, who was selecting Frankfurter's law clerks for him, and others, such as Herbert Wechsler and Harry Wellington. Courts should not, they argued, infringe upon the domain of agencies and the legislative process equipped with the particular expertise to interpret rules, regulations, and statutes. This brake of judicial restraint ensured the integrity of the democratic process, which would otherwise be threatened by the nonmajoritarian nature of judicial review. Courts should intervene only to apply neutral principles of law, that is, principles that decided issues without regard to particular outcomes. The explicit contrast was with the Legal Realists, who looked to outcomes first and reasons second, if at all. The success of judicial opinions was determined, the theorists contended, by, in the phrase of the day, the reasoned elaboration of principles. Craftsmanship for these critics mattered.

The Legal Process school advanced Frankfurter's distinguishing jurisprudential values, which emphasized judicial restraint, craftsmanship, and the deliberative process. It enjoyed remarkable success, setting the tone and substance of constitutional law taught in law schools for a generation. Wechsler provided the classic statement of the theory in his seminal "Neutral Principles of Law" article in 1959, the most cited law review article of all time,[51] while his casebook with Hart in the previous year facilitated the dissemination of the theory.[52]

The target of the Legal Process school, the activist Warren Court, was clearly identified in articles such as Bickel and Wellington's attack on Douglas's majority opinion in the *Lincoln Mills* case,[53] described by some as the classic indictment of the Warren Court,[54] and in Henry Hart's 1958 entry in the influential series of annual *Harvard Law Review* Forewords describing and characterizing the previous term of the Supreme Court in which he scathingly criticized the Court for the poor use of its time as part of his general argument that the Court was failing to honor the values of the Legal Process school.[55] This series of Forewords during the 1950s and 1960s was distinguished, not surprisingly, by its argument for the values of the Legal Process school.[56]

Frankfurter, for his part, kept in touch with the *Review* and tried to influence it by suggesting scholars the editors should publish.[57] The Legal Process school here and elsewhere advanced its position with a vengeance and was distinguished by the scorching tone of its criticisms. Anthony Lewis noted of the criticism that "the strictures are so harsh, the language so sweeping as to give the impression that the craftsmanship of the Court is at an all-time low."[58] That the Legal Process school should adopt such a strident voice suggested that more was at stake for it than just legal theory. For Hart, Sacks, and the others, reputations were being defended and attacked.

Ironically, given the long-term and pervasive success that Frankfurter had in enhancing his reputation with his Harvard affiliation and his acolytes and their Legal Process theorizing, he may well have worked against himself in the revealing, self-serving diary he kept to vindicate himself and his jurisprudence. As a resource, Douglas's interviews with Walter Murphy in the early 1960s perhaps reveal more about the workings of the Court and its various personalities, but Frankfurter's diary, in addition to describing the Court at work, presents an unparalleled picture of a justice at work. Frankfurter only sporadically kept his diary, but when he did he routinely gives full descriptions not only of what he did and those to whom he talked but also the details of the conversation and his assessment of all that has happened, albeit in fulsome, self-serving terms. Frankfurter was no ordinary justice. The diary in part serves to confirm his place as someone within the storm center of governmental and political affairs.

Consider 1943. Although 1943 is a truncated diary year ending on June 17, the entries for it are both the most detailed and the most numerous. Events taking place on the Court made 1943 no ordinary year for Frankfurter, but from the point of view of his social calendar and the web of his influence, it is a representative year. Looking at just its first week, which begins with the January 4 entry, we find, on the social side, a whirlwind of activity.[59] Frankfurter has dinner with Jean Monnet and others discussing supply needs for the war effort. A full analysis is provided. He spends ninety minutes with Kavalam Madhare Panikkar, constitutional adviser of the Indian princes "on all the phases of the Indian situation." Details are provided. He dines with Samuel Eliot Morison, newly named naval historian, only to be interrupted by a phone call from secretary of war Henry Stimson, who, feeling "rather low and need[ing] some comfort," joins them. He spends nearly two hours with Richard Casey, the minister of state for the Middle East, discussing "Anglo-American relations and the relations of Great Britain and this country to Russia." He then dines with Isaiah Berlin, who brought his "usual whimsical and wise comments on the universe" to the table. The French problem, among others, was discussed and a solution provided. He dines with Harold Butler, the British minister, at the home of the head of the delegation of the Fighting French. After dinner he has "a rather full talk [with his host] about the North African situation," which he then summarizes.

He meets with Charlie Poletti, special assistant to the secretary of war, who needs advice, provided in detail, on a number of matters. Richard Casey, the Middle East minister, again calls on Frankfurter seeking advice on matters involving the British. After giving the advice, Frankfurter "then tried to make Casey comprehend something of the position of the Jew in history," which leads to the history of Palestine and other related matters. He lunches with Archibald MacLeish, which he summarizes, surprisingly, in only one paragraph. He meets with a former Harvard Law School student, who gives him a malice-filled description of why he left his government post; MacLeish calls before dinner seeking advice "regarding the conflict of authority as between the OSS and the OWI, and more particularly the proper distribution of authority regarding responsibility for so-called political warfare as between civil and military authorities." North Whitehead, an adviser on American affairs in the British Foreign Office, then comes for dinner, with the talk centering mainly on Anglo-American relations.[60]

This, for one week, was Frankfurter's social side. The entries for the rest of the year are equally impressive as a demonstration of Frankfurter's involvement in governmental and political affairs.[61] They provide a lengthy list of notable personalities and political leaders. Frankfurter meets with, lunches with, or dines with, among others, Dean Acheson; the Australian prime minister; the Canadian prime minister; Sam Rosenman, former judge and presidential counselor; journalist I. F. Stone; religious and social thinker Reinhold Niebuhr; journalist Edward R. Murrow; and President and Mrs. Roosevelt, separately and together.

He tenders advice to all, with the exception of Acheson, with whom he has a friendly, personal relationship. He seems reluctant to tell all only in his dealings with Roosevelt. Here he seems sensitive to how his frequent meetings appear and goes out of his way to indicate that he has little contact with Roosevelt now and that this contact is not initiated by him. "[W]henever the President wants to talk to me about anything about which I am free to talk, I shall tell him frankly what I think," he tells Sam Rosenman after Rosenman exhorts Frankfurter to give the president directly the advice he had been giving him, "but it is not my business to volunteer views although of course you are free to tell him the substance of our conversations."[62]

Frankfurter had less to say in this diary week about his own work on the Court. He summarizes the issues in a few cases and describes the conference discussion. In a case involving the Kickapoo Indians, Frankfurter adopts the tone he consistently employs in Court entries: "I had studied the matter a good deal and more particularly the status of lands held in severalty by [them]. It fell to me to talk about it at some length."[63] Knowing that Chief Justice Stone would be sensitive to the issue, Frankfurter, both mischievous and priggish, recounts how he "got the expected rise out of Stone" by citing in a dissent a Holmes opinion that had embarrassed Stone when the two served together.[64] Unrelenting in his criticism of Stone, Frankfurter describes a late conference session and makes clear that the best use is not being made of the conference. "Conference, which lasted until 6:15 P.M. This partly is due to the habit of Stone, unlike Hughes' behavior, of carrying on a running debate with any Justice who expresses views different from his. The result is not only the usual undesirable atmosphere created by contentious debate, but lack of that austerity of atmosphere which I thought so admirable in a scrupulous observer of each man's saying his say in turn without an interruption, as Hughes conducted in Conference, but also an inevitable dragging out of the discussion."[65]

In a described exchange with Frank Murphy during an oral argument session, Frankfurter makes a point of indicating that he is closer to the president than Murphy is. He criticizes Douglas for his political ambitions and implicitly chastises Murphy for not recognizing them. Then, apparently without recognizing his hypocrisy, he condemns Douglas for not giving up all political aspirations. "When a priest enters a monastery, he must leave— or he ought to leave—all sorts of worldly desires behind him," he sermonizes. "We are all poor human creatures and it's difficult enough to be wholly intellectually and morally disinterested when one has no other motive except that of being a judge according to one's full conscience. And the returns are all in on judges of this Court who, while on the Court, have had conflicting political ambitions. We know all the instances and the experience is unedifying and disastrous."[66]

The balance of Frankfurter's Court-related entries for the first six months of 1943 are especially illuminating. He worries about the growing strength of Black and Douglas and works up arguments for himself and others against their distressing success.[67] He laments the turn of events with Jackson, already an ally, who agrees entirely with him. He reports that Roberts also worries about their strength and that even the chief justice seems concerned about the trend as well, though he seems to pass on the matter with humor in his reference to the "Axis" moniker that is now attached to Black and Douglas and the group they lead.[68] Conferences are growing longer and are increasingly unmanageable, Frankfurter reports. Black shows signs of dominating not only the votes of some of his brethren but the conference as well. He is a force for the wrong reasons. He describes Douglas's approach of persuading his brethren to follow him and roundly condemns it.

After hearing from Roberts about Douglas's attempts at persuasion through flattery, he writes, again without any recognition of irony, "I enlightened neither to the Douglas technique. Except in cases where he knows it is useless or in cases where he knows or suspects that people are on to him, he is the most systematic exploiter of flattery I have encountered in my life. He tried it on me when he first came on the Court—every opinion of mine he returned, he returned with the most extravagant praise, all of which ceased after I left him in no doubt that I did not come on to the Court to play politics but to vote in each case as my poor lights guided me."[69]

Finally, he mentions the pivotal Second Flag Salute case toward the end of the diary year, but only in reference to working on the opinion and to the reservations Murphy and Rutledge have about the now famous opening lines in which Frankfurter inserts himself personally into the opinion.[70] He knows that the Court has spurned him and is setting up defenses he will never abandon. "The sentences will stay in," he writes, "because they are not the products of a moment's or an hour's or a day's or a week's thought—I had thought about the matter for months and I deem it necessary to say and put into print in the U.S. Reports what I conceive to be basic to the function of this Court and the duty of the Justices of this Court."[71]

Joseph Lash, the diary's editor, was more than right in noting that Frankfurter's supporters would be surprised by some of the invective they would find springing from him in these entries.[72] Not surprisingly, this unattractiveness made the critical reception of the diaries less than enthusiastic. Representatively, the *New York Times* wrote that "Frankfurter comes through in these pages as a caricature drawn by his worst detractors—overbearing, pompous, sanctimonious, petty, patronizing, malicious, disingenuous, conniving and insensitive to both the personal and civil rights of others."[73] Even former law clerks, such as Joseph Rauh, were hard-pressed to like what they read.[74] The problem, though, was not that they did not recognize these unflattering aspects of the Frankfurter of the diaries. It was that they were so well detailed, so pervasive.

The Frankfurter who appears in his correspondence is little different from the Frankfurter of the diaries. His extensive correspondence while on the Court was of two types. Frankfurter the political and governmental maven had a range of correspondents equaling that of the visitors and friends in Washington seeking his advice, while Frankfurter the jurist wrote revealingly to just a cadre of correspondents about the Court and its personalities. He wrote most often to Charles Burlingham, Learned Hand, and Paul Freund. He was, in part, looking for someone who would be sympathetic to what he was enduring on the Court as he battled Black and Douglas and stewed in his leadership exile. He wrote to Freund, for example, "[w]hy do I write to you. Well, it's because it is a comfort occasionally to talk into the ear of a scholar as well as someone with understanding of what is meant by the cliche that the function of this Court is one of judicial statecraft."[75]

He let loose with Hand with his frustrations, cataloging the sins of his brethren and tingeing nearly every letter with resentment. He touches on the widest range of Court-related topics with Burlingham. He embraced his role as the heir to Brandeis and Holmes and sprinkled his letters with nuggets of insider information about them and the brethren of their day.[76] He explains why he has taken particular tacks with his own brethren, such as why he chose to concur in the *Steel Seizure* case;[77] he discusses their mutual friends, such as Learned Hand and the suggestion that Hand lacks self-love;[78] and he enjoys himself as he assumes an Olympian pose with a non-Olympian correspondent.

He writes loftily to Burlingham, the doyen of New York lawyers, in a way he could not write to Hand, that "the fact of the matter is that the lawyers with whom talk was exhilarating are men of wide cultivation— Holmes, Brandeis, B. Hand, Gus Hand, John Davis, Charlie Hough, Bob Jackson, Hughes, Cuthbert Pound, Cardozo. No, I do not include Stone, because while he was a man of some reading and wider interests, he was too insufferably vain to make conversation with him a particular pleasure. . . . Stone was a judge of considerable quality, but he was a small man."[79] Frankfurter makes the case for his own sizable dimensions by working the twin themes of his independence and disinterestedness. He mocks others, such as Black, for being influenced in their votes by their own backgrounds. "[*Cloverleaf*], as you probably know, has always stuck in my crop. Particularly did I feel puzzled by Black, J.'s position because it went against what one had a right to suppose was his general outlook on the problems of that case. His behavior in that case and in *Bethlehem Steel*, at about the same time, were among my great eye-openers. In a moment of candor he explained why he knocked out the Alabama statute, and this is it: 'When I was a boy I worked in a grocery store and I learnt that the poor people down there could only buy the kind of renovated butter that the statute barred.'!!!"[80]

Alexander Bickel, Philip Kurland, and Mark DeWolfe Howe became frequent correspondents on Court matters in the post-1954 years. Frankfurter bombards Kurland with ideas and information on the biography he is writing on Jackson, sometimes rising from troubled sleep to outline his thoughts.[81] He assumes his role as keeper of the flame for both Brandeis and Holmes. With Bickel, a Court historian, he provides elaborate explanations and defenses for Brandeis when Charles Wyzanski's *Atlantic Monthly* article on Brandeis is less than fully flattering and accurate in its details.[82] As for Holmes, Frankfurter wrote to Howe, former law clerk to Justice Holmes, about their common interests in Holmes and the Harvard Law School and urged him repeatedly to try to get the Harvard University Press to keep Holmes's essays in print.[83]

Frankfurter, described by his wife as a man with two hundred closest friends,[84] did not have close friends off the Court. An exception might be Dean Acheson, once a student of his at Harvard, with whom he famously walked to work each morning. Then there is Learned Hand. Theirs was a friendship spanning more than fifty years. They shared a love for the intricacies of law and a willingness to disparage those pretending to be their equals. Frankfurter, nonetheless, considered Hand senior to him. He deferred to him on matters of law and generally wrote with the hope that Hand would corroborate his take on other matters. Frankfurter unfailingly spoke highly of Hand to others and pushed for his appointment to the High Court. In fact, Roosevelt said, perhaps jokingly, that the reason he did not appoint Hand was because Frankfurter had lobbied him so hard for it.[85]

Hand, for his part, did not always sing Frankfurter's praises. Douglas, who knew Hand well, perceptively thought that "they were very close in a way, and yet [Hand] knew the weaknesses of Frankfurter,"[86] an assessment borne out in Hand's 1957 oral history interview. There he provided, at the age of 84, a revealing, compelling description of Frankfurter that deserves attention because of the length and depth of their friendship. He points, without provocation, to Frankfurter's faults and provides insights not found elsewhere. From a man fully conversant with Shakespeare, we find in his startling comments echoes, perhaps unintentional, of Caesar's "sleek-headed men" speech in *Julius Caesar,* in which Caesar says he fears Cassius

in part because he loves no plays and hears no music.[87] The interviewer is
Louis Henkin of the Columbia University Law School, a former Frankfurter law clerk.

> *Interviewer:*   I have a feeling from what I've heard that Brandeis suc-
> ceeded in limiting himself more, in confining himself more within
> his job, much more so than Frankfurter has been able to do.
> Frankfurter, it is said, makes a more charming companion.
>
> *Hand:*   Why, he doesn't have many outside interests, does he?
>
> *Interviewer:*   Not in the sense of activity, but in the sense of reading
> and people.
>
> *Hand:*   Does he? Is he widely read?
>
> *Interviewer:*   Oh, yes.
>
> *Hand:*   Well, I didn't know that.
>
> *Interviewer:*   Tremendously—he reads all the periodicals, and—
>
> *Hand:*   He doesn't give you a sense of being widely acquainted with
> letters.
>
> *Interviewer:*   No, that's true. He isn't acquainted in the classics.
> He's a brilliant political and social analyst, very much aware of and
> interested in what's going on today all over the world.
>
> *Hand:*   That is true. He has very—I was going to say discordant
> interests, but that isn't it. His periphery, and the angles of recep-
> tivity, are too large, really. That is true. And yet he never seems to
> be acquainted—I don't think he has any care for beauty. I never
> saw it.
>
> *Interviewer:*   He listens to music.
>
> *Hand:*   Well, does he enjoy it?
>
> *Interviewer:*   I think so.
>
> *Hand:*   I don't think he has any eye whatever, has he? I never saw it.
>
> *Interviewer:*   He has a lovely wife.
>
> *Hand:*   That's really irrelevant. But I never saw him show any sensi-
> tivity to the arts, to the plastic arts. Did you? Or to the dramatic
> arts. I never heard him mention a play. Nor does he ever to me
> give any evidence of interest in literature.
>
> *Interviewer:*   It's spotty, perhaps.
>
> *Hand:*   Well, I didn't even find the spots.
>
> *Interviewer:*   His chief interest is in human beings. He's got a genius
> for friendship, and for knowing what goes on in the world.
>
> *Hand:*   Makes some good enemies, too.
>
> *Interviewer:*   Yes, there's no doubt.
>
> *Hand:*   No, I've come more and more to respect him and have
> affection for him. But he's contentious, too. Now, this comes to

me—I hadn't thought of it before—it's hard to leave a matter in balance with him, without a little residuum of feeling. That I miss a good deal. If you disagree—well, you must take a positive position, for or against. Well, that interferes with intimacy, doesn't it?

Interviewer: Perhaps he spreads himself out. For a man who does that, he does very remarkably, but still he's spreading himself out.

Hand: Do you know—well, I wasn't thinking just of this. I was thinking that in his intercourse with people, things are brought too much to a conclusion, one way or the other. [His wife] is said to have said: "Do you realize what it is to live with a man who's never tired." Is he never tired?

Interviewer: Never tired. We had a dinner the other night, and at 2:00 o'clock in the morning, most of us wanted to go home, but we had to take him home. He was ready to go on.

Hand: I never saw him really drunk, or anything like it. I've seen him when the liquor hit him some, but not really.

Interviewer: I don't think he has any real interest in that.

Hand: Well, does that do anything to him. I thought it did.

Interviewer: He doesn't really care about it.

Hand: Well, it changes him somewhat. I don't think it lifts, I don't think he has a load of melancholy, or has he?

Interviewer: Not that I know of.[88]

Frankfurter's relationships with his law clerks may have been his most successful. Some have suggested that the clerks adopted some of Frankfurter's personality traits and in their dealings with other clerks became larger versions of their diminutive, at five feet five inches, boss. They did his bidding in trying to persuade the law clerks of other justices that their bosses should follow him. They worked tirelessly for him, and they remained loyal to him, as shown in part by the number of law clerks who wrote articles and books extolling his virtues. But while one law clerk has written that Frankfurter recognized the growing stature of the law clerks and the changes that this brought to the relationship with Frankfurter, so that "once a law clerk, forever a colleague and friend,"[89] his extensive correspondence with Philip Kurland and Alexander Bickel over the many years following their clerkships suggests that with them Frankfurter maintained his role as justice and as former teacher.

As a related matter, Frankfurter did not have uniform success with those law clerks who had been his students at Harvard and whom he had placed as clerks with those justices for whom he regularly supplied clerks. The most telling example was Tom Corcoran. Following his clerkship Corcoran had stayed in Washington and acquired enormous influence as fix-it man in the Roosevelt administration, though ultimately he pressed his advantage too far and was ostracized. Frankfurter had been close to Corcoran but had a falling out with him and stopped speaking to him. Frankfurter even worked to keep Corcoran from being appointed solicitor general.[90] Corcoran's view was that Frankfurter could not accept him as anything but a former law clerk, which led him to remark famously that Frankfurter was incapable of having adult relationships.[91]

Nor could Frankfurter count many of his brethren as friends. Even when he had what seemed to be a friendly relationship with a colleague, it is difficult to know the genuineness of his friendship. He seemed to some to have had an affectionate, friendly relationship with Stanley Reed, for example, but Frankfurter's interest seems to be primarily in Reed's vote and in overcoming the opposition he presented. He wrote, for example, an inordinate number of notes and letters to Reed—more than half of the number of notes and letters he sent to his brethren combined—invariably trying to bring him, as a key swing vote, into line.[92]

In contrast, he less often tried to influence Robert Jackson, who was thought to be his closest friend on the Court, though his relationship did not appear uniformly warm. It seems, at best, a complicated matter. Frankfurter once described Jackson as a delectable colleague.[93] Jackson, for his part, certainly considered Frankfurter his closest friend on the Court.[94] He consistently voted with him at a relatively high rate,[95] but Jackson did not blindly follow Frankfurter. They disagreed on many important issues and were not infrequently on opposite sides in majority and dissenting opinions.[96]

Frankfurter was perhaps the only person to whom he confided details of his feud with Black, revealing to him weakness that he revealed nowhere else.[97] Frankfurter, for his part, encouraged Jackson in taking the line he did by corroborating his take on the facts and by agreeing with his fundamental premise that Black was manipulating the process in the *Jewell Ridge* case.[98] Some, such as Douglas, speculated that Frankfurter was using Jackson to advance his campaign against Black.[99] Aware of this speculation,

Frankfurter wrote to Black to disclaim any role in acting against his interests during the *Jewell Ridge* affair.[100]

But even while he created the impression on some fronts that he supported Jackson, Frankfurter at the same time distanced himself from Jackson in correspondence, going so far as to disclaim any understanding of what Jackson was up to in the feud.[101] In a similar way, he sometimes undercut some of his lavish praise of Jackson's writing gifts. He wrote that Jackson was "by long odds the most literarily gifted member on the Court and the most deeply versed in English literature, which enabled him to command so easily apt quotations,"[102] but at the same time he belittled Jackson's prose in a letter to Douglas, for example, a Jackson enemy, describing it as "popular rhetorical stuff."[103]

Ironically, Frankfurter's legacy rests not on his articulation of judicial restraint but on his strategy of infusing memorable language into his opinions. This language, not surprisingly, links him to Holmes in that it is a mixture of the magisterial, the aphoristic, and the epigrammatical. Frankfurter well knew that it is with language that reputations are built. He had written Charles Burlingham, for example, that "judges with literary facility—the relatively few judges that have that—have a way of embalming themselves in history."[104]

Frankfurter's memorable language of choice was figurative language, especially the epigram and the aphorism. A sampling of Frankfurter's frequently quoted opinions suggests the dimensions of this approach. Consider his observation that "a timid judge, like a biased judge, is intrinsically a lawless judge";[105] that "the notion that because the words of a statute are plain, its meaning is also plain, is merely pernicious oversimplification";[106] that "wisdom too often never comes, and so one ought not to reject it merely because it comes late";[107] that "the history of liberty has largely been the history of the observance of procedural safeguards";[108] that "the fact that a line has to be drawn somewhere does not justify its being drawn anywhere";[109] that "disinterested zeal for the public good does not assure either wisdom or right in the methods it pursues";[110] that "the history of American freedom is, in no small measure, the history of procedure";[111] and that he does not "use the term 'jurisdiction' because it is a verbal coat of too many colors."[112] And on mens rea we find, "a muscular contraction resulting in a homicide does not constitute murder."[113]

We know that the Court in time rejected Frankfurter's positions on the preferred position and incorporation doctrines through its adoption of the selective incorporation approach. That it did so does not by itself raise questions about the sincerity with which Frankfurter advanced his positions. They arise instead because the contradictions in the positions he took on these issues in various cases were so powerful as to suggest that they were advanced for personal rather than ideological reasons. When Frankfurter made his stand against the preferred position doctrine in the Second Flag Salute case, for example, he looked to Holmes for support and premised his argument in large part on the idea that the Constitution did not distinguish between its rights and that individual liberty rights could therefore make no special claim for preference.[114]

However, when he wrote at length about the preferred position doctrine six years later in *Kovacs,* he changed not the fact of his opposition to the doctrine but the underpinnings to it.[115] He now acknowledged that certain rights had enjoyed preferential treatment in the Court's jurisprudence. He went further and now took the position that Holmes himself had made this very distinction between economic and individual liberty rights. Then, astonishingly, he cited to his own writings on Holmes to support this position, making the reader of the Second Flag Salute case wonder how this same Frankfurter could have ignored what he now claimed to be a position he had himself written about.[116] Now Frankfurter's objection to the preferred position doctrine in *Kovacs* was with the difficulty of its application. His message was that doctrine could be made into an effective constitutional tool but only with great care, such as the care he brought to the matter.[117]

The contradiction in Frankfurter's response to the incorporation doctrine was equally glaring. In *Adamson* in 1947 he ridiculed the proposition that provisions of the Bill of Rights could be selectively incorporated into the Fourteenth Amendment, mockingly wondering aloud how these incorporated provisions would be chosen.[118] But in *Wolf v. Colorado* just two years later, Frankfurter wrote the majority opinion in which he held that the Fourth Amendment's prohibition against unreasonable searches and seizures was incorporated into the Fourteenth Amendment and made applicable to the states.[119] He did this with remarkable ease. First, he established the premise that rights basic to a free society are evolving as of any one moment. This then lets him argue that "the security of one's privacy against arbitrary intrusion by the police—which is at the core of the Fourth Amendment—is basic to a free society. It is therefore implicit in 'the concept of ordered liberty' and as such enforceable against the States through the Due Process."[120] So much for rejecting selective incorporation because it relies on subjectivity.

More to the point, Frankfurter in *Adamson* and his other incorporation opinions contradicts publicly what he had said privately. When discussing Black's belief in total incorporation in 1939, Frankfurter wrote him, "perhaps you will let me say quite simply and without any ulterior thought what I meant to say and *all* I mean to say, regarding your position on the 'Fourteenth Amendment' as an entirety. (1) I can understand that the Bill of Rights—to wit Amendments 1–9 inclusive—applies to State action and not merely to U.S. action, and that *Barron v. Baltimore* was wrong. I think it was rightly decided. (2) What I am unable to appreciate is what are the criteria of selection as to the nine Amendments—which applies and which does not."[121] Seven years earlier Frankfurter had asserted the same position publicly, making his about-face even more puzzling. In a *New York Times* editorial occasioned by the Court's reversal of the infamous *Scottsboro* case because the defendants had been denied counsel and due process of law under the Fourteenth Amendment, Frankfurter wrote that the Fourteenth Amendment imposes a broad limitation on state action. "The assertion of the limitation is a study of the federal judiciary, and a right of defendants under the federal Constitution."[122] That the Court had come to this view, was for Frankfurter, "a notable chapter in the history of liberty."[123]

In large measure Frankfurter's debacle in the Second Flag Salute case determined his subsequent strategy and tactics in his relations with his brethren. Within the confines of the Court itself, Frankfurter worked hard but without much success to persuade his brethren to follow him. His professorial persona flourished during Court conferences. He would hold the floor for fifty minutes at a time, the length of the Harvard seminars he had run for many years. He thought it was his obligation to assume the role of teacher and to treat his brethren as his students. Others saw his teaching more as advocacy. For Douglas, Frankfurter was always proselytizing. "I mean, every case for him is a cause. He has a missionary zeal about even a stinking little tax case. He wants everybody to vote his way."[124] Frankfurter employed a filibuster strategy, for example.[125] And when this approach failed, he employed personal attacks on his brethren in conference. Douglas, in his early 1960s interviews, said that Frankfurter would bait some of his brethren and insult both their intelligence and integrity, on one occasion nearly instigating fisticuffs. Reed and Vinson were his favorite targets. Douglas recalled that Frankfurter

> was very, very bitter about Fred [Vinson]. Fred had a capacity, of course, to be bitter. Everybody has that, every human being has that capacity. Fred once in a while would get bitter. I mentioned the time during conference when the result of slighting remarks made by Frankfurter reflecting upon Fred Vinson's character, integrity. He just got out of the chair and came around the table with a clenched fist. He would have knocked Frankfurter's teeth out if he hadn't been stopped by his colleagues. Of course, that wore off in a few hours and Fred was once more the polished gentleman that he basically was. Frankfurter had a habit of baiting Vinson. He saw Vinson as a man of rather pedestrian mind and Frankfurter could trip him up, could show how the step he proposed was false or treacherous. Fred didn't have the mental facility that Frankfurter had. Those relations between Vinson and Frankfurter are probably worse than the relations between Jackson and Black. Frankfurter took Vinson on as a lumbering dodo.[126]

The problem that Reed posed for Frankfurter, Douglas speculated, was that he was too much like him and that subconsciously at least Frankfurter resented him for this. This, in turn, led to demonstrable displays of bitterness and anger. Douglas writes that Frankfurter,

> conference after conference, day after day, week after week, term after term, sitting there and seeing, in Reed, the embodiment of the thing that he, Frankfurter, really was, became more and more incensed and aroused and opposed and antagonistic towards Reed. Because he was very vitriolic to Reed in conferences, scathing remarks that nobody would stand for. They never even ruffled Reed. He would just, he

would smile and bow and be very gracious and take all the vitriol that Frankfurter would pour on him, Frankfurter making all sorts of denunciations of Reed as a stupid man, as a dishonest man, and so on. I think that Reed and Frankfurter actually were so close together philosophically, but that Reed became somewhat of a living symbol of Frankfurter's subconscious, at least of the thing that he, Frankfurter was, and therefore, I think in some curious way blocked the worst side of Frankfurter out, which was sort of a gossipy, evil person out of control of his conversation, making all sorts of accusations. Reed was his main target of denunciation in the twenty years I sat with him on the Court together."[127]

Eugene Gressman, a leading scholar on practice before the Supreme Court and a law clerk for five years to Justice Murphy in the 1940s, corroborates Douglas's description of Frankfurter and turbulent conferences, writing that "on a few occasions I inadvertently overheard snatches of his shrill, table-pounding lectures to his brethren in Conference, as his cries emanated through the thick walls of the Conference room."[128]

Frankfurter pursued one-on-one tactics to gain votes after conference discussions. Douglas gives the worst spin to Frankfurter's efforts, describing Frankfurter as a malicious gossip whose general strategy was to divide and conquer. He said in his interviews that Frankfurter "spent his time going up and down the halls putting poison in everybody's spring, trying to set one Justice against another, going to my office and telling me what a terrible person Reed was or Black, going to Reed's office telling Reed what a stupid person somebody else was, and so on."[129]

More charitable versions of the Frankfurter strategy had him seeking out his brethren and trying to overwhelm them with his trademark mode of argumentation. He was famous for his vicelike grip of the opponent's arm and an unrelenting, buzzing-bee verbal assault. Consider, for example, the description that one of Justice Reed's law clerks gives of Frankfurter's attempts to persuade Reed to follow his position. Here the emphasis is as much on Reed's disposition as it is on its striking contrast to Frankfurter's. "[Reed] used to drive Felix Frankfurter absolutely up the wall," we learn. "[Reed] was uniformly gracious, uniformly courteous, uniformly polite. Never disputatious. Always the posture of courteously listening to somebody else's views about whatever, and then doing exactly what he wanted to do with a quiet smile, on the basis of the way he saw it. . . . Felix would come in all hotted up and charge in to talk with Stanley Reed to lobby him and try to persuade him of something or other. Felix would have seventeen arguments and be talking like a machine gun and just brandishing his intellectuality and his citations and his European rhetoric and his epigrams. And it was like talking to Buddha. And I've watched this happen so often and Felix was tiny, small, whirring around like a hornet or like a bee, whirling around this sort of Buddha-like figure . . . watching, listening, with a kind of bemused smile. At the end of which, he would say, 'Thank you very much Felix. I appreciate your spending the time with me.' And he would never, really, engage or respond to any of this and it just drove Felix crazy."[130]

A look at the ugly side of Frankfurter's efforts at proselytizing comes from another one of Reed's law clerks. The subject of the anecdote is Reed's unflappable personality; the villain is Frankfurter.

> But I never saw him ruffled except once. Justice Frankfurter, whom Justice Reed admired greatly, almost extravagantly, came into Justice Reed's office one day, and my office which was adjoining his, the door was left open for some reason and I overheard the conversation. It wasn't a conversation so much as a lecture on the part of Frankfurter to Justice Reed. And Frankfurter literally dressed Justice Reed down for something he had said or written or done on a point of law. It wasn't a personal matter. He was, in effect, saying to the justice he didn't know what he was talking about and didn't he understand this and he was treating Justice Reed almost like a student of Frankfurter's. And I came in afterwards and Justice Reed was flushed and obviously very upset. And I, being young, said, "Mr. Justice, how can you let that man talk to you that way?" And Justice Reed, still looking a bit crestfallen, said, "Well, you know, you have to understand that Felix Frankfurter is a great man, a brilliant man, and a little temperamental."[131]

Frankfurter could be equally ugly in inter-Court correspondence when his brethren resisted him. In a letter to Rutledge, for example, Frankfurter exasperatingly wrote that "if I had to expose all your fallacies [regarding a 1946 term opinion] I would have to write a short book on (1) federal jurisdiction (2) constitutional law (3) procedure generally."[132] Frankfurter thought he had a double-barreled advantage over his brethren that placed him beyond question as a justice. There was his pedigree, but beyond that there was his training period at Harvard. He was as unrepentant an academic as he was arrogant. "It is the lot of professors to be often not understood by pupils," he characteristically wrote to Reed, "so let me try again."[133] "I am an academic," he wrote to Reed, "and I have no excuse for being on the Court unless I remain so."[134] After all, he thought that "not even as powerful and agile a mind as that of Charles Evans Hughes could, under the pressures which produced adjudication and opinion writing, gain that thorough and disinterested grasp of these problems which twenty-five years of academic preoccupation with the problem should have left in me."[135]

There were recognizable patterns in Frankfurter's relationships with his brethren. New appointees to the Court were subjected to heavy doses of Frankfurter flattery as a way of winning them over. He would write embarrassingly flattering comments on opinions they circulated. He appealed to their vanity and to their egos by frequently suggesting that only they would have been able to so neatly and judiciously arrive at their conclusion. He wanted the objects of his attention to think that he took them seriously as thinkers and would provide recommended reading lists for them, often promoting his own books and articles. Few justices failed to recognize Frankfurter's motives, however, and they discounted his flattery and other cajoling tactics accordingly. Invariably, following Frankfurter's courtship of them, the new justices took courses declaring that they were going their own way. Frankfurter then let loose with his true view of the justice's qualifications or work.

Just as he could be condescending and insulting in finding fault with his brethren to their face, Frankfurter was vicious in his comments when he wrote about his brethren to those closest to him. To understate the point, Frankfurter, as a general matter, did not think highly of his brethren. Here we hear echoes of the assessments Brandeis gave Frankfurter of his brethren in those conversations Frankfurter had memorialized. He wrote of Stone, for example, that he was one of the three vainest men he knew and that he, Stone, needed to elevate himself by pulling everyone else down.[136] About Vinson he complained of his hot temper, his touchiness, and his ignorance.[137] He wrote Hand that he was sad to see Burton leave the Court. As far as character went, he said, Burton was unexcelled in his experience."[138]

But again, Burton did not measure up. Frankfurter wrote Hand and exclaimed, about Burton, that "Harvard Law School's marking system is vindicated; he is a low-C man!"[139] "[Burton] is the most open-minded colleague. . . . One has easy and inviting access to his mind. The difficulty is with what one finds when one is welcomed to enter it."[140] "Reed," he wrote to Hand, "is largely vegetable—he has managed to give himself a nimbus of reasonableness but is unjudicial-minded, is flagrantly moved, at times, by irrelevant considerations for adjudication, as any of them. He has a reasonable voice in the service of the dogmatic, worldly timid mind."[141]

Frankfurter reserved his harshest criticisms for Black and Douglas. The question here was not their intellects or competence. Frankfurter acknowledged that Black and Douglas were bright. Rather, it was with their character and their motives as judges. "Hugo," he wrote to Hand, "is a self-righteous, self-deluded part fanatic, part demagogue, who really disbelieves in Law, thinks it is essentially manipulation of language. Intrinsically, the best brain in the lot—but undisciplined and 'functional' in its employment, an instrument for supporting a predetermined result, not a means for responsible inquiry."[142] Douglas was "the most cynical, shamelessly amoral character" he had ever known. "With him I have no more relation than the necessities of court work require. He is too unscrupulous for any avoidable entanglements."[143] He thought Douglas was one of the "two most completely evil men I have ever met."[144] Frankfurter despised Douglas for his political ambitions, which he saw as a corrupting influence on his judging. In a diary entry, Frankfurter recounts telling Roberts that "not long after Douglas came on the Court it was plain as a pikestaff to me that he was not consecrated to the work of this Court but his thoughts and ambitions were outside it. And for me such ambition in a man corrupts his whole nature— especially if he is a judge."[145] Black, the former Senator, failed Frankfurter's judicial motivation test because he could not free himself of the forces of populism, which, while perhaps acceptable for a legislator, were not fit for the judicial temple.

Ideology and motives aside, Black and Douglas stood no chance with Frankfurter after the Second Flag Salute case because they unabashedly sought to influence the Court, which he recognized would come at his expense. They were usurpers who operated without proper regard for the values Frankfurter held dear. They were pretenders to the judicial wisdom he had gotten from Brandeis and Holmes. They lacked that which he valued most—adequate judicial cultivation. Frankfurter wrote to Hand that Black and Douglas, along with Warren, were all "undisciplined by adequate professional learning and cultivated understanding."[146] The irony of course is that it was Frankfurter who was undisciplined, though in a different way. Frankfurter could never discipline his hatred of Douglas and Black and instead let it determine his jurisprudence. As Edward Pritchard Jr., an early law clerk and longtime intimate noted, "Felix hated [William O.] Douglas so intensely that he just naturally goes into opposition to Douglas in practically all instances."[147]

Whether Frankfurter had in fact shed his past liberalism for conservatism became a subject of interest from the time of the Second Flag Salute case. Journalists during the 1940s depicted both a struggle on the Court between Black and Frankfurter and between hardening factions, with Black and Douglas on one side and Jackson and Frankfurter on the other. Herman Pritchett's 1947 study of the voting patterns of the justices made clear, in both statistics and accompanying argument, that Frankfurter had positioned himself as a conservative on most of the issues coming before the Court. Frankfurter's voting patterns, in the liberal/conservative dichotomy, were at best erratic. In discrete cases they could be, Pritchett more pointedly wrote, "paradoxical."[148]

Looking at the trends in Frankfurter's voting record more generally, John Frank, a Black advocate and Court commentator, was by the end of the 1940s writing in his annual surveys of the Court's work that "after years of appearing at most a moderate on issues of civil rights, [Frankfurter] has again been made into 'a liberal' by the majority's turn to the right."[149] Frankfurter defender Louis Jaffee rebutted this by redefining the issue as one of fidelity to principle, not fidelity to ideology. He wrote that if the test is the extent to which a judge can be expected to implement a particular legislative program, then Frankfurter, in fairness, could not be considered a liberal. But at the same time he could not be considered a conservative either because "it is the very essence of his judicial philosophy that his role as a judge precludes him from having a program couched in these terms of choice."[150]

The argument over whether Frankfurter abandoned his liberalism did not end with his death. Those trying to shape his image needed to address in some way the notion that Frankfurter had changed in the way his critics alleged. From the beginning Frankfurter's supporters were on the defensive. In the memorial Supreme Court proceedings honoring Frankfurter, Dean Acheson, as chairman of the Resolutions Committee, argued that only in the area of reapportionment, with the Court's latest pronouncement in *Baker v. Carr,*[151] did Frankfurter fall behind in the Court's liberal march, and even there, he intimated, Frankfurter might yet be vindicated. By omitting any discussion of Frankfurter's opposition to the preferred position and incorporation doctrines, Acheson was able to present a Frankfurter having it both ways. Frankfurter, he said, met the dilemma posed by the unconstitutionality mantra of the Old Court by abandoning old constitutional restraints on social and economic reform, while at the same time leading the Court, "after his fashion, subject to the cautions and restraints that were deeply imbedded in his view of the judicial function and in his philosophy of history and of government," in "new and important lines of influence under the First Amendment, in the administration of criminal justice, and in effectuating equal treatment of the races."[152] In his remarks, attorney general Katzenbach recognizes that judicial restraint meant not getting involved but argues that this could be seen as a virtue. Frankfurter's judicial restraint thus rested on "not so much a negative view of the Court's power and competence, but more on an affirmative faith in reason, democracy, and the genius and fortune of the American political system to secure just solutions for essentially social or political problems outside the judicial arena."[153]

Albert Sacks and Paul Freund, who wrote entries in the two leading biographical dictionaries, present Frankfurter's position as Frankfurter himself would have presented it. Sacks in *The Justices of the Supreme Court* makes the arguments for Frankfurter's view of federalism and its attendant consequence for the review of state and federal legislation affecting individual liberties. Freund in his *Dictionary of American Biography* entry accurately states that Frankfurter in civil liberties cases distinguished between the broad guarantees of the Fourteenth Amendment and the enumerated provisions of the Bill of Rights, but Freund does not provide a relative context and locate Frankfurter among his brethren on these fighting issues, leaving the reader with a better-than-warranted feeling about Frankfurter and civil liberties.[154]

Philip Kurland in the commentary to his collection of Frankfurter cases does not consider whether Frankfurter abandoned liberal values in favor of conservative ones and simply presents Frankfurter as a conservative. He sets out Frankfurter's jurisprudential values and defiantly suggests that the Court has erred in not following them. Frankfurter through Kurland becomes the protest justice. Frankfurter's "may be only a voice from the past," he writes, only eight years after Frankfurter's retirement from the Court. "With any luck, it could be a voice for the future."[155] Frankfurter for him becomes "the latest of the great keepers of the legend: a legend of a nonpartisan Supreme Court dedicated to the maintenance of a government founded on reason and based on a faith in democracy."[156] Kurland makes clear that he does not like what has happened to the Court and looks for the coming of a second Frankfurter.

Joseph Rauh, Frankfurter's first law clerk, has a different take on the subject and provides informed candor in his 1975 Biddle Lecture at the Harvard Law School. He was the first of the sympathetic Frankfurter chroniclers to confront what he describes as the tragedy of the Flag Salute cases. There was, in fact, a double tragedy. The tragedy was not just that Frankfurter lost his chance to lead the Court. It was that, in the way he reacted to rejection, Frankfurter lost his chance ever to lead again. Rauh writes that Frankfurter resented his brethren when they deserted him, and he tended to impugn their motives. With Black taking the liberal leadership of the Court, Frankfurter, Rauh writes, "became more personal and more defensive, too often letting his feelings towards his colleagues cloud his judgments." He concludes, "It was in a sense Frankfurter's failure to respect [his brethren's] views that deprived him of the chance he might have had to regain their confidence in his leadership."[157]

Frankfurter's judicial career was ultimately defined by his arrogance and a series of ironies flowing from it.[158] That Frankfurter was arrogant can hardly be denied. Arrogance here is distinct from ego and from vanity. Frankfurter had these traits in spades also, as did many of his brethren, but in arrogance Frankfurter had no peer. The test of Frankfurter's arrogance is that he would have wanted, if it were possible, to arrogate to himself the task of judging. He believed that he alone was best suited to do the Court's work.

His brethren were not up to the challenge of judging on the highest level because they were either not smart enough or because their motives were tainted. Ironically, however, Frankfurter was not up to his own standard of disinterestedness. As Douglas put it, "no one poured his emotion more completely into decisions, while professing just the opposite."[159]

Frankfurter's self-image was so finely tuned and so deeply ingrained that he likely saw none of the contradictions that his life presented. Not one to gaze introspectively, though he could look penetratingly into the psyches of others, he never sought to explain to himself what was obvious to others—the connection between his personality and the lack of success he had with his colleagues on the Court. He likely believed himself when he castigated his brethren for grouping together and advancing a particular ideology, while at the same time he praised himself for his supposed disinterestedness in judging—this even though he was trying his best to influence others and advance his own brand of intellectual leadership. Frankfurter created for himself the most effective tools for rationalization and justification he could find in explaining his life and work on the Court. The direct lineage that he traced from himself to Brandeis and Holmes—his giants of the Supreme Court—meant that he acted not for himself alone but for them as well. Arrogance compelled him to follow the path he did in rejecting the Court once it rejected him as its leader.[160]

Perhaps the grandest irony here is that the positions Frankfurter urged in the defining debates over the preferred position and incorporation doctrines fostered not the judicial restraint he urged but what he considered to be the evil of greater judicial discretion. Frankfurter was surely right in identifying the paradox of divided government and its reliance on a judicial branch that is inherently antidemocratic because it is not accountable, at least not directly, to the electorate.

But if he wrote penetratingly about the possibilities of mischief in judicial unaccountability, the protection against this unaccountability for which he argued ironically provided more room for mischief. Black and Douglas wanted to pin judges down to the defined rights of the Bill of Rights, while Frankfurter wanted to roam the landscape of fundamental fairness and identify breaches of that fairness. The fundamental fairness standard of the due process clause for which he argued was in fact more flexible because it left judges without any precise guidelines to determine if it had been breached. Judges were, to use Frankfurter's phrase, to divine the scope of these rights.

Frankfurter, of course, had a stake in arguing that judges should be relied upon to plumb the depths of social consciousness and divine answers to the questions relating to fundamental fairness. As the heir to Holmes and Brandeis, Frankfurter believed himself to be best qualified for this task of divining. Finding breaches of the fundamental fairness would of course be rare, however, given the narrow exception to the rule of states' rights sovereignty, which in effect would result in the abrogation of judicial responsibility. In wanting to judge so limitedly, Frankfurter did not want to judge at all.

It is no defense to argue, as Frankfurter supporters have, that even if Frankfurter was "expansive, vindictive, and narcissistic," this could not be enough to condemn him since that "diagnosis would also be an accurate one of at least half the faculty and student body at Harvard Law School."[161] That students and faculty may well have this described arrogance is not relevant because it is only arrogance on the High Court that matters. Arrogance on the High Court has special meaning because it relates to the essence of the Court's function. Arrogance runs counter to the Court as an institution because the Court's work is premised on the idea that each of the nine justices has come to the Court by his or her own route and is entitled to the respect that comes from the mere fact of having been appointed.

Frankfurter might write in his diary that the conference discussion was meant to facilitate the equal voice of each justice,[162] but through his actions at conference, such as by holding the floor for extended periods and treating his brethren as his students, he provided overwhelming evidence that he could not have believed what he was writing. Ironically, in linking respect, or the lack of it, to what he set out as the qualifications of his brethren, Frankfurter revealed a fundamental failure to appreciate the nature of the Court. This is grandly ironic since Frankfurter had so often said that no justice had come to the Court with a fuller knowledge and better appreciation than he had of the Court and its justices. His diaries and correspondence make painful reading because Frankfurter's arrogance cannot be hidden or be given an ameliorating gloss. That he believed that the Court wrote its opinions for lawyers and others educated in the law rather than the average person is another damning example of Frankfurter's lack of respect for the Court's function.[163]

Frankfurter was perhaps at his best in a case such as *Rochin* with its Olympian statement and then resolution of the issue. There a defendant in a drug prosecution had swallowed the evidence and then had it dredged out of him. After setting out the fundamental fairness standard of the due process clause of the Fourteenth Amendment, Frankfurter wrote, in his best magisterial mode, that "we are compelled to conclude that the proceedings by which this conviction was obtained do more than offend some fastidious squeamishness of private sentimentalism about combatting crime too energetically. This is conduct that shocks the conscience. Illegally breaking into the privacy of the petitioner, the struggle to open his mouth and remove what was there, the forcible extraction of his stomach's contents—this course of proceeding by agents of government to obtain evidence is bound to offend even hardened sensibilities. They are methods too close to the rack and the screw to permit constitutional differentiation."[164]

Eloquence, however, did not move Frankfurter any closer to explaining why pumping a stomach to recover evidence on the one hand constituted conduct that shocked the conscience, while, on the other hand, permitting the executioner a second go at his subject when the electric chair did not do its job the first time around, as in *Francis v. Resweber,* did not violate that same fundamental fairness standard.[165] Moreover, Frankfurter's eloquence in *Rochin* could not distance him from his sharpest critics, Black and Douglas, who were nipping at his heels though they concurred, with Black, in particular, making the convincing argument that Frankfurter's exercise in judging, in "divining" fundamental fairness, was an ironic exercise in constitutional usurpation.

Frankfurter never addressed the fundamental inconsistency that his approach to constitutional interpretation presented. He recognized that the judiciary had an inherent antidemocratic element to its nature, and he sought to restrain that element as much as possible. What he never explained was how this attitude toward judging could be reconciled with arguments that gave judges more rather than less discretion in interpreting the Constitution. Putting aside the notion that Frankfurter felt free to stray from his own principles when he felt the need, the very nature of this contradiction suggests that Frankfurter's insistence on judicial restraint was rooted not in principle but in his reaction to being rejected by the Court.

The result is that he worked against himself and the Court and cut himself off from the Court's response to the different set of problems it faced during the 1941–54 period. Frankfurter's fight could hardly have been worth the candle. The federalism he championed could not be sustained in the face of the undeniable disadvantage states imposed when their rights were judged in relation to the corresponding federal rights. Frankfurter was damned either way. Whether he misjudged the relative value of these rights in light of federalism or whether he was forced to advance the position knowing better because he could not find a way to save face, Frankfurter distinguished himself and his career with futility and misspent energies. All would have been different if Frankfurter had not been so arrogant, but with his arrogance Frankfurter gave himself little chance of success on the Court.

≫

CHAPTER 4

Hugo Black & the Perils of Literalism

With Hugo Black we come to a rare example of a Supreme Court justice doubling as a national hero. In the twentieth century only Oliver Wen-
dell Holmes and Earl Warren have had greater public recognition for their
role as justices, and in the case of Chief Justice Warren not all of the public's sentiments were complimentary. Not so with Hugo Black. He was
beloved, as was Holmes. Both served well until old age—Black until he was
eighty-five years old and Holmes until he was ninety-one—and both were
known as dissenters whose dissents were later vindicated. That, at least, is
how Black portrayed himself in 1968 when he had the chance near the end
of his career and life to be interviewed on national television by Eric
Sevareid and Martin Agronsky.[1] With their help, he portrayed himself as
the champion of civil rights and individual liberties. His was an unwavering
commitment to a strict interpretation of the Constitution and all the protections it afforded, especially the First Amendment and its directive that
"Congress shall make no law . . . ," which Black took literally and
absolutely.

And it is of course true that Black was a leader in the Court's civil rights
revolution, though perhaps not in the way that most Americans understood. There is, in fact, a central paradox about Hugo Black and the liberal
credentials that helped make him a national hero. He was without question
the leader of the liberal faction during the principal 1941–54 period under
review here. This liberal faction, however, was more a dissenting than
majority voice, however, once the Court moved to the right with Truman's

four appointments. Somewhat surprisingly, given the liberal positions he had staked out in the 1940s and 1950s, when the Court later hit its full liberal stride in the early 1960s, Black was not leading the liberals as his earlier credentials might suggest that he would. This was not only due to the appointment of Earl Warren as a strong, liberal chief justice. It was because Black, by this time, had taken a principled, contrarian stand and refused to follow the Court in expanding constitutional rights beyond the literal language of the Constitution.

The irony of Black's career is that the Court did not follow him in the 1941–54 period in either of his signature arguments—(1) that the First Amendment imposed absolute limitations on the government's right to silence free speech and (2) that the Due Process clause of the Fourteenth Amendment incorporated all of the Bill of Rights and made them applicable to the states—because both arguments too liberally interpreted the Constitution. The Fourteenth Amendment incorporation argument did in fact help lead the Court to expand the application of federally guaranteed rights to the states, though under a different theory, one that Black resolutely opposed but nonetheless took credit for in his last years because it brought to the states the federal rights he had championed for a career. Black himself conveniently overlooked this grand irony when he made the case to the country in his television interview that he rather than Earl Warren was the great liberal leader, and in so doing he tried to obscure the fact that for the last decade of his career he tried to erect roadblocks to the expanded liberalism that Douglas, Warren, and others were trying to advance. For Black, in the end, his literalist, sometimes idiosyncratic view of constitutional interpretation tested whether his approach to judging was as principled and as objective as he consistently claimed it to be. And unfortunately the test finds him wanting, due largely to his inability to deal with advancing old age.

Born February 27, 1886, in rural Clay County and raised in Ashland, Alabama, Hugo Black was raised in relative prosperity made possible by his father's success as a merchant, amid the county's poverty. His father's alcoholism, however, brought Black embarrassment and made him determined to always be in control of his mind and body. In contrast, his mother provided a different sort of motivation. She was an indefatigable believer in his promise, something that always stayed with him. The steel will that would come to define him as a lawyer, senator, and justice revealed itself early on. For example, he and his sister Daisy were both students at the misnamed Ashland College, which was really a high school, when Black was all of fifteen and the principal, to Black's mind, unfairly disciplined his sister. To punish Black's grumblings of unfairness, the principal then took a switch to Black. Black resisted and destroyed the principal's tool of oppression, and when the principal found other switches, Black broke them as well. He left school with his family's consent, never to return to Ashland College or any other high school.

Yet not having a high school diploma did not stop him from first trying medical school for a year at Tuscaloosa before settling on the two-year law program at the University of Alabama and its two-member faculty. Black first began the practice of law in his hometown of Ashland, but when a fire destroyed the office that he maintained above a grocery store, he took his practice to Birmingham, where it steadily grew. With a brief stint in his mid-twenties as a city police court judge handling minor criminal matters and later as the county prosecutor for three years, Black began to prosper. He specialized in personal injury cases, always on the plaintiff's side. An effective, zealous advocate, Black played to juries and all their biases, including racial biases, to secure large awards for his clients. He was by all accounts a dazzling trial lawyer, one who understood trials as theater and juries as just a group of regular people who can be persuaded to do the right thing with the right kind of advocacy.

He capitalized on his financial success and local prominence to run a grassroots campaign for the U.S. Senate in 1926 and surprised many by winning. In Washington, he continued the populist themes with which he had identified himself as both a plaintiff's lawyer and a candidate, though he was a Democrat rather than a populist in the strict sense. He also brought the passion of his advocacy to the Senate and, though he did not speak often, gave memorable speeches on the floor. He began to distinguish himself in his second Senate term, sponsoring what became the Fair Labor Standards Act and chairing a committee that investigated subsidies to the Merchant Marines and the airlines, finding corruption in airmail and oceanmail contracts.[2]

Black's success in the Senate and his credentials as a New Dealer led to his appointment to the Court in 1937, at the age of fifty-one, though not without a stumble and not without grander ambitions. Just confirmed by the Senate, his nomination was attacked when it was revealed that he had joined the Alabama Ku Klux Klan in the 1920s. His response was to give a nationwide radio address in which he explained but did not repudiate his association with the Klan. He pledged his commitment to racial justice and with this took his seat on the Court.

Some have speculated that Black, the first of Roosevelt's eight appointments to the Court, was sent there to send a message to the members of the Old Court that, even though they had begun to ease their record in finding New Deal legislation unconstitutional, Roosevelt preferred to have more of Black's type of activism. He quickly began to distinguish himself from his Old Court brethren, issuing a record number of solo dissents. Substantive due process, Black would later say, was "why I came to the Court. I was against using due process to force the views of judges on the country."[3] Black served thirty-four years and retired from the Court in 1971 at the age of eighty-five. He wrote 481 majority, 88 concurring, and 310 dissenting opinions.[4] He did not take easily to loosening his reins and only grudgingly retired on his deathbed.

In an interesting twist, it had also taken him several years at the beginning of his tenure to give up the political bug, a rather striking contradiction for a justice who argued that "once someone is appointed to this Court, he should stay here."[5] Black biographer Roger Newman reports, for example, that a journalist friend of Black's said that "there was no way you could tell him that he wasn't going to be president. He just had it in his head." Some of his Alabama friends believed that Black went to the Court thinking it was a way to the presidency. According to Newman, Black went so far as to tell Roosevelt in 1940 that he would resign from the Court to run with him. Black apparently did not recognize that he had no chance in 1940 because of the lingering effects of his KKK association, and while Black did recognize that he had no chance as well in 1944 and 1948, he nonetheless continued to see himself as a potential candidate for president.

Journalists covering the Court in the 1940s invariably marked Black as the leader of the liberal block of justices, if not the entire Court. This status derived both from his actual leadership and from partisans taking up his cause in the same way that Frankfurter's partisans took up his. Black supporter Fred Rodell, for example, did his best to elevate Black and to bury his two principal rivals, Frankfurter and Jackson. Merlo Pusey's take on Black, also in the *American Mercury* of about the same time, is, in contrast, strikingly different. His approach is to compliment only after criticizing. "Justice Black is the leader of the court's liberal wing," Pusey writes, before recalling Black's great Ku Klux Klan embarrassment. "Black has worked prodigiously for six years to counteract the furor his appointment caused. In that he has partly succeeded."[6] As to his judicial ability, Pusey again undercuts, writing that "by burning midnight oil Black has also greatly extended his legal knowledge. Once he was accused of writing such blundering opinions that they had to be rewritten by other justices. Now he is something of an expert in maritime law. But Black was never a scholar by habit, and there is no reason to suppose that his mental brushing-up will make him a great judge."[7]

Louis Jaffe, a Frankfurter supporter, took the contest between Black and Frankfurter further in the *Atlantic Monthly* and settled for his side the question of which justice had the greater claim to the great prize of being associated with Holmes and his liberalism. "Recently Fred Rodell has been pleased to bestow on Black the mantle of Holmes," Jaffe writes derisively before restating the question as to the extent to which a justice's commitment to liberalism stays within the "traditional limits of the judicial process."[8] Black, he argues, eschews Holmes's approach and moves pell-mell toward liberalism. Frankfurter, on the other hand, respects precedent, as did Holmes, thus linking him more closely to Holmes.[9]

It was for Arthur Schlesinger Jr., the best informed and most neutral journalist to write on the Court during this period, to memorably sketch its personalities and divisions in a 1947 *Fortune* article.[10] He decides the Black-Frankfurter contest by declaring a tie. "Two of the Justices—Frankfurter and Black—are men of unusual intellectual ability and personal force," he writes. "Each leads his own faction on the Court. Black has a trenchant intelligence and is quiet, somber, hardworking, politically savvy, and extremely forceful in his advocacy."[11] He writes that for Black the defining debate is usually framed between activism and restraint, but the division turns more on what is to be gained through activism. Frankfurter is an activist in his own right, Schlesinger writes, on issues dear to him, but, without judging the appropriateness of activism, he indicates that Black, seeking to secure a wider agenda of civil liberties, is the greater activist of the two.

᠅

Black left his clearly recognizable jurisprudential mark during the 1941–54 period in a number of areas. In his best-known cases in the civil liberties field he moved at the end of the period toward the absolutist approach to the First Amendment, which he later championed. Until then, he recognized limits on First Amendment rights and employed the Court's traditional balancing tests. As he evolved in his thinking, he could accept some restrictions on time and place, but none on content. As would be the case with Douglas, Black during the early 1950s saw an increasing need to draw bright lines and recognize the government's encroachment on First Amendment rights through loyalty oaths and the like.[12] His response was to declare that the language of the First Amendment was for him clear and definitive, which in turn led to his absolutism of a few years later.

He was a friend to labor as well, not only in the application of federal regulatory laws but also in the First Amendment aspect inherent in picketing. During the period he consistently voted with picketers and distinguished between the speech and conduct components of picketing. In religious cases, he interpreted the establishment clause narrowly and distinguished between legislation to promote social welfare and legislation to promote religion. On the criminal side, Black from the beginning believed in the right to appointed counsel but had doubts about the scope of the Fourth Amendment's search and seizure provision. In maritime cases he enhanced the ability of seamen to sue by eliminating jurisdictional conflicts between state and federal courts.[13] He believed in the expansive power and application of the commerce clause to federal legislation, but at the same time he believed in the rights of states to regulate their own commercial interests when there was little or no impact upon national commerce. He also believed in the vigorous application of federal antitrust laws.

Black continued to build his liberal credentials in the years following the 1941–54 period and was recognized, along with Douglas, as a great civil libertarian. He spelled out his credo of constitutional interpretation in his 1960 James Madison Lecture, fittingly entitled "The Bill of Rights."[14] Douglas responded with a contrary declaration of his own three years later in his own Madison Lecture, pointedly entitled "The Bill of Rights Is Not Enough," making it clear that there was fundamental disagreement between the leaders of the liberal camp.[15]

Black believed that the only legitimate way to read the Constitution was to read it literally. He professed that such an approach would enlarge the scope of some liberties, such as the rights of the First Amendment, with its definitive "Congress shall make no law . . ." language, which Black interpreted to mean exactly what it said. But at the same time a literal reading recognized the limits of the Constitution, that rights not detailed within it could not be read into it. "It is my belief that there *are* 'absolutes' in our Bill of Rights, and that they were put there by men who knew what words meant, and meant their prohibitions to be 'absolute.'"[16] Douglas took the more expansive view that the Constitution need not be read literally to give it its intended meaning and that judges were obliged to adapt it to the times.

As prefigured by this declared dissonance between Black and Douglas, each went his own way during the 1960s. Black could not find references to wiretaps in the Fourth Amendment and could not follow the Court in *Katz*. Nor did he find, in the most celebrated case of the decade, *Griswold v. Connecticut*, the zone of privacy Douglas said was to be found in the penumbras of the First, Fourth, Fifth, and Fourteenth Amendments. He could not follow the Court in the sit-in cases,[17] where, in a mechanical if not reductionist fashion, he distinguished between speech and conduct and could find no constitutional protection for the conduct of the protesters. Black's liberal status in his last decade on the bench was under attack. His string of disagreements with the liberal wing of the party led some commentators to suggest that he was invoking a reflexive conservatism that aberrantly betrayed his own voting record and the Court's evolving civil rights jurisprudence. Michael Klarman, for example, has written that "Black, a hero (along with Douglas) to millions of mid-century political liberals, compiled a voting record during his half dozen years that can only be described as reactionary."[18]

Black's most significant and recognizable jurisprudential contribution during the 1941–54 period was in his advocacy of the "total incorporation" doctrine, which held that the due process clause of the Fourteenth Amendment incorporated and made applicable to the states the provisions of the first eight amendments of the Bill of Rights. In a historic clash with Frankfurter in *Adamson v. California*,[19] and in cases both before and after it, Black urged the expansion of the Court's authority in the relationship between the federal government and the states. His pitch and manner were matched only by Frankfurter's advocacy of a federalism that deferred to the states. In their clash Frankfurter and Black were fighting over nothing less than the soul of the Court.

In the Fourth Amendment case of *Rochin v. California,*[20] just five years later, the Court revisited the "total incorporation" theory, and Black, again dissenting, made his most pointed and effective attack on Frankfurter and his fundamental right analysis of the "selective incorporation" doctrine. He pointed to the unlimited discretion at the center of the analysis and found it inconsistent with the Constitution. That the Constitution speaks in unqualified language on its Bill of Rights by itself indicates that the Framers did not contemplate the exercise of discretion, especially given that the Constitution does not provide for judicial review at all. In his concluding lines he describes his great fear to be "the use of the philosophy [of fundamental rights analysis] to nullify the Bill of Rights." He wrote, "I long ago concluded that the accordion-like qualities of this philosophy must inevitably imperil all the individual liberty safeguards specifically enumerated in the Bill of Rights. Reflection and recent decisions of this Court sanctioning abridgement of the freedom of speech and press have strengthened this conclusion."[21]

Black did not take well to criticism that he had abandoned his liberalism. He argued instead that his constitutional credo did not permit him to play favorites in its application. He prided himself on his intellectual integrity, telling his law clerks on the occasion of his eightieth birthday, for example, that one reason he had lived so long and could sleep each night with a clear conscience was because he had chosen the path of intellectual honesty.[22] He was the same in the 1960s as he had always been, bound by his conviction that judges were not to exercise discretion or engage in balancing tests. It was only incidental that he was now accusing the liberal members of the Court rather than his great rival, Frankfurter, gone from the Court since 1962, of arrogating to themselves too much authority. The principle he was advocating was the same. For him, judges were limited by the express language of the Constitution—no more, no less. He had come onto the Court criticizing the way the Old Court had employed the due process clause to reach desired goals. Now, in the 1960s he was criticizing the Court's promiscuous inclinations of the same type. That the first attempts at misusing the due process clause had been anathema to liberals, while the second were a celebration of progressive thought, did not figure in his calculus.

Means not ends mattered most for him. He had written in dissent in *Griswold*, "I realize that many good and able men have eloquently spoken and written, sometimes in rhapsodical strains, about the duty of this Court to keep the Constitution in tune with the times. The idea is that the Constitution must be changed from time to time and that this Court is charged with a duty to make those changes. For myself, I must with all deference reject that philosophy. The Constitution makers knew the need for change and provided for it. Amendments suggested by the people's elected representatives can be submitted to the people or their selected agents for ratification."[23] This led him to note, "I like my privacy as well as the next one, but I am nevertheless compelled to admit that government has a right to invade it unless prohibited by some specific constitutional provision.[24]

With only slight variations in the last years, Black's agreement with the majority declined steadily throughout the 1941–54 period, moving from agreement rates nearing 90 percent in various years between 1941 and 1945 and slightly more than 60 percent in the first years of the 1950s.[25] The break between an agreement rate near or above 80 percent and a rate of 70 percent or less came in 1949 with the addition of Truman's last appointments, Clark and Minton. A listing of the rate with which Black agreed with the majority of his respective brethren shows not only that Clark and Minton are at the bottom but also that his long-recognized allies Murphy, Rutledge, and Douglas are at the top.[26] Black's votes with the majority opinions of Frankfurter and Jackson over the period have a familiar pattern, with greater agreement in the beginning and less toward the end.[27]

Black brought a strong, direct, and plain style suited to the articulation of point-by-point argumentation that distinguished his opinions. In some of his best opinions, such as *Gideon v. Wainright*,[28] he empathizes with the appellant and writes so as to allow the reader to identify with the appellant's feelings of helplessness and isolation when caught up in a process gone awry.[29] He could, in a different style, write as though he were still a trial lawyer when he wrote paragraphs that read as though they were meant for a jury.[30]

Black frequently said that he wrote to be understood by laymen. He could write memorable, forceful declarations of law and principle, and while some topics brought his passions to the surface, he did not often write with either the felicity or figurative language that attracts those looking for quotations. Black once told his son that he did not like to use figurative language because it lacked the precision he was looking for.[31] His son was right in responding that this was a shame because Black was so good at using such language. Indeed, two of Black's most memorable opinions use powerful figurative language. In one, for example, Black writes that "the freedom to speak and write about public questions is as important to the life of the government as is the heart to the human body. In fact, this privilege is the heart of the government. If the heart be weakened, the result is debilitation; if it be stilled, the result is death."[32] And in the other he writes that "today, as in ages past, we are not without tragic proof that the exalted power of some governments to punish manufactured crime dictatorially is the handmaid of tyranny. Under our constitutional system, courts stand against any winds that blow as havens of refuge for those who might otherwise suffer because they are helpless, weak, outnumbered, or because they are non-conforming victims of prejudice and public excitement."[33]

Generally, he seeks to impress in his arguments with the concrete and the factual and was right, given his objectives, in shunning figurative language. His is a prose of bluntness shaded by eloquence, with those issues dearest to him bringing out the best of this combination. He writes in a free speech case, for example, that "if the inference of conflict . . . be correct, the issue before us is of the very gravest moment. For free speech and fair trials are two of the most cherished policies of our civilization, and it would be a trying task to choose between them."[34] His forceful tone only occasionally dips into the personal, such as when Black in chastising Frankfurter wrote that "for judges to rest their interpretation of statutes on nothing but their own conceptions of 'morals' and 'ethics' is, to say the least, dangerous business."[35]

Books written on either side of Black's career have helped shape the way Black and his work have been interpreted. The first books on Black's life and jurisprudence described him as an agent of change on the Court. John Frank's 1949 volume explicitly sought to quiet some of the controversy swirling about Black and the Court, first by acquainting the public with an insider's knowledge of Black the man and the judge and second by offering a selection of Black's opinions on a variety of topics.[36] Frank drew heavily upon his personal relationship with Black in his hundred-page introduction to Black's life and set as his central theme Black's understanding of the common man. He was, for Frank, the common man transcendent. He coupled it with an emphasis on Black as a hardworking and compassionate justice. He brought Black's Alabama upbringing to life and sketched Black more as a man than as a justice, describing controversial incidents in Black's life, such as his involvement with the Ku Klux Klan, in a light most favorable to him.

The opinions Frank chose looked broadly at Black's record on civil rights and on the control of the economy and more specifically at Black's views on the relationship between the federal government and the states on business regulation and taxation, on the due process clause and its relationship to the full incorporation theory, on the enforcement of labor statutes, on criminal statutes and procedures, and on the First Amendment's free speech and religion clauses. Frank argued that Black, with the exception of his restrictive view of the Fourth Amendment, sided with the common man and was a sentimentalist about people in deciding their cases. Without apology, Frank considered Black a hero and wanted the country to see him in the same way.

Charlotte Williams's early academic study of Black in 1950 locates him amid the profound changes on the Court that had begun with his appointment in 1937 and the breaking up of the Old Court.[37] She recounts Black's Senate career and his Court appointment before turning to his jurisprudence and identifying it as the most dynamic force in the reshaping of the Court. She, like Frank, stresses Black's identification with the common man and his understanding of federalism, with its emphasis on a limited interpretation of the Constitution and the recognition of states' rights. She returns to her theme of change on the Supreme Court by identifying the fundamental issue on the Court as the clash, not between the Old Court and the new, emerging Court, but as the clash between Black and Frankfurter over issues such as the "preferred position" and the "total incorporation" debates.

The first book-length study to appear after Black's retirement from the Court was from a former law clerk, Howard Ball, who sought in his *The Vision and the Dream of Justice Hugo L. Black* to examine Justice Black's

unwavering vision of the law, which he does by outlining Black's understanding of democracy as set out in his opinions.[38] Black for him is the
restrained activist, reading the Constitution expansively when needed, so as
to give meaning to those rights set out in it, restraining whatever impulse he
might have as a judge to do good unless it is constitutionally authorized.
The fundamental distinction in reviewing the constitutionality of legislation is between economic legislation, which is given a wide berth, and legislation affecting individual rights, which comes in for closer scrutiny.

What is implicit in Ball's volume—that Black is a central figure in the
changes brought about in American society in the last few decades—
becomes the central theme of Gerald Dunne's 1977 *Hugo Black and the
Judicial Revolution.*[39] Detailing the history of what Justice Abe Fortes
described as "the most profound and pervasive revolution ever achieved by
substantially peaceful means,"[40] Dunne marks Black as the catalyst for the
Court's developing jurisprudence in the area of individual rights and criminal procedure and, with a mixture of biography and Court history, explains
to the general reader the constitutional times and the forces at work within
the Court that produced tension and then the ultimate liberal victories.
Black for him is the populist hero, with his book updating the themes that
Frank had set out in his 1949 profile of Black as a populist on the Court and
that Charlotte Williams had continued in her study.

Interest in Black has not flagged in recent years. James J. Magee's 1980
academic study of Black continued the theme of earlier books by identifying Black's absolutism and detailing its development, doctrinal underpinnings, and fullest expressions in his First Amendment and Fourteenth
Amendment positions.[41] Roger Newman then accorded Black his first complete biography, a full-blown, adoring volume of seven hundred pages
trimmed with the occasional acknowledgment of Black's flaws, foibles, and
inconsistencies.[42] Newman culled research libraries throughout the country
for new material and interviewed hundreds of friends, relatives, and others
who knew or worked with Black as he takes his subject from birth to death
in sometimes excessive detail. He argues that Black's Ku Klux Klan association was as innocent as Black made it out to be in his speech to the country
in 1937; he identifies and fleshes out Black's political ambitions; and he
describes Black as a stern parent and as an uxorious but domineering husband. Black's flaws, such as an intolerance toward significant changes in the

social fabric in the 1960s, are not so much minimized by Newman as they are noted without looking to consequences.

The result is that Newman's is both a story of Black's and the Court's triumphs, and as such it links him with Frank's and Williams's initial studies of Black. Former Black law clerk Howard Ball, perhaps the most active Black proponent, just two years after Newman's biography brought out his own, though here the life is sketched rather than fully presented. Once he gets to Black's Court years, which take up more than two-thirds of the book, Ball integrates discussions of key Court cases into the narrative of Black's role in the evolving Court. He, like the others, considers Black the most important agent in the Court's jurisprudential revolution, which for Ball makes Black a hero to the nation.

Black sought to control what was known of him on and off the Court. In his strongest measure he took the unusual step of directing his son Hugo Jr. to destroy his Court papers. Black, unlike Frankfurter, Jackson, and Douglas, did not memorialize his life as they had with their diaries, oral histories, and/or autobiographies. The most he did was to write a brief remembrance of his Alabama years for a law review and a longer, but still brief, memoir written in 1968 of his career until 1921, which was published as part of his second wife's journal entries of their marriage.[43] The little we can glean from the autobiographical sketches results from our interpretations of the way Black presents himself. He acts honorably on all occasions, is proud of helping his friends, of not gossiping maliciously, of being admired by others, and of working hard at everything. But we also see that Black sees himself as invariably right on all matters, that he likes getting even with his opponents, and that he likes being vindicated.

Black was not a revealing extrajudicial letter writer. He had few close correspondents, and even with them he did not reveal much about himself on the Court, the workings of the Court itself, or his brethren. He maintained a lengthy correspondence with Fred Rodell, as had Douglas, but here Black provides few clues as to what animates him personally. An example of Black writing in his warmest, most revealing mode shows, first, that he identifies traits in Rodell that he had himself and, second, that a Southern gentleman's sensibility of graciousness and modesty shapes nearly all of his thoughts. Rodell in one example has sent Black a copy of a recent flattering article he had written about Black, to which Black responded: "It is not for me to say whether what you wrote about me is true. I can repeat, however, what I have told you many times, that you are *some writer!* You write not only with the kind of terse style I like and use the kind of simple English words I think you should, but when you want to do so you can touch the hearts and arouse the emotions of people. I am sure that you found this out from the letter Elizabeth went to her typewriter and wrote you instantly after reading what you had said about me in the *American Law Review* article. In addition to all that I have just said, I know that you are one man in the world who never writes anything he does not believe. This is the kind of intellectual honesty that is worthwhile. I want you to take care of yourself, not merely because you are my friend but because people with your sturdy intellectual integrity are needed."[44]

For insights that Black did not provide personally, we have instead his second wife's journal entries and a memoir of him written by his son Hugo Jr., which provide rare access to Black's personality and life outside of his chambers and conference.[45] His son's warm, loving memoir variously presents him, either unwittingly or with absolving qualifications, as a parental taskmaster, as a stern disciplinarian, and as one determined to be in control of both people and events. As a parent he could punish errant behavior harshly, such as locking his son in the attic for a week when he once ran away from home as a teenager. He insisted that his sons adopt his values on important issues such as hard work and would find fault with them whenever they underperformed. He expected nothing short of consistent achievement of the highest order, so that if Hugo Jr. came home with perfect grades for several semesters and then followed with a stray B on a report card, Black would criticize him for being merely streaky as a student. Black took this approach because he believed that the way to motivate his children was to assault their self-esteem, expecting that they would then begin to perform as he expected so as to get into his good standing.

Hugo Jr. had been a fine student, for example, and had been accepted at the Yale Law School, but for Black this was not enough. He told his son, after learning of the Yale admission, that his son knew nothing, that he was lazy, and that he would not contribute financially to his legal education. Black changed his mind only when Hugo Jr. agreed to work with him during the summer and follow a course of instruction that Black himself would supervise to enable him to compete at Yale. In their daily study sessions, Black would berate the young Hugo Jr. for his inability to penetrate to the core of books such as Blackstone's *Commentaries.*

But Black went further and frequently embarrassed Hugo Jr. as a spur to his development, though sometimes the embarrassment seems born of ignorance and smacks of cruelty. He would, for example, criticize Hugo Jr. for having acne, saying that he could not understand why his son had it when he had been acne free as a teenager. Hugo Jr.'s anger at being treated this way is pointedly described in the memoir, with the recollection that at times he wanted to kill his father for so embarrassing him. This is the exception, however. Trained to blame himself, Hugo Jr. finds fault with himself rather than with his father. He tells of often having let his father down—by not getting perfect grades, for example—but he then exculpates his father by asserting, ultimately, that even if his father had expected too much, it shouldn't be considered a fault because the great success his father had made of his own life explained and justified his behavior.

Black's first wife, Josephine, died in 1951 at the age of 52. By all accounts their marriage and his home life were strained by her illness in her last years. He married again in 1957, choosing his secretary, Elizabeth. She kept extensive journals from 1964 to Black's death in 1971 and published excerpts of them in 1986. These entries are a remarkable portrait of Black not only as a justice and as a husband but also as an elderly man. Elizabeth was an unabashed Black hero-worshiper, granting him liberal allowances for behavior that would not go unchecked in others. Put in its mildest form, Black was a loving but domineering husband. He subscribed to an older Southern tradition in treating women, including his spouse, as inferior and subordinate. Perhaps unwittingly, Elizabeth Black portrays Black as a rather insistent man in his encounters with the everyday world. She writes, for example, "Hugo can be so dumb about mechanical things. He doesn't understand them at all, and he pinpoints and confuses store clerks with a number of staccato cross-examining questions. If I open my mouth he silences me with 'Let her explain it' (if she can, is implied). If I didn't know he was the smartest man in the world . . . I'd think he was pretty dumb."[46]

In a more important way, she reveals Black's domineering personality and means of dispute resolution when she writes generally about their disagreements. She writes in 1965 that "the raw naked force of Hugo's intellect and will is usually concealed beneath that kind, gentle exterior, but, believe me, on the few occasions we have had a clash of wills since we first met, I have seen the County Prosecutor, the Senate Investigator, the Attorney Cross-Examiner, and the Justice's analytical powers all rolled into one. Although I thought, and still do think, that I had a justifiable complaint, I ended up apologizing to Hugo. I asked him for an apology, but I never got it. However, when he summed up our conflict, he did it so sweetly by saying, 'I have told you and others many times that the period I have been married to you has been the happiest period of my life.' After that, I just melted right down."[47]

Black was a reader, both before coming to the Court and throughout his time there. He was determined once he was elected to the Senate to become better read and embarked on a program of reading political, historical, and legal works that in significant ways distinguished him personally and as a justice.[48] The ancient Greeks and Romans were his favorites. He read them for enduring lessons in human nature, which he thought was unchanging, and their applicability to current problems. Edith Hamilton's *The Greek Way* was his principal guide to the ancients and was perhaps his favorite book. He urged it upon his law clerks along with a bevy of classical texts. After telling a law clerk on one occasion that Tacitus had the answer to the problem he and the law clerk were trying to sort out, he remarked, upon learning that the law clerk had not read Tacitus, that one could not be a lawyer without having done so.

He was also fond of British constitutional history, and on this side of the ocean he preferred Jefferson above all, having read all of him. There was little American history that he had not read. The Harvard Classics made up one of his favorite sets of standard authors. He marked them as he did many other books in his library of some thousand volumes, most of which had been accumulated between the mid-1920s and mid-1940s.[49] He underlined important passages, wrote substantive marginal notes, and sometimes even indexed the texts for further reference. He read carefully and often reread books of particular significance to him.

He had no interest, though, in whole areas of literature, such as modern fiction or scientific writing. The sweep of what he rejected in modern liter-

ature suggests, however, more than just a lack of interest. His son Hugo Jr.
wrote in his memoir that "according to my father, Dostoyevsky,
Kierkegaard, Mann, Hemingway, and Joyce were worthless, and Melville,
Proust, Kafka, and Camus were bores, whose mission, if any, seemed to be
to corrupt humanity." He avoided law review articles and seemed to have
little interest in contemporary writing about law.

He had his particular interests and pursued them. His reading seemed to
touch him personally. Black once spent the larger part of an evening reading aloud to a law clerk the account of Plato's death in the *Phaedo.* He also
drew from his reading and sprinkled his opinions with references to historical voices and commentators. Among his hundreds of opinions are dozens
of references to figures such as Tacitus, Plutarch, Plato, Jefferson,
Macaulay, *Pilgrim's Progress,* and the Bible.[50] To the end, he incorporated
reading that had moved him. Having read Will and Ariel Durant's *The
Lessons of History* in 1968, when he was past eighty years of age, Black, in an
opinion involving a boundary dispute between Louisiana and the federal
government, for example, quoted a detailed passage from the book on the
flux of the sea and the land.[51]

Black seems to have written his own opinions, though there was some
question about his first years on the Court. Charlotte Williams argued that
Tom Corcoran was ghostwriting some of Black's better opinions,[52] though
Corcoran laughed off the suggestion.[53] Ironically, the generally recognized
poor craftsmanship of Black's early opinions suggests that he wrote them.
Justice Stone was reportedly so concerned about the poor quality of these
opinions that, in addition to bringing his concerns directly to Black, concerns that Black took graciously to Stone's face while rejecting them otherwise, Stone tried to arrange for Frankfurter, then still a law professor at
Harvard, to tutor Black in the craft of opinion writing.[54]

Of the 1941–54 period, Professor Daniel Meador, Black's law clerk in the
last year of the period, reports that Black wrote the first draft of his opinions
and presented the clerks with typed drafts. The clerks studied the drafts,
made notes on them, and then met with Black to discuss them, usually line
by line. The process was then repeated for each additional draft that was
needed.[55] John Frank, a Black law clerk for the 1942 term, reports similarly
on Black's writing habits, emphasizing the line-by-line review and the
ongoing give-and-take between Black and his clerks. As Frank wrote, "the
law clerks and the Judge worked over and debated the drafts of opinions,

line for line, hour after hour, either at the Judge's desk in the Supreme Court building, or in his study at home. Much of the work was done at home in the study, with long hours of drafting and debate over points of law in a library lined with the learning of Greece and Rome. These sessions often ran until midnight, with words added, but usually dropped . . . The clerks had no real effect on the work; as one of them said, 'although he sometimes let me practice writing an opinion before I read his first draft, the finished product always strongly resembled his first draft and seldom had any resemblance to my effort.' No one, after the incredulity of his success in the first year, ever seriously suggested that the Judge's opinions were anyone's but his own."[56]

Black was adored by his law clerks and got along extremely well with them, most of whom were from Harvard or Yale. He developed close personal relationships with them and saw his role as an educator in the affairs of law and life. He played tennis with them, refusing to lose to them as he refused to lose to everyone else. He often had them to his house for dinner and, except for his unquestioned obligation to make the ultimate decisions, treated them more as associates than as subordinates. They, in turn, remained fiercely loyal to him, perhaps to the point of distorting history to maintain their hero worship.

When many of his law clerks from his last decade on the bench were contacted and asked whether they thought that Black had toward the end of his career begun to grow rigid in his positions and to shrink from the liberalism he had marked out earlier in his career, to a clerk they responded emphatically that Black had not changed. The Court had changed, some argued, while others thought that Black's votes and opinions in the later civil rights cases were misunderstood. All championed what Black had argued was his great virtue—consistency of conviction. Not one thought that the growing jurisprudential gap between Black and the majority headed by Warren, Douglas, and Brennan reflected badly on Black. Those justices had strayed, the argument went, from Black's core principles. His principles were found in the Constitution, while the principles of the liberal majority were not.[57]

Black prided himself on his manners and on his relations with his brethren. He never spoke ill of them publicly and in only the rarest of instances did he express disenchantment with them, even when they had spoken ill of him or worked against him, taking to heart, perhaps, an observation he had underlined in his reading: when Diogenes was asked how to be revenged upon an enemy, he said, "the only way to gall and fret effectively is for yourself to appear a good and honest man."[58]

Douglas said of Black that he "always got along well with everyone. He is a very polished person with all the proprieties and the protocol of the South ingrained in him."[59] Black never commented, for example, during Jackson's attacks on him when Jackson was in Nuremberg and felt slighted at being passed over for the center seat. Nor did he treat Stone differently when he learned that Stone had been belittling his abilities to a Washington journalist, who then put Stone's gossip into print. According to Douglas, "Black never, in the years I was with him in conference, never once spoke an unkind word, never spoke a mean word or a malicious word. That's not to say that he didn't present powerful advocacy. Hugo Black is and always has been a great advocate. And he feels very deeply and he speaks with great intensity. But never so far I had observed has that involved any personal animosity to Stone as an individual."[60]

As for his Court friendships, it is often written that Douglas was Black's closest friend on the Court. Certainly both men said and wrote at various times that each was the other's closest friend. Douglas, for example, in his 1980 autobiography wrote that Black was "my closest friend on the Court and my companion in many hard judicial battles."[61] Black, for his part, in 1968 inscribed his gift copy of *A Constitutional Faith* to Douglas with "to my good friend Bill Douglas, my close working colleague for nearly thirty years, a genius in his own right, a man of indomitable courage, unexcelled energy and to whom I am indebted for his contribution to the formulation of many of the constitutional principles expressed in this book."

Looked at in the context of what their friendship had been like through most of their careers, these sentiments, representative of what the justices were saying about each other at the end of their careers, suggests that each was looking beyond truth to history. The two were perhaps closest during the 1940s, when they saw each other off the Court often, for example. This changed in the beginning of the 1950s. Black did not countenance Douglas's marital difficulties or the differences that were developing on substantive issues. Now they rarely spent time with each other at the Court, sometimes not speaking to each other for long stretches of time. Black's disenchantment with Douglas's extrajudicial activities—the traveling, the book writing—made matters worse, as did the break between the two in the 1960s on profound substantive issues, such as the right of privacy as found by Douglas in *Griswold v. Connecticut.* But even before *Griswold,* the degree to which Black and Douglas disagreed on issues and the way they expressed these disagreements made clear that, while they remained two of the Court's leading liberals, they were at odds with each other.

In a water rights dispute between Arizona and California, for example, Black wrote the majority opinion and Douglas in dissent made the stinging charge that, in siding with the federal bureaucracy despite the absence of congressional authorization, the opinion in the case "will, I think, be marked as the baldest attempt by judges in modern times to spin their own philosophy into the fabric of the law, in derogation of the will of the legislature."[62] Wife Elizabeth recalls in her journal that Douglas "literally spit out his words" in anger when he read his dissent in Court.[63] Revealingly, Douglas in his interviews with Walter Murphy in 1962 downplayed the depth of their personal friendship and gave what is probably the most accurate description of a friendship that, except for public posturing later, continued to deteriorate. "Actually," Douglas told Murphy, "personally, Black and I have never been very close. I very, very seldom see him. We're very seldom together socially. It's just more happenstance, I think, that we have found generally some kinship, although Black and I very often disagree on important matters."[64]

Black created the image of himself as someone who could distinguish between arguments and personalities and who did not let his affection for a person get in the way of standing on principle, whatever the fallout. The incident as recounted by Douglas surrounding Owen Roberts and the retirement letter that Chief Justice Stone wanted to be sent to him provides an illustration here. It was Black who led the revolt among some of the brethren when Roberts retired and Stone wanted language in a farewell letter that Black could not countenance. Even though he had been good friends with Roberts, visiting him on weekends at his milk farm in Pennsylvania, for example, and even though he did not hold it against Roberts that he had mistakenly, due to Frankfurter's influence, blamed him for leaks to the press about the outcome in certain cases, Black refused on principle to go along with a farewell letter that suggested a spirit of cooperation in Roberts that he thought did not exist.

He could do this on the professional side and at the same time Douglas could explain in 1962, "Hugo Black to this day would put down Roberts as, not the man he admired most, by any means, but the man whose company he enjoyed most of almost anyone that he had met."[65] He could feud with Frankfurter but at the same time think highly of him personally and recognize his importance to the Court. He lamented Frankfurter's retirement in 1962, writing him that "we're going to miss you on the Court because we need you. When some of my friends say to me 'things will be easier on the Court now,' I tell them they couldn't be more wrong."[66] He cried upon learning the news of his death and wrote in a memorial tribute that Frankfurter was a formidable adversary who thrived on argument and that his "initial respect and friendship for Felix survived all differences of opinion, [and] in fact grew with the years."[67]

Black seemed to have two personalities, the one known to most and the one that sometimes emerged when he felt he had been crossed. Justice Goldberg noted that "when Hugo was in agreement, he was a sober fighter . . . when he was in disagreement, he was a terrible and vigorous adversary. He was a gut fighter."[68] Chief Justice Warren observed that on occasion Black said and did things that did not "represent the better part of his nature."[69] Frankfurter, for one, felt the strength of Black's convictions and resistance when, on one occasion at least, they nearly came to blows at conference.[70]

Black was a proselytizer on the Court. Douglas ranked him with Frankfurter and Stone as the Court's most persistent proselytizers. At conference Black brought not just the passion of his convictions and a desire to convert but also impressive advocacy skills to complete the job. "Black is a very forceful pleader," Douglas explained to Walter Murphy. "He's one of the two or three men on the Court that has been a very active exponent of his point of view. He has an evangelistic fervor."[71] Anthony Lewis noted that "Hugo Black—and I say this in an admiring way—may have been the most relentless person I ever met in my life about getting his way. He did it with much more casualness, friendliness, easiness, and I'm sure was a more pleasant companion."[72]

His success, perhaps more than the passion he brought to his positions, made relations difficult with both Frankfurter and Jackson, each of whom resented Black's attempts to lead the Court. Frankfurter, at least in private, reviled Black and considered him unfit not only for the leadership role but for the role of judging itself. He pointed to Black's willingness to stray from the rules of neutral, principled decision making. In his diary, Frankfurter writes of Black that "every time we have that which should be merely an intellectual difference gets into a championship by Black of justice and right and decency and everything and those who take the other view are impliedly always made out to be the oppressors of the people and the supporters of some exploiting interest."[73] In one entry he describes Black in conference discussion as having "blazing eyes and ferocity in his voice";[74] in another, "Black [is] at his worst, violent, vehement, indifferent to the use he was making of cases, utterly disregardful of what they stood for, and quite reckless when challenged once or twice regarding the untenability of what he was saying."[75] Jackson's dislike for Black went beyond the private and expressed itself most notably in conference, where Jackson treated Black with disrespect and even contempt. Douglas's descriptions of Jackson's conduct toward Black reflect both Jackson's weakness in failing to control his emotions but also Black's strengths as an advocate to have so inflamed the passions of his opposition.

Black responded to the Court's individual rights jurisprudence of the 1960s with obstinate resistance. In a series of strongly worded and often impassioned dissents he repeatedly inveighed against the Court's willingness to go beyond the literal language of the Constitution. As one of Black's 1969 law clerks put it, "at times, the judge was obstinate and unwilling to explore contradictory viewpoints . . . [this was] a result [of] his intense beliefs in certain principles."[76] Some commentators have seen him as intransigent. Maurice Kelman, in his study of dissenters and dissenting opinions on the Court, described Black this way and as the century's foremost dissenter. For Kelman, Black rejected precedent that did not conform to his literalist reading of the constitutional text in the freedom of speech cases, for example, but at other times and with other constitutional issues he confoundedly appealed to stare decisis and surprised with his willingness to accommodate others, if at least temporarily.[77]

Black, as suggested by his wife Elizabeth's journal entries, refused to recognize that he had been wrong about anything. At the very outset of his career, he refused to acknowledge that he had been wrong in becoming a member of the Ku Klux Klan in the 1920s. Certainly, Black never apologized for his membership or said that if he had it to do again he would not have joined. It is of course possible that Black refused to acknowledge making a mistake because he believed that he had not made one.

In the same way, Black could well have believed that he had not made a mistake in the *Korematsu* case, in which he wrote the majority opinion upholding the constitutionality of the Japanese internment camps during the Second World War. We know that nearly thirty years later, just a month before he died, Black still defended his opinion in *Korematsu*.[78] Douglas, on the other hand, later came to acknowledge that he had made a mistake in voting to uphold the government's action, but Black said he would have done the same thing again. That Black never retreated from his position on *Korematsu* and would have done the same thing all over again was something not lost on a recent conference on judicial biography; it reinforced the notion that Black's star has dimmed, despite efforts by biographers Newman, Ball, and Dunne to cast Black as an American hero and despite Bernard Schwartz's rating of Black as the eighth of the ten greatest Supreme Court justices.[79]

Pride—perhaps overweening pride—and what some have called old age combined to present a different image of Black toward the end of his career. "Black has hardened and gotten old," Chief Justice Warren said in 1966, "It's a different Black now."[80] A fierce desire to see that he got what he considered his due grew to such a level that he even risked alienating friend and ally Chief Justice Warren. He bristled at the "Warren Court" appellation both behind the scenes and publicly. The liberal Court for which Warren was getting credit had begun with him, he believed. With this complaint, Black was conveniently overlooking the increasingly obvious point that as the majority grew more liberal—especially in adopting the unenumerated rights jurisprudence best represented by *Griswold*—Black voted with it less and less often.

Old age transformed Black and perhaps best explains his petulance at not getting the credit he thought he deserved for shaping the Court. Black had turned eighty in 1966, and his last five years on the Court were distinguished by classic signs of old age—physical frailty, fatigue, irritability, and forgetfulness.[81] His behavior even took on elements of the bizarre, such as when he, as Newman puts it, "kept a lawyer arguing a case [in 1967] well beyond the allotted time by repeatedly demanding that the attorney agree with his view of the case."[82] That Black got old was also not lost on commentators. Distinguished political scientist Glendon Shubert, for example, described the Hugo Black of the national television interview in 1968 with Eric Sevareid and Martin Agronsky as "a rigid, crotchety, dogmatic old man." Connecting style and substance, he noted that Black had been put on the Court to break up the conservatism of the Old Court but that in a stroke of great irony, he ended up animating a conservatism of his own that was fundamentally at odds with the liberalism of the New Deal.[83]

His civil rights jurisprudence became more and more a jurisprudence that insisted on his narrow reading of constitutional provisions. He condemned new challenges to his "total incorporation" theory, even from friendly, that is, liberal, sources. His relationship with Justice Fortas deteriorated in large part because Black took personal umbrage at Fortas's advocacy of the fundamental rights jurisprudence that he, Black, had argued against for so long. That Fortas was a member of the new, increasingly liberal majority represented the absolute death of Black's "total incorporation" theory. The result was increasingly stern, strident, and even condescending Black dissents when the majority enacted its understanding of the jurisprudence of fundamental rights.

The long view left Black with only one option. If he did not want to let Chief Justice Warren get credit for what the Court was doing and what the country was embracing, then he needed somehow to align himself with that new, increasingly liberal majority. This required the brazen skills of Hugo Black the politician and Hugo Black the lawyer who played to juries. It required the skill to argue that black is white and that white is black.

For their part, Black's supporters have sometimes contorted themselves to defend their man. Black's 1960s insistence on literalism at the expense of liberalism has presented his biographers with the difficulty of reconciling this last period of his career with the earlier periods. Roger Newman thinks Black's contributions as whole are significant enough to outweigh a stumbling finish. He admitted that which can hardly be denied: that Black in his last years became increasingly unwilling to move with history. He writes that "Black's Constitution had become all anchor and no sail, all umbra and no penumbra. As he aged and his tendons shrank, so did the joints in his Constitution lose their elasticity."[84]

Others have not been so candid. Black's other recent biographer, Howard Ball uses Black's refusal to follow the Court on the sit-in cases, on the privacy issue in *Griswold,* and on a number of other cases, as proof of Black's constancy and fidelity to principle (as had Gerald Dunne in his 1977 biography). For them, the fact that he did not vote with the Court shows the depth of Black's commitment to principle. The biographers also add that personal reasons may have had something to do with Black's votes, but not so much so as to call Black's fidelity to principle into question. They recount that Black feared the breakdown of the social fabric and that he could not divorce this feeling from his response to the sit-in cases, which he saw as illustrations of lawlessness.

G. Edward White and David Currie, the two leading commentators on the Court generally and on the period specifically, have gone beyond the biographers and have in varying degrees explained and defended Black against the charges of inconsistency. Both are Black admirers. Currie takes the approach Black himself would take and argues for principled consistency.[85] In Black's opinions in the sit-in cases, for example, the distinction between speech and conduct is not disingenuous but is instead rooted in principle. Nor for Currie is it inconsistent that Black would dissent in *Griswold,* since it is plain that the Constitution does not detail a right of privacy for the use of contraceptives. If anything, Currie argues, Black's opinion in *Griswold* shows his jurisprudential consistency. Black meant what he said in 1947 in *Adamson* when, in the context of the "total incorporation" doctrine he was describing, he also argued that the rights made applicable to the states needed to be interpreted narrowly. If the right was not explicitly described, it did not exist.

White, like Currie, finds consistency in Black's jurisprudence, though in doing so he sometimes strains.[86] For White, the essence of Black's jurisprudence was that it allowed him on the one hand to find absolute values in the Constitution, but at the same time to find flexibility—albeit a linguistic one—there as well. When the Framers did not foresee and provide for a particular right, or for the particular application of a right, Black, in White's view, felt justified to fashion his own gloss on the Constitution. In this way he reconciled the two strains in his thinking. He could, for example, provide a gloss to speech as described in the First Amendment to include radio broadcasting, something not contemplated by the Framers. But he could also interpret speech narrowly and distinguish between protected speech and conduct, such as in a sit-in or picketing, that was masquerading as speech.

The argument seems to be that if the premise is broad enough, consistency can be found if we look hard enough for it. It is not manipulation of the Constitution when the goal is just, as it was for Black. It is manipulation, however, when White describes Black finding in the Constitution a right not actually there—the right to vote and Black's agreement with the majority in *Baker v. Carr*[87]—that his argument of internal consistency seems especially tenuous. The solution for him is to describe Black's vote in *Baker v. Carr* as an aberration.

The full arc of Black's career, however, suggests that Black was not as principled as he claimed to be. Black, despite denials to the contrary, seems to have engaged in one of the great inconsistencies in the Court's history. On the one hand, he argued that what could be found in the Constitution was only what could be found in its language, while on the other he argued for an interpretation of the due process clause of the Fourteenth Amendment that was wholly without textual support. If those who drafted the amendment had wanted its provisions to incorporate all of the Bill of Rights and be made applicable to the States, as Black argued they did, then they simply would have written such an intention into the amendment. They did not, but Black was willing to search the legislative history until he found what he claimed supported his total incorporationist view. But, as one scholar has noted, Black's use of history in this regard valued expediency rather than honesty.[88] What can hardly be denied was in fact denied by Black throughout his career on the Court—that he was reading a political or judicial philosophy into the Fourteenth Amendment and that he resisted or ignored contrary views because he was determined to bring to the states the values found in the Bill of Rights, regardless of whether the drafters of the Fourteenth Amendment intended such a result.

Black was principled when it was consistent with his objective. The best example of this comes with his commitment to the incorporation doctrine on the one hand and the federalization of the provisions of the Bill of Rights on the other. Black maintained to the end that an approach that fell short of the total incorporation approach he was advocating was wrong, if for no other reason than its apparent sanctioning of the great evil in Black's judicial universe, judicial discretion in the application of the due process clause of the Fourteenth Amendment.[89] But at the same time, of course, Black not only signed on to the spate of opinions selectively incorporating various provisions of the Bill of Rights and making them applicable to the states, he wrote some of those decisions using the dreaded language of fundamental fairness.[90] The goal of federalizing the provisions of the Bill of Rights loomed larger than the means. To achieve his objectives, Black accommodated others on the Court and subsumed his tenacious belief in total incorporation.

Black, however, exercised discretion in his willingness to go along with the Court to meet his objective. The best illustration of this comes in Black's argument for the total incorporation theory. At first he had felt compelled to be consistent in his debates with Frankfurter over the doctrine, as when it came before the Court a few years after *Adamson* in *Wolf v. Colorado,* an important search and seizure case.[91] Here Frankfurter used his fundamental right analysis to conclude that, while the suppression of evidence under the Fourth Amendment had been applied in federal criminal trials, the Fourteenth Amendment did not incorporate the amendment's provisions and make them applicable to the states. Douglas in dissent was quick to point out that without the complementing suppression provision, the Fourth Amendment's protection would do little for state citizens.

Black, like Douglas, thought that the Fourth Amendment was applicable to the states under the full incorporation theory, but because he read the Fourth Amendment literally and could not find the suppression provision within it—it being a creature of judicial creation—he concurred while Douglas dissented. Principle gave way, however, when the suppression issue came up again a dozen years later in another important search and seizure case, *Mapp v. Ohio.*[92] Black this time could not be left behind. He still doubted whether the Fourth Amendment standing alone would be enough to suppress the evidence at issue in state trials, going so far as to quote the reasons he had set out earlier, but now, "reflection on the problem . . . in the light of cases coming before the Court . . . had led him to believe that without suppression the Fourth Amendment guarantee was hollow."[93] If such a change in thinking were part of a larger scheme of reconsideration, it could be called growth. But as an example of otherwise unexplained revisions, it represents only inconsistency.

To rebut the charge of inconsistency and to help secure his credentials as the leader of the Court's liberal jurisprudence, Black adopted an ultimate strategy of revising the Court's jurisprudential history. That he bristled at the credit Chief Justice Warren had received at his expense in shaping the Court indicated that Black had retreated to the notion that the Court was not being properly understood, and that if it were, his leadership would be recognized. The most striking illustration of Black's insistence on being the Court's hero came in a nationally televised interview at the end of his career in which he remarkably took credit for the revolution in individual rights by arguing that his dissent in *Adamson* had been vindicated. Black did not misrepresent his dissent in *Adamson.* Instead, he misrepresented, to a national audience, its significance. Eric Sevareid, developing the theme that, like Holmes, Black had been a great dissenter whose dissents later became law, asked: "I think that more of your dissents have later become majority opinions and the law of the land than is true of any other Supreme Court justice. What's the most important of those dissents that later became law?" To this Black answered, "Adamson against California. That's the case where I asserted at full length for the first time my belief that the passage of the Fourteenth Amendment made the Bill of Rights applicable to the states."[94]

This assertion is vital to understanding Black because it makes his inconsistency plain: He had, on the one hand, repeatedly and forcefully distinguished between the total incorporation doctrine he advocated and the selective incorporation doctrine he deplored. But, on the other hand, in this chance to present himself to the nation he conflated the two doctrines and misled the national audience as to his role in the Court's liberal jurisprudence. Black's *Adamson* dissent, of course, had never been adopted by the Court. To the contrary, the argument for total incorporation that the dissent set out had been repeatedly rejected by the Court. That it had been repeatedly rejected while Black was sitting was the very reason he unflaggingly argued that the "selective incorporation" doctrine was wrong. Black had ultimately followed the path of "selective incorporation" only as a means of last resort to see that various individual rights were made applicable to the states.

Black, in this chance to present himself and his career on the bench to the nation, did not assert his dedication to principle and seek to distinguish himself from the unenumerated rights jurisprudence that he had inveighed against. Rather, he jumped aboard the bandwagon and took the reins, claiming that he had been driving all the while. It is as though through an act of will Black could revise history and make himself the leader he insisted on being. None of Black's recent biographers have made the argument that Black made to his national television audience. Only John Frank, his first and greatest academic supporter, has made the argument. For him, in a recent essay on Black's contribution to contemporary jurisprudence, "selective incorporation" and "total incorporation" are but the same doctrine when, with only minor exceptions, "selective incorporation" leads, as it has, to the application to the states of all of the rights found in the Bill of Rights. The principled distinctions Black insisted on honoring have been swept away, ironically, in his name.[95]

That Black should attempt as he did to shape his image for the nation with his televised interview should perhaps come as no surprise. He had, after all, followed a similar strategy immediately following his confirmation to the Court when he addressed the nation on radio regarding the disclosure that he had once been a member of the Ku Klux Klan.[96] His seven-minute radio address to the nation and an audience of forty million is a remarkable rhetorical performance distinguished by Black's admission of his membership, his statement that he terminated the membership, and then the complete absence of any discussion of what most listeners would have most wanted to know about—what connection there might be between Black's membership and his views on race. Instead, Black merely stated, albeit forcefully, that he was firmly committed to the freedoms of speech and religion.[97] His commitment to equal justice was beyond reproach, he implicitly argued, because he said it was so. Obstinacy had led to ipse dixit reasoning. In doing this he declares the matter closed, having shaped the issue's discussion, or lack of it, only to suit his purposes.

In light of Black's obvious but unacknowledged transformation on the selective and total incorporation doctrines, his refusal to follow Douglas and the Court on the individual rights issues of the 1960s suggests that Black might have insisted on principle not for the sake of principle but as a pretense to justify conclusions based more on a personal response than a judicial one—his dislike of antiwar protesters and his fear of the lawlessness of sit-in protesters. Loosed from this fundamental form of judicial restraint, obstinacy when coupled with overweening pride, as described by his wife Elizabeth, could become both the best defense and the best offense.

What Black did not see was the irony of his ultimate position. He could find fine distinctions to justify his reluctance to follow the majority in the liberal decisions of the 1960s (as some of his admirers did). But for the common person he ostensibly represented, the fine distinctions translated into distinctions without differences. Black, as he grew increasingly distant jurisprudentially from Douglas in this last decade, did not appreciate what Douglas recognized as the essence of judging: to recognize that in the conflict between the spirit and letter of the law, justice rested with the spirit (see chap. 5). It is to Douglas's credit that we find in him what the Court stands for in its outline of personal freedoms, but it is also, unfortunately, a commentary on Black's failings.

Black's adventures with "total incorporation" and "selective incorporation" did have a satisfactory if not happy ending as they related to his insistence on literalism. "Selective incorporation," as he argued in one of his last cases, was not all that he desired, leaving as it did the incorporation of various Bill of Rights provisions to an ad hoc process too dependent on judicial discretion,[98] but the doctrine had brought about Black's desired goal, the federalization of the Bill of Rights. What we better appreciate, after looking at Black's 1941–54 period and the self-abnegatory result of his concurrence in *Wolf,* is that his 1960s insistence on literalism ended badly, with Black unable to recover his perspective and find a way to accommodate the Court's evolving liberal jurisprudence, one that in any other context he would have embraced. He had gestured this way once, getting right in *Mapp* what he had gotten wrong in *Wolf,* but his willingness to accommodate principle to result would take him no further.

‑‑‑

CHAPTER 5

William O. Douglas
Judging & Being Judged

While there has been some controversy about some of the details of William O. Douglas's life, at least as he recounted them, the degrees in the arc of his career of high achievement are well known. The details of his personal life aside, his enduring legacy comes in the contrast between Douglas as he is generally known today and his contributions to the Court during the period of 1941 through 1954. This early period shows us that we need to see the Court and the job of judging less in terms of the application of pure reasoning and neutral principles, as the Legal Process theorists preferred, and more in a political context in which personality and fundamental philosophical predispositions determine results.

To consider Douglas's career is to consider the way we see and evaluate the Court and its justices. Ironically, the recent biography of Douglas by Bruce Murphy, which details a host of Douglas's personal failings, such as his coldness, selfishness, and self-serving self-creation myths, has prompted us to ask questions about the significance of these details and to look to where Murphy did not have much interest, that is, in Douglas on the Court and the way he responded to the obligations of his office. We recognize, when we approach the matter this way, that, despite the compelling nature of their details, Douglas as a historical figure is far more than the sum of his personal imperfections. On the Court they did not get in the way. The irony of Douglas's personality, maligned as it has been, is that when his career is contrasted with those of Jackson, Frankfurter, and Black we recognize that Douglas did not, as they did, indulge the pettiness of personality

failings when it came to his commitment to the Court and to his jurisprudential development. Whatever his failing as a person might have been,
Douglas understood his role as a justice. In that role Douglas blazed a path
on the Supreme Court that we are still following today.

The standard version is that Douglas's life was one of achievement. Born
October 16, 1898, to poor parents in Minnesota and transplanted to Washington state at the age of four, Douglas lost his minister father at the age of
six. With the family poorer still, he was then beset with infantile paralysis,
which he overcame with a combination of rigorous outdoor exercise and
daily and even hourly ministrations from his devoted mother. The burning
desire he brought to conquering his physical disability carried over throughout his life to success on all fronts. As a youth it brought him top honors as
a high school student and as a college student at Whitman College. He followed a two-year hiatus as a local school teacher with a trip East and enroll-
ment at Columbia Law School. He continued as a top student, but with a
lone C he dropped from first to second place in his law school class and lost
out on a chance to clerk for Harlan Fiske Stone, the Columbia dean now
sitting on the Supreme Court. He went to Wall Street rather than to Washington and spent two years at a blue-chip law firm learning the intricacies
of railroad reorganizations.

He put his knowledge of corporate business practices to good use when
he moved uptown as a new Columbia Law School faculty member. He pursued the theme of Legal Realism in his research into the quotidian mechan-
ics of corporations and bankruptcies and delivered his conclusions in articles distinguished by their clarity and their direct, forceful, and nearly
antiacademic prose. Disputes between the faculty and the administration
over the school's philosophical directions led Douglas to the Yale Law
School. He continued his own brand of legal scholarship there and became
an academic leader not only at Yale but throughout the world of legal scholarship.

Moving at full stride as an academic, Douglas in the 1930s began to apply
what he had learned from his close examination of the business world. He
first moonlighted with the Securities and Exchange Commission, conduct-
ing hearings and producing a pathbreaking seven-volume report on Wall

Street's often unsavory practices. Douglas in 1934 then took a leave of
absence from Yale and signed on as an SEC commissioner. He helped root
out some of the securities industry's offenders, such as Richard Whitney,
and came to the attention of Franklin Roosevelt and his administration.

His fruitful work and an ever-increasing web of personal contacts soon
had Douglas as chairman of the SEC and as a Roosevelt intimate. He wrote
speeches, gave advice, drafted legislation, and played an impressive game of
poker as a member of Roosevelt's brain trust and inner circle. Few in the
administration were closer to Roosevelt, and none was more able or more
ambitious. Having been offered the Yale deanship, Douglas met with Roosevelt on a fateful day in 1939 hoping he would be able to turn down whatever new job Roosevelt wanted him to take on. He said goodbye to academic life, however, when he left with an offer to join the Court, at forty-one,
as the youngest justice ever. He left the Court thirty-six years later as its
longest-serving member, having written 524 majority, 486 dissenting, and
154 concurring opinions.[1]

It had been clear by the end of Douglas's first decade of service that the
Court could not cabin him. Beginning almost with the date of his appointment, Douglas was rumored to be a candidate for high political or
appointed office. Roosevelt thought him presidential timber and advanced
his cause, both floating suggestions of Douglas as a member of the Democratic presidential ticket and considering him for a series of cabinet or high-
level administration posts. When a roomful of Roosevelt's top advisers had
narrowed the choice in 1944 to two, Roosevelt chose to run with Truman
rather than with Douglas, though he said he would have been happy running with either. Douglas did little to discourage speculation about him as
a politician, telling close friends that he would be willing to leave the Court
to be either secretary of state or war if the conditions were right.

The chance of a high administration post died in 1945 with Roosevelt's
passing, but speculation continued on Douglas's chances on a national
ticket. There were rumors that Douglas would run with Truman in 1948,
but Douglas seemed to have no interest in the job, perhaps because of Truman's poor chances of reelection. Douglas himself finally put an end to his
speculative career in national politics by telling the country in 1952 in a letter to the *New York Times* that he had no interest in politics and that he
would spend the rest of his career on the bench. By the late 1940s he had
already begun to shift gears by embarking on extensive domestic and inter-

national travel that would in part distinguish him. Moreover, by 1950 he had written the first of more than twenty books about his own life, travel, politics, law, culture, and the environment that marked him, by the end of his career, as an environmentalist, wilderness maven, First Amendment defender, and multidimensional maverick of a sort never seen before or since on the Court. The early 1950s brought as well the end to his thirty-year marriage. He would marry and divorce again two more times before marrying a fourth time in 1966 and finally finding happiness. His fourth wife, like his third, was one-third his age.

Douglas achieved legendary status by the time he retired from the Court at the age of seventy-seven following a debilitating stroke. His votes and opinions, primarily in the second half of his career, on a wide array of civil liberties issues—such as his landmark opinion in *Griswold v. Connecticut* on privacy as it related to the sanctity of the bedroom and the right of couples to use contraception—brought his clear and direct judicial voice to the attention of an entire nation.[2] Along with his ally Hugo Black, Douglas held an essentially absolutist view of the First Amendment. He was an integral part of the Warren Court's effort to extend fundamental constitutional rights in the area of criminal procedure to the states by way of the selective incorporation doctrine, and he was foursquare with the Court as it broke new ground in the areas of political enfranchisement and racial equality.

He almost never voted with Warren Burger, on the other hand, Warren's successor. And, as the last remaining New Deal official following Black's retirement in 1971, he rarely agreed with new appointees such as William Rehnquist. In his last years on the Court, in *Roe v. Wade*,[3] he brought to fruition what he had put in place in *Griswold* and its predecessor, *Skinner v. Oklahoma*,[4] on the Constitution's protection of unspecified fundamental rights. In a concurring opinion in a companion case to *Roe* he made clear what had only been implied until then when he cataloged the rights he considered fundamental, rights not to be found, his academic and political critics had been pointing out for years, in the explicit text of the Constitution.[5]

He coupled his judicial activity of the 1960s and 1970s with calculated image making. This included books that appealed to mass audiences with increasingly simplified solutions to problems and an increasingly radical authorial voice. He became a lightning rod in the 1960s and 1970s for reactionary and sometimes even mainstream conservatives for all that was wrong with an activist Court. Some members of Congress went further in

1970 and sought impeachment, but the attempt disgraced itself and failed. To his death on January 19, 1980, Douglas continued to shape his image, first with an unprecedented 1975 volume of autobiography, *Go East, Young Man,* and then with a posthumous second volume in 1980, *The Court Years, 1939–1975.*

As was true for nearly everyone else, Douglas went through an adjustment period on the Court. He explained that little could prepare a justice new to the Court for the breadth and the technical nature of the Court's work.[6] It was not until problems had come around a second or third time for a justice that he could begin to feel comfortable. He did not begin to find his stride, he said, until he had been there two or three terms.[7] Until then he was inclined to follow Chief Justice Hughes's votes. For Douglas, feeling comfortable on the Court coincided with the beginning of the 1941–54 period and the 1941 term. By then he was his own justice.

The rate of Douglas's agreement with the majority during the 1941–54 period illustrates the Court's conservative and liberal dynamics at work. Douglas on average agreed with the majority three-fourths of the time, but this figure is misleading. The degree to which Douglas voted with the majority divides sharply into two phases. During the first, from 1941 through 1946, Douglas voted with the majority at least 80 percent of the time each year. Beginning with 1947, however, and continuing through the balance of the 1941–54 years, Douglas's agreement with the majority never went beyond 73 percent, dropping as low as 50 percent in 1952.[8] Not surprisingly, Douglas's increasing dissatisfaction with the Court's direction with Truman's more conservative appointments of Vinson (1946), Burton (1945), Clark (1949), and Minton (1949) finds its way into his voting patterns with his individual brethren. His patterns in agreeing with the majority opinions of his individual brethren reveal a liberal/conservative schism. Douglas agreed least often with Truman appointees Burton and Minton, and with Frankfurter and Jackson least often after them.[9] In contrast, he voted with the majority opinions of Murphy, Black, and Rutledge most often.

But beyond this basic division, Douglas was less inclined to vote with Jackson, Frankfurter, and Black in the second half of the period. He agreed with Frankfurter and Jackson less often during this second phase. He had consistently disagreed with each during the first half of the period, but during the second Douglas's dissent rate for each erupted and was indiscriminate. They seemed to agree on nothing of importance. Douglas's agreement rate dropped even for Black during the second half of the period. While he had agreed with Black, for example, nearly all of the time during the 1941–46 period, during the 1947–53 phase there were glaring examples of fissures between the two.[10] He agreed with him on only four of ten occasions in 1952 and only five of nine occasions in 1953.[11] He dissented with an opinion sixteen times of the twenty-nine times he did not vote with a Black majority opinion. The dissents were primarily in the areas of administrative and regulatory law, tax law, and labor law.

For a justice with a strikingly low agreement rate with the majority opinions of certain of his brethren, Douglas, surprisingly, secured unanimous opinions during the 1941–54 period at the highest rate on the Court.[12] Given the alliances and conflicts between Douglas, Black, Frankfurter, and Jackson, it is not surprising that Frankfurter and Jackson, aside from the ever-dissenting Roberts, disagreed most often with Douglas's majority opinions.[13] Their agreement rate of only 70 percent was strikingly low. Even Truman appointees Minton and Burton agreed with Douglas approximately 85 percent of the time. Clark and Vinson, apparently untroubled by the frequency with which Douglas disagreed with their respective majority opinions, were even more drawn to him, voting with his majority opinions at a 90 percent rate. Black, clustered with a group of others, agreed with Douglas nearly 90 percent of the time.[14] The year-by-year votes of these justices with Douglas's majority opinions provide no surprises.[15]

Douglas did not arrive at the Court as the great civil libertarian he became. During the 1941–54 period he evolved toward the position for which he is now primarily known, but the evolution was hardly consistent and uniform. He was more than willing to defer to the government's alleged interest in the Japanese internment and related military cases of the Second World War, for example. Douglas in these cases followed the balancing test, which suggested that the mere reasonableness of the governmental interest would always trump the individual's liberty interest.

Only much later did Douglas come to the view that the government needed a compelling reason to infringe upon the individual rights that he so easily yielded on in the wartime cases. Moreover, Douglas on both the establishment and exercise clauses of the First Amendment's religious protections followed the Court in its application of a balancing test in the establishment clause cases, only later coming to a near absolute position on the issue. In the same way, Douglas's first religious exercise cases had him applying a balancing test during the 1941–54 period, often holding against the individual and drawing distinctions between acts, which the state could regulate, and beliefs, which the state could not. After the 1941–54 period, however, little regulation of religious acts could survive.

Douglas's jurisprudence in the free speech area during the 1941–54 period also differed strikingly with what followed. He later became a near-absolutist, eschewing the application of a balancing test to determine whether the government's or the individual's interest should prevail. The Framers of the Constitution had already done the balancing with the directives of the First Amendment, he would argue. During the early part of the 1941–54 period he was, however, more attuned to governmental interests, especially the interests of the federal government during wartime, and accepted the Court's cautious approach to free speech values. He accepted as well the idea that certain types of speech, such as obscene speech, were not entitled to constitutional protection, but here too his jurisprudence evolved, following the 1941–54 period, to a near-absolutist approach, one that held that all speech, commercial and obscene, enjoyed protection.

But while Douglas's views were in step with the Court's during the first half of the 1941–54 period, during the second half he wanted to provide greater protection to speech and applied the clear and present danger test of Holmes to do so. This is the meaning of *Dennis*. In dissent, Douglas applied the Holmes test and could find nothing to fear in the communist ramblings of the defendants.

Later Douglas would himself abandon the clear and present danger test and, in moving toward the absolute protection of speech, argue that the only speech not protected by the First Amendment was speech brigaded with illegal action. In the obscenity case of *Roth v. U.S.*, Douglas in dissent argued that "government should be concerned with antisocial conduct, not with utterances. . . . The First Amendment, its terms absolute, was designed to preclude courts as well as legislators from weighing the values of speech

against silence. The First Amendment puts speech in a preferred position.
. . . Freedom of expression can be suppressed, if, and to the extent that, it is
so closely brigaded with illegal action as to be an inseparable part of it."[16]
Douglas, who had started the 1941–54 period believing in the government's
right to regulate speech, by the end of that time would have none of it. Censorship had become anathema to him. As he said in one case, "in order to
sanction a system of censorship I would have to say that 'no law' [as found
in the First Amendment] does not mean what it says, that 'no law' is
qualified to mean 'some' laws. I cannot take that step."[17]

Douglas's most significant contribution to the area of civil liberties, if not to
the Court generally, came with his bold pronouncement in *Skinner v. Oklahoma* of the strict scrutiny equal protection doctrine as it related to fundamental rights. At issue in *Skinner* was an Oklahoma statute that permitted
the sterilization of habitual criminals, defined as those convicted of two or
more felonies involving moral turpitude. Excepted from the list of eligible
crimes, however, was the crime of embezzlement. The defendant argued
that this exception meant that he was not being treated equally under the
law, since there was no difference in the nature of the crime between someone convicted of larceny and someone convicted of embezzlement.

It was not necessary for Douglas to consider the other arguments the
defendant made, such as the claim that the statute violated his right to due
process under the Fourteenth Amendment, or that sterilization should be
prohibited by the cruel and unusual punishment clause of the Eighth
Amendment. In an opinion of striking simplicity, Douglas announced a
new doctrine to review claims such as the defendant's. The right to procreate was a fundamental right, Douglas wrote, and as such state legislation
such as Oklahoma's sterilization statute had to be subjected to what Douglas termed "strict scrutiny." The phrase had been used in only a handful of
cases prior to *Skinner,* and never in the way Douglas applied it.

For Douglas, any legislation that treated one group differently from
another creates discrimination. Legislation treating persons convicted three
times of grand larceny differently from those convicted three times of
embezzlement cannot stand. "When the law lays an unequal hand on those
who have committed intrinsically the same quality of offense and sterilizes

one and not the other, it has made an invidious discrimination as if it had selected a particular race or nationality for oppressive treatment. Sterilization for those who have thrice committed grand larceny with immunity for those who are embezzlers is a clear, pointed, unmistakable discrimination."[18] That Oklahoma could offer no reason based in eugenics or in the inheritability of criminal traits to distinguish between the two crimes clinched Douglas's argument that, since the two crimes were otherwise treated similarly by the Oklahoma penal code, the statute necessarily discriminated blatantly against one group, the grand larceny group.

The Court's equal protection jurisprudence had fallen into disuse and even contempt before *Skinner*. Paraphrasing the derisive observation that patriotism is the last refuge of the scoundrel, Holmes had gone so far as to quip, in the sterilization case of *Buck v. Bell,* that the clause was the last refuge for those bringing constitutional challenges.[19] But just a little more than a decade later, the Court in *Skinner* had little trouble in following Douglas's reasoning and his revival of the equal protection doctrine. Douglas reports that Roberts disagreed with the results of the case but agreed to keep silent, while Stone opted in his concurrence for due process rather than equal protection reasoning. Jackson in his concurrence went even further and speculated that the Oklahoma statute could well be unconstitutional under an Eighth Amendment cruel and unusual punishment analysis. The rest of the Court was firmly with Douglas. As he explained it, "It was a Court where there was a unanimous vote to draft a cert. and a unanimous vote to reverse. Stone and Roberts, in particular, being very doubtful about the equal protection point. But Murphy and Black and Frankfurter, Reed and I were very clear on the equal protection point from the beginning."[20]

Douglas's *Skinner* opinion—with its identification of a fundamental right, of groups being treated differently, and the application of strict scrutiny to determine whether the state's interest is sufficiently compelling to outweigh the individual interest at stake—became the fountainhead of the Court's contemporary equal protection jurisprudence. Some have argued that *Skinner* is really a due process case rather than an equal protection case, but there is every reason to believe that Douglas meant equal protection when he invoked that analysis. When justices in later years cited to *Skinner* in due process cases, Douglas was consistent and principled in his argument that *Skinner* was an equal protection case.[21] The distinction was important to Douglas because he opposed using due process reasoning on

the grounds that it commits too much discretion in determining and applying the standard of fundamental fairness as a way of determining whether it
had been violated in a particular case. Douglas preferred the more narrow
limits of equal protection. As he had written in 1952, whether rights existed
should turn on the Constitution rather than on "the idiosyncrasies of the
judges who sit here."[22]

Douglas's reputation on the Court among both critics and the public has
been distinguished more by criticisms aimed at what he represented—as a
moving force in the increasingly activist Warren Court—than by his contributions to the Court as an institution. Criticisms of Douglas's jurisprudential habits were criticisms by association and did not begin until the late
1950s when proponents of the Legal Process school began their assault on
the Warren Court and its activist justices. But inasmuch as Douglas helped,
along with Brennan and Black, to form the core of that activism, the criticism was surely meant for him.

That conclusion could hardly be escaped, for example, with the Bickel
and Wellington 1957 attack on the *Lincoln Mills* case. Douglas wrote the
majority opinion, which the Legal Process theorists found wanting on
every front, and Frankfurter, their ally and Douglas's adversary, had written the dissenting opinion that, in contrast, represented what the theorists
advocated.

Henry Hart's famous *Harvard Law Review* Foreword of 1959, in the same
way, could be seen as an attack on Douglas. Hart's argument was that the
Court was wasting its deliberative time on inessential cases and that it was
not taking adequate care, at the same time, to produce well-crafted opinions. Douglas, everyone knew, not only wrote his opinions quickly, he also
thought the Court barely had enough work to keep it busy four days a
week. Moreover, he also, it was well known, expressed his disenchantment
with the collegial and deliberative aspects of the Court's work by leaving for
his summer vacations once he had finished his own opinions, usually well
before his brethren had finished their work. That Douglas published a 1960
article in the *Cornell Law Quarterly* defending the Court's use of its time
certainly suggests that Douglas took Hart's article personally and that he
felt the need to defend both himself and the Court.[23]

General criticism of Douglas's work in the wake of the Legal Process theorists became explicitly specific in 1964 with an important article by University of Chicago political scientist Yosal Rogat in the *New York Review of Books*.[24] The article was occasioned by two newly published Douglas books, *The Anatomy of Liberty* and *Freedom of Mind*. Rogat charged that the Douglas in these books offered embarrassingly simplistic analyses and solutions to the political, cultural, and legal problems he sketched. The books were worth examining, Rogat contended, only because they were written by a Supreme Court justice and because they helped expose the recklessness of Douglas's judicial philosophy. It was reckless because it was so simpleminded and so detached from rigorous analysis.

Douglas was the Legal Realist come to power, the superlegislator fashioning antimajoritarian solutions without accountability to precedent or legal doctrine, Rogat said. The case of Douglas well illustrates the problems that arise when the Legal Realists have a chance to act on their belief that law is little more than politics. Without the accountability inherent in legal analyses premised on precedent and doctrine, there are no brakes on a judge's political judgments, and when the judgments, as in Douglas's case, are simpleminded, our worst fears are realized. Using the language of the Legal Process theorists, Rogat argued that what was needed instead was "the importance of arguments, the constraints of legal doctrine, the goal of neutrality, and the distinctive resources of legal institutions."[25]

But while Rogat's argument was hardly new in light of the Legal Process theorists' criticisms of Douglas, the article had significance for two reasons. First, it brought the criticism to a larger, more general intellectual audience than had the academic criticism. And second, it included the explicit charge that Douglas wrote careless opinions. Confining the observation to a footnote, Rogat took the position that would so dominate discussions of Douglas in the future, that however admirable and courageous Douglas's opinions may be, how Douglas decided was more important than what he decided.[26]

Intended in part to be a critical assessment of Douglas and his work on the Court, James Simon's 1979 biography was the first full-scale effort.[27] Simon's biography, written for a general audience, used archival material but relied primarily on secondary sources and on interviews with nearly everyone who knew or worked with Douglas throughout his various careers. He presents the full story of Douglas's life and career, educating the reader to the academic, government, and judicial worlds that Douglas occupied, though his treatment of Douglas's judicial life is necessarily briefer than it would be in a judicial biography. Moreover, Simon stresses the latter half of Douglas's judicial career and the great civil libertarian that Douglas came to be. His is a full-scale biography that presents Douglas much as he would have wanted: as the rugged individualist who achieved at the highest levels throughout his life.

He devotes equal attention to Douglas's public and privates lives and follows Douglas's ambition and his rise through the levels of his careers. He provides details for Douglas's marriages and divorces and his few successes and many failures as a parent. He examines his finances, chronicles his excursions, and notes his many books. Simon describes the effort in 1970 to impeach Douglas and details, unsparingly, Douglas's last years on the Court, including his illness and then death. Simon clearly admires Douglas, generously describing the great friendships he developed and the devotion many had toward him, but his biography points to the inconsistencies between the facts of Douglas's autobiographical tall tales and the actual facts. Simon could get Douglas himself to say only a little about his life in the one interview he had with him, and of that nothing was new. Simon apparently did not have access to the Murphy interviews and, as a result, provides a view of Douglas on the Court that conforms with the view that had already been taken. He follows the Rogat lead and notes that the quality of Douglas's opinions began to drop and that one of his distinguishing traits as a justice was writing hastily prepared, shoddily constructed opinions. Simon dates the drop-off in quality at approximately ten years into Douglas's tenure. He, like others, admired Douglas's civil liberties positions and his willingness to dissent, sometimes strongly, in cases threatening those liberties.

G. Edward White followed Rogat's attack and Simon's biography with a chapter on Douglas entitled "The Anti-Judge: William O. Douglas and the Ambiguities of Individuality" in the revised edition of his important book *The American Judicial Tradition* in which he makes the Legal Process argument. At fifty-one pages, it is the most significant and most sustained critical analysis of Douglas's life. Douglas for White is the anti-judge in his series of portraits of appellate judges beginning with Marshall that aims to articulate and develop the fundamental tension in appellate judging between the judge's objective and subjective influences in rendering decisions and writing opinions.

White's argument has three elements. First, White recites a number of Douglas's comments and examples of his behavior relating to the Court to portray Douglas's anti-Court sentiments—that judging was only a four-day-a-week job; that law clerks were not needed; that conference discussion rarely changed the minds of the brethren; and that he spent his time during oral arguments doing his own research. He then takes a number of inconsistencies and discrepancies, some first mentioned by Simon, between the stories Douglas told about himself and actual fact to argue that, in creating the image of himself as the rugged individualist who constantly bristled at authority and convention, Douglas revealed himself as a man consumed by personal demons. Finally, he argues that Douglas disdained precedent when the occasion suited him and that his opinions were unprincipled and antidoctrinal.

Amplifying Rogat, he argues that there was little difference, if any at all, between Douglas's judicial writing and his extrajudicial writing, which for White stands as proof that Douglas rejected his judicial obligation. The opinions invariably arrived at the right result, White concedes, but because they were not moored in recognized doctrine, they were spurious. The general argument, made explicit by the end of the chapter, is that the subjective, individualist, and unrestrained tradition of appellate judging, as illustrated by the extreme example of Douglas, is inherently unreliable and should be rejected in favor of the appellate judging tradition in which judges are restrained by the obligation to follow precedent and to write doctrinally rooted opinions that explain the reasoning leading to a result.

In fairness to Douglas, Bruce Murphy's obsessively detailed account of Douglas's personal life hardly adds to earlier assessments of Douglas's work on the Court. It certainly does not add to what can be seen in Douglas's papers—for example, that he had a capacity for great friendship, which we see in his letters to Fred Rodell and to others. He argues that Douglas's personal flaws made him an all-around failure—as an indifferent parent, a serially unfaithful husband, a tyrannical employer of law clerks, an inveterate fabricator and embellisher of his own history, and most damning, an indifferent justice. The judicial life went out of him, Murphy contends, when Douglas's political ambitions foundered in the 1940s. But what Murphy never reconciles are the acknowledged facts of how hard Douglas worked on the Court and how deeply committed he was to liberal principles, which he then put into jurisprudential action. For Murphy, as for many others, the test of Douglas's commitment to judging lies in the quality of his judicial opinions.

Turning to Douglas on the Court, we note first that he was its most prolific writer.[28] His average of 17.9 majority opinions per term for the 1941–54 period is even more impressive given that Douglas was hospitalized for most of the 1949 term with a riding accident and missed nearly the entire term, writing only 4 majority opinions. He wrote on all subjects but was the Court's workhorse, because of the training and experience he brought to the bench, in the areas of corporations and bankruptcy. His opinions are on average shorter than those of his brethren. With only few exceptions, he documented them fully. Unlike Frankfurter, Douglas concurred only infrequently. He did, however, dissent frequently. He ranks behind only Roberts and Frankfurter in the number of dissents per term. If these rankings are readjusted to consider Roberts's artificially high number of dissents due to his anger at the Court for his perceived mistreatment during the last terms of his tenure, then Douglas would rank behind only Frankfurter as the Court's most frequent dissenter during the 1941–54 period. Not surprisingly, given Douglas's record in agreeing with the majority, his dissents were most frequent during the second half of that time.[29]

Douglas wrote his own opinions, secluding himself in his office, spreading his books out in front of him, and writing in longhand on yellow sheets of paper. He would then dictate what he had produced to his secretary.[30] One of Douglas's first law clerks paints a compelling picture of the justice at work. "I see him as a man focused on his work, absolutely determined to get through and get through fast. The books would be brought down. . . . He would close the door [and work]. If you went in, you felt you were interrupting him. He would look up and seem to say, 'Why did you come in?' It wasn't put that way, but that was the feeling that was conveyed. There he was, working with the yellow sheets of paper and with the books spread out in front of him, writing everything in longhand and then he would call his secretary, Edith Waters, and he would dictate, piece by piece. But he was hard at work every moment of the time. This was not a man who took lightly the burden he had assumed getting on the Court."[31]

Warren Christopher, a Douglas law clerk in the 1949–50 term and future secretary of state, recalls that Douglas wrote his own opinions in longhand in green ink that came out quite crystalline; that the law clerks checked citations, made suggestions, and occasionally contributed a "talking footnote" or a discrete section; and that the opinions did not go through many drafts and were not much revised. He reports that he never knew anyone who wrote as well or as quickly as Douglas.[32]

Douglas had something of a wizard's touch with opinion writing. His brethren in their reminiscences routinely recalled that he wrote with blinding speed. A study of the Vinson Court confirms that Douglas was the Court's quickest writer.[33] The brethren were dazzled by the speed with which he would produce his dissenting opinions, writing them sometimes, as did Holmes, even before the majority opinion writer had circulated his opinion. One of his last law clerks remembers that Douglas waited impatiently for the chief justice to assign majority opinions and that he literally began to write his own once he had received his assignment.[34] "I had never had any experience before writing for the Court, opinions of any court," Douglas told Walter Murphy. "I had written, of course, many briefs and so on, many law review articles and whatnot. I think, due to the fact that I was a commuter in the early years out of New York City, I learned to write with a pencil or pen on a yellow pad on my lap and that is the manner in which I have done all my work on the Court. Writing, taking briefs and records with me on airplanes, and writing opinions as I cross the country, or out in the desert in Arizona, where I try to go in the wintertime, or wherever I might be."[35]

There seemed to be nothing beyond Douglas's talents. He had once, he confided to his law clerk, gone so far as to complete a most unusual double play, writing both the majority and dissenting opinions in what Douglas described as a trivial tax case.[36] He had circulated his dissent, and when the majority opinion writer said he was having trouble with the reasoning of the opinion, Douglas took it over and became a ghostwriter. His speed in writing was the outward flourish of a dazzling mind capable of mastering the most complex fact patterns and legal issues and reducing them to sturdy, illuminating, and straightforward prose. But two decades after his appointment, the speed with which Douglas produced his opinions began to take on a different gloss. Douglas's 1959 law clerk reports that "[m]any [of Douglas's] opinions were drafted in twenty minutes. Some were written on the bench during oral argument. Editing was minimal. His published opinions often read like rough drafts."[37] That Douglas wrote so quickly, some have argued, explains in part the notable absence of solid doctrinal underpinnings for his opinions. The other reason, supporters and critics seem to agree, is that Douglas had something of a cavalier attitude toward the use of precedent and was more interested in the result than in the reasoning. As he famously noted when he had reached his sought-after legendary civil libertarian status, he would rather create a precedent than use one because creating one shows that the law is being used for current circumstances.[38]

Douglas's problem with opinions, to the extent that he had one, stemmed, one knowledgeable insider has observed, not from his indifference but from unrealistic expectations of his audience. Professor Walter Murphy, who had the chance to get close to Douglas in the series of oral history interviews he conducted, argues that it was Douglas's inability to recognize that others could not see what was so apparent to him that kept him from sometimes taking an extra step or two of explanation in his opinions. He writes that "Douglas's intellect was swift, able to cut through a mass of data like a laser to reveal the core of a problem. He was not, however, inclined to philosophize or even play with ideas. Rather, he saw and within milliseconds understood a problem, considered alternative solutions, and made a judgment. Moreover, he was impatient both in analysis and explanation. Seldom did his opinions lay bare much of the basis of his decision. I once mustered the courage to suggest that more careful explanation might convince readers, on and off the Court. He looked at me disdainfully and replied that anyone who read his opinions could see the basis of his reasoning; thus lengthy exegesis was a waste of time. He was wrong, of course, but he never fully grasped that most people were not as quick as he."[39]

⇗

Douglas's judicial opinion prose style is distinguished by clarity, directness, and simplicity. He fully and objectively sets out the underlying facts before taking up the argument. He presents his points with complete confidence as to the adequacy of the conclusion. Rather than suggesting the difficulties that the case presents, he gives nearly every case a sense of ordinariness with the confident, workmanlike analysis he brings to it. He renders the complex apprehendable. Only infrequently does he turn to eloquence to help him make his point. This is especially true about his majority opinions, but even in dissent Douglas only infrequently used eloquence. He was, however, capable of writing with it. In one privacy case, for example, in which Douglas made use, as he frequently did, of Brandeis's often-quoted remark that the right of privacy in part is the right to be let alone, Douglas eloquently sets out his views on the case's essential point. In rejecting the majority's conclusion that bus riders could be subjected to radio messages, Douglas wrote that

> when we force people to listen to another's ideas, we give a propagandist a powerful weapon. Today it is a business enterprise working out a radio program under the auspices of government. Tomorrow it may be a dominant political or religious group. Today the purpose is benign; there is no invidious cast to the programs. But the vice is inherent in the system. Once privacy is invaded, privacy is gone. Once a man is forced to submit to one type of radio program, he can be forced to submit to another. It may be a short step from a cultural program to a political program. If liberty is to flourish, government should never be allowed to force people to listen to any radio program. The right of privacy should include the right to pick and choose from competing entertainments, competing propaganda, competing political philosophies. If people are let alone in those choices, the right of privacy will pay dividends in character and dignity, the resourcefulness, and the independence of our people. Our confidence is in their ability as individuals to make the wisest choice. That system cannot flourish if regimentation takes hold. The right of privacy, today violated, is a powerful deterrent to any one who would control men's minds.[40]

Douglas's direct style states matters both plainly and bluntly. He uses figurative language sparingly but effectively. In explaining the purpose of the federal version of worker's compensation for railroad employees, for example, he writes, "The Federal Employers' Liability Act was designed to put on the railroad industry some of the cost for the legs, eyes, arms and lives which it consumed in its operations."[41] In another opinion, he writes, "[The veteran] does not step back on the seniority escalator at the point he stepped off. He steps back on at the precise point he would have occupied had he kept his position continuously during the war."[42] His terseness sometimes gives way to aphorism, as when he says that "the power to tax the exercise of a privilege is the power to control or suppress its enjoyment."[43] He can be epigrammatical: "The question here is not what the government must give, but rather what it may not take away";[44] "The emergency did not create power; it merely marked an occasion when power should be exercised."[45]

Douglas's prose was more often dotted with brilliant flashes after the 1941–54 period than during it. Conflicts seemed sharper, distinctions in starker relief. Especially with the advent of the new conservatism of the Burger Court, Douglas's voice grew sharper. Of the period generally, for a sampling consider: "The Eighth Amendment expresses the revulsion of the civilized man against barbarous acts—the 'cry of horror' against man's inhumanity to his fellow man."[46] "The powerful hydraulic pressures throughout history that bear heavily to water down constitutional guarantees and give the police the upper hand."[47] "The function of the prosecutor under the Federal Constitution is not to tack as many skins of victims as possible to the wall. His function is to vindicate the rights of people as expressed in the laws and give those accused of crime a fair trial."[48] "People live or die [with the unchecked discretion of the death penalty] dependent upon the whim of one man or of 12."[49] "At the constitutional level speech need not be a sedative; it can be disruptive."[50]

Douglas seems to have been difficult to work for. Former law clerks, in an unprecedented fashion, have described the particular challenges Douglas presented these newly minted lawyers.[51] They describe being more or less ignored by Douglas when they first arrived at the Court and then throughout their year with him. He is the taskmaster, impatient with any effort that does not equal his own. He had only one law clerk into the 1960s, and once he decided to go to two he more or less forbade them to talk with each other, seeing it as a frivolous excess. Some fondly recall examples of Douglas's empathy and kindness, but most remember Douglas working them relentlessly and, perhaps explaining some of their lingering resentment, confining them to research tasks. He did not allow them to write his opinions, in part or in whole. When the issue came up, Douglas reminded the clerks that it was he who had been appointed by the president and confirmed by the Senate.

With the obvious exception of Frankfurter, Douglas got along well with his brethren. He was often at odds with Jackson, but there is little evidence that Douglas either disliked him or had trouble working with him, perhaps because they had both been intimates of Roosevelt and had gotten to know each other in the executive branch. He considered himself very close to Jackson in their early years together on the Court.[52] He thought himself close as well to Hughes and to his successor, Stone. With Stone, it was something of a continuation of the student-professor relationship the two had at Columbia.[53] He, like many of his brethren, including Black, Jackson, and Frankfurter, spent time with Roberts on his milk farm in Pennsylvania until Roberts's belief that Black and Douglas were leaking information about him to the press turned him inward and isolated him on the Court.[54] Douglas said that during the time they served together, he was closest to Frank Murphy, spending more time with him outside of the Court than anyone else.[55] He was generally thought to be closest to Black, at least in part because they voted together so often and formed the core opposition to Frankfurter and Jackson, and though Douglas and Black did see each other a good deal during the 1940s, by the early 1950s their friendship had changed for the worse, with most speculating that Douglas's troubled marital life cooled Black's friendship with him.[56] Without providing details, he explained in 1962 that while he and Black were often allied ideologically, they were not personally close.[57]

Though they had started out on friendly terms when they were both academics, Douglas and Frankfurter soon parted ways once on the Court. Douglas dates the split from the Second Flag Salute decision and points to Frankfurter's intellectual dishonesty as the cause.[58] Relations between the two on the Court were often strained. Douglas had no fear of Frankfurter's famed intellect and resented his attempts at browbeating him. He chafed at Frankfurter's attempt to dominate the conference, and he would, ultimately, go so far as to write the chief justice in 1960 an undelivered note in which he declared that, due to Frankfurter's belligerent conference behavior toward him, he would no longer participate in conference so long as Frankfurter was there.[59]

During the 1941–54 period, however, strained as their relations were, Douglas seems to have been able to cut through the tension with humor.

When it was rumored in 1949, for example, that Frankfurter and Douglas were no longer speaking to each other, Douglas found occasion to make a joke out of it at, of course, Frankfurter's expense, saying in conference that, with Frankfurter sitting between Black and Douglas at the conference table, a nutcracker effect was achieved. Douglas, recognizing the Frankfurter method of intimidation at conference, would blunt his thrusts at every turn. When Frankfurter would engage in his harangues or lectures, Douglas would sometimes leave his seat and either take a reading chair in the conference room or simply leave the room, telling the chief justice that he would be back when Frankfurter finished. On other occasions Douglas would fight it out with Frankfurter, with explosions between the two the result.

On the bench, Douglas asked relatively few questions and would interpose himself in an argument only as a way of balancing the questions of another justice, usually Justice Frankfurter. He kept up with oral argument, as he put it, by listening with one ear. He occupied his time by continuing with his research on the case being argued or, in the Holmes tradition, by writing letters to friends. Douglas also did not have much to say at conference. His papers at the Library of Congress show that he did, however, take copious notes on the cases under discussion and the positions taken by the brethren.

When the discussion came to him, he would state his vote and the reasons for it. He did not think that it was a judge's job to change the minds of his brethren and, as a result, did not use the conference as a proselytizing pulpit in the way that others did, such as Frankfurter, Black, Jackson, and Stone. He thought much time was wasted under Stone and Vinson, who felt compelled to answer the contrary arguments of the brethren, and much preferred the Hughes approach.

At the end of his career, his colleagues report, on those occasions when he sat in for Chief Justice Burger he would, in the Hughes tradition, succinctly state the case at hand, give his vote, and only briefly explain the reasoning behind the vote before going around the table for the views of the others. Douglas summed up his approach to judging when he said in his Murphy interviews that, while Black, Frankfurter, and others eagerly sought votes in and out of conference, "most other judges have not been evangelists for their own particular point of view. And most of them make up their mind and then when they make up their mind they think their job is over. That's always been my philosophy. So I have never gone up and down the hall trying to get votes and very few judges on this Court have."[60]

Though he thought conference discussions had limited value, they were nonetheless important to Douglas. In one letter rebuking Frankfurter, for example, he invokes the dignity of the enterprise. "Today at Conference," he wrote in 1954, "I asked you a question concerning your memorandum opinion in Nos. 480 & 481. The question was not answered. An answer was refused, rather insolently. This was so far as I recall the first time another member refused to answer another member on a matter of Court business. We all know what a great burden your long discourses are. So I am not complaining. But I do register a protest at your degradation of the Conference and its deliberations."[61]

As a letter writer, Douglas wrote frequently and revealingly to a wide range of correspondents on an equally wide range of subjects. He wrote touching, empathetic letters to people he did not know. One law clerk recalls that after telling Douglas that a relative was having an operation to implant a pacemaker, Douglas wrote a three-page letter to her describing the procedure and his own experience with it as a way of easing her fears of the procedure.[62] With the exception of Fred Rodell, he seemed most at ease with people he did not know or know well. There is an element of awkwardness in Douglas's letters to friends with whom he corresponds infrequently, with Douglas lapsing into recitations of his activities.

With his children there is a different awkwardness. Here he is restrained and more formal than we would expect. The tone suggests not only that he is not comfortable writing to them but also that he is at a loss to understand the nature of their relationships and why they so frequently seem to be failing.

With strangers it is different. Without regard to the posturing that distinguished his autobiographical writings, for example, he could better describe the essence of the wilderness experience in a brief letter to a schoolgirl in Seattle than he could in all of his published writing on the subject: "[A] person's experience on a mountainside turns so much on his own personality. For myself it is a testing ground of my strength and endurance, a pitting of finite man against one of the great rigors of the universe. It is an interesting testing ground. A man—or girl—can get to know himself—or herself—on the mountain. He gets to know his inner strength—the power of the soul to add to the power of the legs and lungs. In the solitude of the mountains—especially on the highest peaks—he is close to the heavens, close to the outer limits of the earthly zone. It is for me easy, therefore, to have communion with God and to come on understanding terms with my own being. Other people might have different experiences. These are the essence of mine."[63]

With Court-related matters he would lavish praise on his law clerks when he wrote on their behalf for jobs and judicial appointments, though he could, at least later in his career, write scathing office memorandums to his clerks finding detailed fault with them. He could write flattering notes to his brethren, some genuine, some not, but he could also bicker in correspondence with Frankfurter over minor legal points, never letting Frankfurter get in the last word. He wrote memorandums for his files to document where he and others stood on particular points he expected would be debated later. Among his brethren, in his early years on the Court he confided only in Black when it came to his political ambitions or the possibility of high administrative appointments. He defended himself with the press on occasion with letters to the editor pointing out, sometimes emphatically, a newspaper's misunderstanding of the judicial process.

Douglas was his most revealing about himself and about the Court and his role on it in his correspondence with Fred Rodell, a former student of his at the Yale Law School who had become a professor at Yale and one of the country's leading commentators on the Court. Rodell wrote specialized articles for law reviews, even though he claimed to have sworn them off in his famous exposé on their weaknesses ("there are two things wrong with law reviews, style and substance," he wrote in "Goodbye to Law Reviews").[64] He had greater influence as a popular journalist, however, writing descriptive, analytical pieces for magazines such as *Fortune,* the *Progressive,* and the *American Mercury.* His 1955 book *Nine Men* was one of the most important studies of the Court.

The Douglas-Rodell correspondence was wide-ranging and frequent. During the 1941–54 years, Douglas wrote Rodell some seventy times, filling the pages with some fifteen thousand words of prose and, on occasion, poetry, as he and Rodell often swapped limericks. Neither seemed to read much that was not related to law. Rodell was the leader and frequently sent Douglas law review articles to read. Douglas, in return, would provide his own commentary, sometimes at length. On the personal side, Douglas provided Rodell whatever measure of comfort he could for the nearly constant strain he experienced as a result of his second wife's illnesses. They saw each other as frequently as they could but not as often as they would have liked. Rodell sometimes joined Douglas on camping expeditions, but, again, not as often as either would have liked. Douglas would provide descriptive commentary for the trips Rodell missed, speaking as fisherman to fisherman.

They kept up on the academic wars at both Yale and Harvard and charted the movements of Frankfurter's troops in the battle over the way the Court and its work should be interpreted. That Frankfurter was using his former clerks and academic friends to promote him and his judicial philosophy was not a secret. Rodell would often note in his letters to Douglas what Frankfurter's minions were up to, and on occasion he would, in reference to something on the Court he was writing, mention that he had to balance the Frankfurter forces.

Douglas confided in Rodell, keeping him abreast, for example, of the possibility of political appointments and ambitions. But while Douglas did confide in him, he did not write to Rodell about the Court as often as the reader either wants or expects. In a letter that touches upon the recent appointment of Fred Vinson as chief justice, however, Douglas did provide Rodell with perhaps his most revealing comment about the Court, in the context of whether the appointment of Chief Justice Vinson will go far in soothing the personality differences between the justices. "The personal friction here has been way over magnified," he writes. "That is not the problem. As you know, the issues are [illegible word] ones (not personalities). A man who is adept can iron out personality issues. But the basic issues of liberalism vs. conservatism cannot be worked out by pleasing personalities. This is a good chance to put the problem in the true perspective. This appointment (any appointment) is important only in terms of balance of power."[65]

The only time Douglas takes the lead and mentions his own work is when he suggests to Rodell that he might want to write an article about the *Hope Natural Gas* case for *Fortune* magazine. "It's a large subject and should prove interesting," he writes.[66] He occasionally mentions that the Court has had some interesting cases and that Rodell would be interested in the divisions among the justices formed by them. He complains about conferences under Chief Justice Stone: "I must go now to a Conference. It seems like we have them all the time these days and they seem eternally long—and often dull."[67] He does, however, frequently describe, without complaint, how hard he has been working. He describes frequent bouts with dizziness and fatigue but does not seem to make the connection between these symptoms and the intensity of duration of his judicial labors.[68] He does not, with the exception of Frankfurter, write much about his brethren. The comments are mixed. He thinks highly of Stanley Reed and wants Rodell to meet him, while a few months into Chief Justice Vinson's tenure he writes of him that "next to Vinson, Byrnes was a Bismarck."[69] He takes Vinson to task in a long letter detailing the special session of the Court for the *Rosenberg* case and his belief that Vinson maneuvered to exclude him from the session.[70]

Douglas recognized Rodell's place as a legal journalist and on occasion sought to provide him with both material and with a motivation to write disparagingly of Frankfurter. When Rodell in 1947 wrote an article that Douglas thinks is not sufficiently tough on Frankfurter, he writes him: "You only consider how the son-of-a-bitch votes." He then sarcastically adds, "You forget how hard he works for the good and the truth, when freed from his judicial fetters."[71] When Rodell expressed interest in the topic, Douglas supplies explication, adding some personal spice to the mix. "The matter of Frankfurter's manipulation of the press is rightly a concern of yours. For you are for whom he has reserved a very special hatred. Somewhere, sometime you must have crossed him. He burns with an intense heat when your name is mentioned."[72] "Frankfurter," he writes on another occasion, "is an interesting character to study. He works at manipulation full time. He never ceases. Every sentence cuts in some direction. All the judges here are of course used to it. He has no friends on the bench except Jackson."[73]

He wanted to be Rodell's guide in assessing Frankfurter. When Rodell sent Douglas an article describing the way Frankfurter used the press to enhance his reputation, Douglas pounced on the issue and all but asked Rodell to take both his opinion and the insider information he gave him to the public. In his first response he wrote, "I think the appraisal of Frankfurter's activities with the press, law journals, authors etc. is a very conservative one. He works at the job practically full time. I mean by that that he is continually inspiring articles in magazines, newspapers, columns, law journals and the like. Part of his endeavor is to get articles written which are derogatory to Black, Murphy, Rutledge and myself. He has done a particularly vicious job on Murphy, whom he ridicules and derides. His hatred of

me is genuine and unqualified. Black and Rutledge are impressive opponents of his point of view on law. For various reasons this is the group he
would destroy. He cannot stand to see the mantle of liberalism go to other
shoulders. That's the main motivation. His technique is superb. He works
through dozens of his students and law clerks, publishers, columnists, etc.
It's common for example to see in editorials of the *Washington Post* on
Monday or Tuesday *the exact words* which he uses in Conference on Satur-
day. In other words, he selects the targets and equips the gang with the
artillery. He's a master at it."[74] A week later, on the subject of Frankfurter's
success at getting the *Washington Post's* Supreme Court reporter fired,
Douglas wrote, "So—a Justice of the Court got a newspaper reporter fired
because he did not like what the reporter wrote! What would the country
think of that! It's a very deplorable state of affairs. Frankfurter has infected
the place with a nasty virus. How ashamed such stalwarts as Brandeis would
be if they had known of such goings-on. It's a mad state of affairs. And
nothing will assuage Frankfurter's thirst for power and approbation."[75]

Rodell wrote several law review articles drawing attention to Douglas's
work on the Court, but more important for Douglas's reputation were the
articles he wrote for national newsmagazines about Douglas and other
members of the Court and his important 1955 book *Nine Men,* which
praised Douglas almost to extravagance.[76] Former law clerk Vern Countryman wrote academic pieces on Douglas and also put together a collection of
excerpts from Douglas's most important cases, doing for Douglas what
Philip Kurland was doing for Frankfurter.[77] Another former law clerk,
William Cohen, later came to Douglas's defense with academic articles
when Douglas's role in the *Rosenberg* case was questioned, on one occasion
by a Frankfurter supporter, in a way that suggested that Douglas was
maneuvering in his conference votes for rehearing to maintain his liberal
credentials while simultaneously abandoning the Rosenberg cause.[78]

Supreme Court commentator John Frank, former law clerk to Hugo
Black, was also a supporter of the Douglas cause. Beginning in the 1940s
and throughout Douglas's career, he consistently praised Douglas in his
yearly overview of the Supreme Court in his law review articles and elsewhere.[79] It was Frank in conjunction with Countryman who wrote the

Douglas entry in the important compendium *Justices of the Supreme Court*.[80] The entry emphasizes the journey of Douglas's professional and personal lives. It highlights his personal courage, his achievements, and his many and deep personal friendships. It links him with Brandeis and argues that Douglas's early views on freedom of speech, rate-making, and antitrust cases extended those of Brandeis.

It argues that he did his most important work, though, in taking his view of a dynamic Constitution and applying it to a variety of individual liberty issues, such as privacy in *Griswold*. Douglas occasionally faltered or simply erred in the beginning, Frank and Countryman note, such as in the First Amendment areas of speech and religion, but when he revisited the problems he corrected himself, always in the direction of expanding individual liberty. As a justice he was, in their view, "an extraordinarily dedicated and effective exponent of individual liberty for all."[81] That his career was not defined by his work on the Court was, they argue, a commentary on the Court, as the Court, ultimately, could not keep the ambitious and supremely gifted Douglas busy enough. His interests in politics, travel, and extrajudicial writing were primarily explained by this fact.

For his part, Douglas tried his hand three times at autobiography. He first wrote about his own life in 1950 in *Of Mountains and Men* but waited until the end of his career to attempt full-scale autobiography with *Go East, Young Man*, published the year he retired from the Court. A posthumous volume, *The Court Years*, followed in 1980. None of the volumes is particularly revealing, either about Douglas or about the Court. As commentators have pointed out, Douglas sought to create a persona of the rugged individualist when he wrote about himself. His struggles are exaggerated, as are his successful responses to the obstacles he encountered. His intensely limned psychological themes, ironically, give insights into only part of Douglas's character and leave unaddressed larger aspects of his life and work. He hardly wants to write about the Court at all, cramming brief observations about his years there into one chapter in *The Court Years*. It is an issue-based book instead, leaving the reader wanting more.

Douglas provided a fuller, if more oblique, view of the way he saw his work on the Court in a series of interviews with Walter Murphy of the

Princeton University Political Science Department in the early 1960s. The interviews provide the most detailed description we have of the Court's work and personalities. His interviews not only give us all the information he withholds in his autobiography, they at the same time present a different Douglas, one deeply connected to his Court work and eager to describe not only its day-to-day operations but also its lifeblood. He gives readers that which he denied them in his volumes of autobiography, especially *The Court Years*. As much as he held back in those volumes, he expansively provides in these interviews.

As Murphy recalls it, Douglas asked him around 1960 if he would come to Washington and go through his papers with him, to pose him the questions that scholars might want to ask.[82] Murphy's working arrangement was that he would send his questions to Douglas, who would then arrange to have the pertinent files laid out for them. They would sit together for several hours at a time going through the questions and the files, with Douglas supplementing the written material with his recollections. The papers on hand acted as a check for Douglas's memory, and it was Murphy's impression that Douglas was being candid in his answers.

The answers were recorded on audiotape and languished for nearly twenty years before Murphy's Princeton University found the money to transcribe the tapes. All but a few of the twenty-four tapes covering nine interview sessions between December 20, 1961, and September 10, 1963, survived for transcription. In the interviews, Douglas both provides extra details on subjects covered in his autobiography and also addresses new topics. He describes nearly all of the justices he served with between his appointment and 1963. For most he provides the details of their appointments, the way they worked as justices, his relationship with them, and their views on the law. He describes at length conference dynamics among the brethren as a group and evaluates and contrasts the management style of the chief justices under whom he served. He describes the personalities of his brethren both in and out of conference. He makes a series of striking, perceptive observations on the way particular justices responded to the Court's work. He describes James Byrnes, for example, out of place away from the legislative process, sitting in his office, "with all these problems in front of him and books staring at him from the bookshelves" waiting for someone to come down the hall with whom he can talk.[83] He provides much of the same material about his own appointment to the Court that he gave in his autobiography, but he supplements it in the interviews with details about the way he approached his work on the Court. He also gives details on the inner workings of his chambers and the Court in response to Murphy's questions about particular cases. Referring to his notes, Douglas recreates the conference votes and subsequent changes.

Douglas looked at many factors in assessing his brethren, including the habits or approaches they brought to conference and to the decision-making process. As to the extent to which a justice argued for a position at conference and sought to persuade the others, Douglas had Chief Justice Hughes as his role model. "Hughes," Douglas told Murphy, "was utterly circumspect, always proper, wholly impersonal, never, never arguing, never, never begging, never pounding on the table, never denouncing another school of thought, never screaming, never raising his voice, never having near apoplectic fits at somebody's view that sounded to him stupid. Hughes, in his management of the conference, was very sharp, precise, succinct. And he would never take more than just a minute or two with every case and then when that discussion of his was over, would go around by seniority, never once would he interrupt, never once would he reply to anything that was said. He would wait until everybody was finished and then say now we will vote. Hughes was very, very opposite from Frankfurter, from Black and from Stone in that regard."[84]

Douglas frequently said that Hughes had helped free him on the bench by telling him that, at the constitutional level at which the Court operates, 90 percent of the decision is made up of emotion,[85] but Hughes's view of his brethren had an equally powerful effect on him. Hughes believed that each of the justices had arrived at the Court under his own steam and that, as a result, they were equally sovereign and not appropriately the subject of persuasion by the other justices.[86] For Douglas and for Hughes, there were limitations on the role of the conference. "After all," he explained to Murphy, "the Justices are mature people. They are not students in the university or college sense of the word. They each of them had studied the cases, had heard the oral argument, and made up his mind. And in my experience on the Court the conferences accomplished very little except to expose a position and indicate what range of the spectrum is covered, where the middle position is, around what point can you get a majority. But the conference is a futility in terms of trying to persuade somebody because everybody has made up his mind before he comes in. Once in a while there is an exception but that's very, very rare."[87]

Douglas accepted his brethren and the different views and approaches they brought to the Court's work. The ever conscientious Rutledge, for example, felt compelled to reinvent the wheel with each heavily footnoted opinion, which Douglas considered to be a useless expenditure of time and effort when the opinion did not require such detailed treatment.[88] Nonetheless, Douglas valued Rutledge's approach to judging. His wheels ground slowly, Douglas said, as Rutledge needed to work all the pieces of the law's mosaic into place. "He was," said Douglas, "a valuable man on the Court because he was provocative. He always came up with ideas."[89]

Douglas insisted only that his brethren be frank and honest in their views. He recognized that the brethren brought their individual life experiences to the Court and that these experiences influenced their judging. About Stanley Reed, for example, he told Murphy that "he was a man like everybody else, with a very definite bend, inclination, a very definite set of prejudices and like everybody else, he catered to those prejudices in all of his work."[90] "But he was, in terms of his personal liberties, he was strangely conservative, strangely conservative because all of his decisions on the First Amendment, the Fourth Amendment, and the Fifth Amendment, were decisions that continued to surprise me because they didn't seem to be in keeping with his character. And I think he believed in that kind of life and society and he lived, he lived the ethic he believed in."[91] "He just frankly was for the kind of society in which the rough and tumble speakers didn't have much of a chance, where a society was more run by the properly-dressed, properly-behaved people. I suppose it was a reflection perhaps of his southern upbringing but a person, of course, doesn't need to come from the South to have that philosophy."[92] Douglas could accept Reed's views on the First and Fourth Amendments because Reed was frank and honest about the prejudices underlying them. In contrast, a justice who failed Douglas's frankness and honesty test was someone like Frankfurter, "who was always protesting that he would like to go the other way but the law prohibited him from doing it."[93]

Douglas disagreed with Frankfurter's judicial philosophy but went further and rejected his approach to judging. He complained that Frankfurter wanted to avoid the very task of judging. He did this two ways. First, he believed, in the spirit of the Legal Process theorists, that the Court should intervene only when it had no other choice. Second, he held on to his opinions in difficult cases for months, facilitating his greater interest in spending his time trying to influence all aspects of government. Douglas, to be sure, levels withering criticism of Frankfurter's approach to judging. He writes to Rodell, for example, that

> [i]n the Frankfurter technique there is little of what I call principle or morality. He teaches and practices the art of manipulation of words, the twisting of meanings, the infusion into law of one's own predilections. It's cute and clever to be able to put a false facade on law. He used to say to us that behind Hughes' beard he could get away with murder. To him the end justifies the means. This is a devastating influence on young men. They get a false standard of values. It is also a baneful influence on our public life. It's the importation of the art of intrigue from the ancient capitals of Europe. It glorifies the art of deceit. It has a devastating influence on the Court. Owen Roberts was a fine man. But Frankfurter got Roberts to believe that the new judges were scheming behind his back, giving stories to the press, and playing politics. While he was doing this to Roberts, he was saying behind Roberts' back, "I would hate to be Roberts. I couldn't sleep nights if I were. I would think his conscience would keep him awake—the way he votes." He once said that to me. He is so intellectually dishonest that I shudder at the effect he has on the Court.[94]

In another letter to Rodell, Douglas contrasts Frankfurter with one of Frankfurter's own idols, Holmes, and writes that "Holmes did not carry his cynical philosophy into the law to any great extent. Frankfurter does. There is no sacred ethical principle for him. Every principle is made for manipulation. It can serve a noble or a tawdry end, so long as it's Frankfurter's end. I would say that Frankfurter's influence has been towards the disappearance of the ethical principle from the law. It has had a devastating influence, not only on the law (which is pretty [illegible word]) but also on the group of young men who have come under his influence . . . It has had a terrible . . . influence on some of them."[95]

There was no single standard for a successful justice. Douglas thought, for example, that Frank Murphy made an important contribution to the Court. He recognized that Murphy was not a scholar on the bench, that he was less a professional lawyer or professional teacher the way others on the

Court had been, but for him Murphy was eminently qualified and one of the best justices Douglas had seen because he had the right temperament and a better grasp of the dimensions of the Constitution and the overtones of the various clauses than justices such as Jackson.[96] Murphy had the right "feeling about the law, and about justice, about people, about the weight of government coming against the individual," he said, all of which for Douglas were "all very important." Scholarship was not unimportant, but in the contrast between Murphy and Frankfurter, the quintessential academic justice, Douglas preferred Murphy.[97]

He also did not have great admiration for Roberts as a jurist, for example, because "his points of reference seemed to me to be fairly movable," he told Murphy.[98] "He would be, it seemed to me, swayed by inconsequential, irrelevant factors to make a decision one way or the other that were very difficult to match up with what he had done before. All of us change in our legal philosophies and the way we look at problems. That's a part of life. What I'm talking about is something different. It was a week to week, month to month, changed back and forth that seemed to be part of Roberts that I could never quite understand."[99]

Douglas's view of judging was preeminently distinguished by the respect he accorded each of his brethren. He believed that each was equally entitled to be there and that each was entitled to his own opinion. Hughes held this view and passed it on to Douglas. It was a view that had shaped Hughes's minimalist conference approach to the job of judging. He would not argue with any of his brethren as he went around the table for their views and votes because he did not think it was his prerogative given their equal status on the Court. For Douglas, "Hughes was a very great man. There was nothing petty about Hughes. He knew that every one of the men around the table got there under his own steam and was not beholden to him and was sovereign in his own rights. And he had great respect for each of them I think."[100] Hughes, whom Douglas says took him under his wing, taught Douglas this important lesson.

Not surprisingly, Douglas understood the Court and its work primarily in political terms. For him the basic issue continually engaging the Court was the conflict between liberalism and conservatism. Appointments to the Court, as he said in a letter to Rodell, are important only in terms of the balance of power on the Court.[101] Douglas decided cases and wrote opinions not so much for the moment but for the time, knowing, believing, and expecting that an opinion's life was determined by the composition of the Court when it next took up the issue. Douglas and Rodell, his principal champion, were of the same mind on the Court. Rodell, when the Legal Process theorists were formulating and beginning to advance their views, argued instead that the Court should be recognized as primarily a political institution whose results were determined more by the backgrounds each of the justices brought to the Court than by anything else.

Former law clerk and Douglas commentator L. A. Powe makes the case that Douglas should have paid more attention to doctrine in his opinions if for no other reason than because those commenting on the Court's work held up fidelity to doctrine as a standard.[102] Douglas knew better and recognized, however, even if the commentators did not have the courage to admit it, that the Court fashioned its results not in the idealized manner of the Legal Process theorists but in a way that looked to results. Even the darling of the Legal Process school, Frankfurter, put results before reasoning. That he argued against the preferred position doctrine for personal rather than jurisprudential reasons shows this. He also manipulated precedent when it suited his purpose, as when he was helping to construct "our federalism."[103] In this regard, criticism of Douglas's approach to judging (such as White's, in which he inveighs against the illegitimacy of *Skinner*) fails to recognize that *Skinner* was embraced not only by Douglas's brethren in their votes but also by the Court as time progressed.

Douglas, to the dismay of many, was willing to point out that the emperor had no clothes. Beyond his Legal Realism, which reflected the Court's political nature, he countered the notion that the Court was overworked by saying that at best it was a four-day-a-week job and that a justice only needed one law clerk. Perhaps more significantly, by writing his own opinions and insisting that it was the justice's job—not the law clerk's—to write, he drew attention to the fact that after the 1941–54 period few if any of his brethren were faithful to the obligation to do their own work. Douglas's opinions were not fashionable to the Legal Process theorists in large part because he did not write them as a law clerk would; the scholarship upon which the Legal Process theorists insisted as part of the craft of opinion writing was a function of the law review experiences law clerks brought to their jobs. And while he did not make this charge himself, Douglas, in

writing his own opinions, drew attention to the idea that the elaborate reasoning and scholarship that has come to mark the law clerk–written opinions of the justices has little relation to the decision itself. Justices are
appointed by the president and confirmed by the Senate, not law clerks.
The justices make law, not the law clerks.

During the 1941–54 period, Douglas was a hardworking justice dedicated
to the Court's work who respected his brethren's sovereignty and did his
own work. He thrived in the 1941–54 period in part because it was a period
in which the political nature of the Court was recognized and accepted.
Both Roosevelt and Truman certainly saw the Court this way in appointing
so many political figures to the Court. Moreover, and perhaps more
significantly, Chief Justice Warren, appointed by Eisenhower at the end of
the 1941–54 period, was a national political figure before going to the Court.
His predecessor, Vinson, had been a political figure, and while Vinson's
predecessor, Stone, was not, Stone's own predecessor, Chief Justice
Hughes, was, like Warren, a political figure of high rank and standing.

Ironically, Douglas's contributions to the Court during the 1941–54
period, before he embarked on a campaign of high profile visibility—with
his speech making, book writing, and magazine writing—were appreciated
and written about during the 1941–54 period by academics-turned-journal-
ists such as Arthur Schlesinger Jr., who recognized the political nature of the
Court. Commentators such as those in the Legal Process school, who
rejected this political aspect of the Court, not surprisingly, gave Douglas
different reviews.

But it was with G. Edward White and his analysis in his *American Judicial Tradition* that Douglas was so distorted as to be unrecognizable. White
was right in looking to personality as an animating force in a justice's work
on the Court, but with Douglas he looked to the wrong measure of personality by simply looking to what he said about himself. In doing this he made
two mistakes that undercut the strength of his analysis and distort Douglas.
First, he failed to appreciate that Douglas, as has been true for others as they
entered the last phases of their lives, engaged in concerted image-making
and became a press agent for himself. Embellished personal anecdotes,
which had once been used to amuse, were now transformed into revisionist
history.[104] Second, White does not go beyond what Douglas said about
himself autobiographically and look to what Douglas said in his interviews
with Walter Murphy and in his letters to Rodell about the Court, his
brethren, and the job of judging. When these sources are considered it is

clear that, at the very least, even if White's argument carries weight for the second half of Douglas's career when he adopted increasingly liberal views, it is not true for the period Douglas served with Black, Jackson, and Frankfurter.

History, however, has been on Douglas's side when the whole of his career is assessed. Douglas did what Black could not and either led or followed the Court in the 1960s in its individual rights revolution, a revolution embraced by the nation. Douglas, like Black, believed in the total incorporation theory, but unlike Black, Douglas did not let the literalism with which Black read the provisions of the Bill of Rights restrict him. He saw the Constitution as a more malleable, expansive document and could find the right of privacy in it when Black could not. *Griswold* could well be said to be a watershed event for both the Court and for the careers of Black and Douglas. The result, reasoning, and spirit of *Griswold* are firmly embedded in the Court's jurisprudence and stand as a landmark of not only the Warren Court but also the contemporary Court. Douglas's opinion had been assailed in all but the loyalist quarters for years, but now it, as is true for Douglas himself, has gained increased respectability. Even Douglas biographer James Simon, who doubled as one of Douglas's sternest critics on the subject of craftsmanship of Douglas's opinions, recently recognized that the opinion had been percolating in Douglas's jurisprudence for more than a decade and that, rather than being just a slapdash effort reflecting Douglas's whim, it reflected the reasoned collaboration of Douglas with other members of the Court.[105]

In something of a surprising twist, given the prevailing view that Douglas was defined as a justice more by his indifference than his dedication, scholars looking to understand the long period he served on the Court have been turning to Douglas's papers generally and his conference notes specifically as a record of the time. These are the same conference notes Douglas had with him and consulted when Walter Murphy interviewed him on some two dozen occasions between 1961 and 1963. These interviews reveal a different Douglas. Certainly during the 1941–54 period, Douglas was fully engaged in his Court work and brought to it both a dazzling intelligence and a vision. This vision, as I've also tried to show, was greater than Black's because Douglas's was not bound by literalism as was Black's.

This is not to say that Douglas was without foible or blemish during his 1941–54 period. It was at the end of the period, as one academic study has shown, that Douglas began his disquieting habit of dissenting without opinion in tax cases involving individuals.[106] While Douglas's papers show, at least to someone such as James Simon, that Douglas was more involved in the group dynamic of the Court than had been earlier thought, Douglas's insistence on going his own way in certain tax cases continues to represent to some the weakness if not danger of vesting justices with lifetime tenure and no check on their voting performance.

There is also some truth to the criticism of Douglas's dedication to the Court during his last years, though it is somewhat overstated. Old age did take its toll on Douglas. As he moved into old age, Douglas began to believe in the image that he had been projecting about himself. He was, he thought, the great libertarian, the great independent thinker and defender of individual rights. He had become, in his mind, the embodiment of the American spirit and needed to be appealed to as such to get his attention. Even a great, good friend such as Fred Rodell needed to pay this kind of homage to Douglas to get his ear. When Douglas in 1968 was considering leaving the Court, in part because of physical infirmities, Rodell wrote to implore him to stay on. "Bill, please get well fast," he wrote, "and PLEASE don't forsake the Court AND US. With Hugo slipping, with the Chief presumably gone, you're the ONLY guy we can always count on. Let me repeat, in case you didn't hear me say it publicly a few times: you're the greatest living American. You're also one hell of a good guy."[107]

Douglas's problem in his last years was consistency of dedication, not consistency of jurisprudence. He could disengage himself from the Court's work by leaving early for summer recess, as so many commentators have noted, and he could also, as just as many have pointed out, write opinions that merely did the job and did not set out doctrine in such a way that the Court in the future would rely on it. David Currie, for example, points out that, when Douglas in 1966 wrote on protecting associational rights in *Elfbrandt v. Russell*,[108] he did such an incomplete job of it that Justice Brennan needed in *Keyishian v. Board of Regents*[109] to say it all again.[110]

The Douglas of old could still be relied upon, though, to do work that only he could do. Even at the end of his career he was looked to as the justice the Court relied upon to take on the most complicated cases, especially those relating to business and regulatory activity. Professor Mark Tushnet, for example, former law clerk to Thurgood Marshall, recalls an instance in the early 1970s involving complex regulatory scheme cases. The Court had gotten cases late in the term challenging new federal Food and Drug Administration procedures. The opinions had to be written quickly, Tushnet recalls, "and the only justice the others had confidence in—to figure out the statutory complexities with reasonable care in the short time available, and to turn acceptable opinions out—was Douglas."[III]

Douglas, unlike Black, did not have a problem with the consistency of his jurisprudence, regardless of the extent to which he applied himself on the Court. He did not conform his jurisprudence to his personality shifts. He throughout maintained and extended his core liberalism, which brought him from *Skinner* to *Griswold* and beyond to *Roe*. Critics might argue that the difference between Douglas and Black is just a difference in values and that to favor Douglas is but to honor Douglas's version of liberalism consistently applied over Black's liberalism qualified by retreat as he grew older. That is true, of course, but what cannot be neglected is that the Court's jurisprudence is laden with values, and those values reflect the nature of our democratic experiment. In this regard, Douglas's values have been the values that have distinguished the Court and the nation.

One aspect of Douglas's contribution to the Court, beyond his opinions and doctrines, was his refreshing willingness to point to the political nature of the Court. The Court, during the time of 1941–54 and beyond, has been influenced by politics in the same way that it has been influenced by the personalities of the justices. This is equally true for self-proclaimed judicial restraint advocates, such as Black, Frankfurter, and Jackson, as it is for someone like Douglas. The country has reason to fear for the fragility of the Court, given that incompetent or mischievous justices can impede the judicial process, but the country had nothing to fear from Douglas.

At the same time that he was willing to point out that the Court is but nine sovereign voices voting as they individually see fit, the example he set during the 1941–54 period and beyond as a talented, dedicated jurist shows that the system thrives when the right sort of justices are appointed. Douglas fulfilled his responsibility on the Court by always doing his own work and, in doing so, providing individual accountability. Ironically, in taking on the full responsibility of the job, Douglas was held up to the wrong standard—the standard of opinions written by law clerks—which is at best wide of the mark. When a more appropriate standard is applied, that of a justice working within the limitations and true nature of the Court, Douglas, as perhaps best shown in his 1941–54 years and in his interviews with Walter Murphy, set his own high standard, one that has rarely been met since his passing.

꩜

CHAPTER 6

Conclusion

The story of Justices Jackson, Frankfurter, Black, and Douglas is really three interrelated stories that affect our current understanding of the Court and its justices. One story is about the Court's evolving civil rights jurisprudence, a jurisprudence that was born in the period that the four justices served together and that had its custody and direction shaped by the debates between the two factions that the four justices were divided into. It is the jurisprudence of unenumerated rights that shapes in significant part the way we live today. The second is about the justices themselves and the capacity each of them had to let bitterness, resentment, and intransigence prompt self-destructive contrariness. That it could happen to them means that it can happen to any of the current justices. The third is about the Court as an institution and its relation to the American public, a public that can find in the Court the paradox of inscrutability just beyond its public face. Knowing how the Court works is as important today as it was then.

There are some contrasts worth noting between today's Court and the Court of Jackson, Frankfurter, Black, and Douglas. In our age the Court is distinguished by an institutional anonymity, fashioned in part through justices who keep a low public profile and in part through the bland, homogeneous, and voiceless prose of the law clerks who write the vast majority of the Court's opinions. In contrast, not only did the individual justices of the group of four have their individual voices, which they expressed with their unsurpassed writing ability, the Court as well had a voice that shunned the institutional. The Court today seems incapable of fashioning the brief, public-oriented opinions that distinguished some of the most important cases of the 1941–54 era. Moreover, the justices of that era were public figures of a sort unknown by today's standards. Several had held high public office before becoming justices, some were mentioned frequently for high public office while still on the Court, and a few engaged in highly visible extrajudicial activities, such as Justice Jackson's prosecution of Nazi war criminals in the Nuremberg trials, that brought them attention off the Court. In contrast, today the justices come almost exclusively from the ranks of federal circuit court of appeals judges, where they are, by nature of that position, anything but well known to the public.

The Court of the 1941–54 era featured human rather than institutional dimensions of judging, again in contrast to the Court of today. Its authority came not just from its institutional role but from the legitimacy each of the justices brought to the Court as individuals. As Justice Jackson wrote about the nature of the Supreme Court's ultimate authority, "[w]e [on the Supreme Court] are not final because we are infallible, but we are infallible only because we are final."[1] That the 1941–54 era Court featured individuals rather than an institution brings into focus the fallibility of those individuals. What we learn about the relationship between personality, friendship, ideology, and judicial behavior helps explain the dynamics of the 1941–54 Court. It helps as well to enlighten us as to the tensions that make up any Court, including our own.

Appreciating the human dimensions of the justices in turn helps us better understand the Court itself by revealing some of its secrets. Court chroniclers such as Michael Kammen have stressed the important point that, for all the public statements that the Court makes in the form of its opinions, the Court is in effect hidden from the view of the public because the judicial process is a secret one.[2] Accountability and trust have been the function of what the Court says in its opinions. For those who want or need more, a look into the way a particular group of justices negotiated their own lives and their relations with their brethren, with the Court, and with the nation provides both the good and bad news that the Court as an institution works and that it is made up of only nine black-robed justices who are, despite or because of their best intentions, as human as the rest of us. Finally, a look behind the scenes tells us that we should consider the source of Court commentary and recognize that reputations, as in the case of Douglas, can sometimes be misleading.

There are, of course, problems in approaching the work of the Court and of its justices as a function of personality. The biggest is that it is difficult to know what role personality actually plays. The nature of the Court's secret conferences means that we will never really know what goes on at them. We are getting more and more reports of what happens there as the papers of more justices are becoming available, but selective accounts are a weak substitute, for example, for transcripts of conference discussions. Moreover, outside of conference dynamics, an approach to the Court rooted in personality rarely, if ever, explains how a particular case was decided. We can see particular cases as turning points in a justice's career, such as the Second Flag Salute case in the example of Frankfurter, but more generally personality helps us understand the arc of a justice's career. Personality affects ideology or jurisprudential positions, as with Jackson, Frankfurter, and Black and the contrarian positions they moved toward.

The problem with assessing personality in the careers of Supreme Court justices is an outgrowth of the problem of deciding where judicial biography ends and constitutional history begins. It's not as though we can consider only doctrine in looking at the Court's work. To look at doctrine is to look at the opinions from which the doctrine came, and in looking at opinions we are looking on some level at an expression of personality. The Court's work is always of a piece with ideas and individuals—and when it comes to individuals, we have to recognize the role of personality. It is certainly not surprising that judicial biography confronts the issue of personality. The now apparently failed effort in literary studies to argue that it is the text alone (without its author) that should be studied has not found converts in legal studies so that we can say that it is only the opinion and not the opinion and its author that matter, though the more that law clerks do the work of their justices the more forceful this argument becomes.

Perhaps the biggest problem with using personality to look at the Court and its justices is that it makes us uncomfortable to recognize that the Court is, in fact, made up simply of nine different individuals. Those who do not want to recognize the role that personality plays will likely argue that it is harsh or reductionist to argue that personality has any direct causal effect on anything the Court decides. But that is not my claim. Of course much of the Court's business is conducted without regard to personality. Justices are not schoolchildren. But at the same time we have to acknowledge that there are patterns in the careers of the justices under review here that are other-

wise difficult to explain and that these justices had grandly felt and articulated personality traits.

Personality may not explain all, but it does prompt us to confront the ele-
phant in the room when it comes to the role of the Supreme Court in the
American democracy. To point out the more human aspects of the justices
and to argue that their frailties can influence something as fundamental as
their jurisprudential positions suggests, ultimately, a fragile aspect to our
democracy. It is fragile, though, only in the sense that it reflects the underlying political nature of the Supreme Court. This we should not be afraid
to consider.

The period under review here demonstrates that results rather than
process matter more. Even the Legal Process theorists had to acknowledge
that the Court got it right in *Brown v. Board of Education,* for example,
despite the variety of ways Chief Justice Warren's opinion for the Court has
been attacked. Warren's forceful personality and political instincts turned
the Court around after Chief Justice Vinson died and *Brown* had not yet
been handed down. For a more recent example of the political element in
the Court's work, we need only glance back to 2000 and the Court's handling of the litigation flowing from the presidential election.

There is no escaping the fact that ours is a judicially tinged democracy.
Sometimes, as with *Brown,* the Court has to step in and do what the legislators are slow or unwilling to do because fundamental fairness is at stake.
Other times, as in *Bush v. Gore,* the Court can impose itself on the democracy, but not to the good. The Court has its political role to play in the
democracy, and the members of the Court are influenced in the way they
perform their roles by their own personalities, maybe not in the short term,
but certainly in the long term. Acknowledging this influence helps us
understand the Court and its role.

＊

APPENDIX

TABLE A1.   Total Number of Majority, Concurring, and Dissenting Opinions of Various Justices, Excluding Byrnes, J., and Warren, C. J.

	Majority	Concurring	Dissenting	Terms	Total Cases
Frankfurter	142 (10.9)	105 (8.1)	190 (14.6)	13	1,503
Jackson	149 (12.4)	36	112	12	1,289
Black	229 (17.6)	20 (1.5)	157 (12.1)	13	1,493
Douglas	233 (17.9)	37 (2.8)	167 (12.8)	13	1,421
Reed	158 (12.1)	17 (.4)	79 (6.1)	13	1,494
Burton	65 (7.2)	8 (.9)	39 (4.3)	9	929
Murphy	111(13.9)	21 (2.6)	64 (8.0)	8	1,127
Vinson	77 (11.0)	0 (0.0)	18 (2.6)	7	716
Rutledge	65 (9.3)	28 (4.0)	62 (8.8)	7	899
Stone	96 (19.2)	8 (1.6)	40 (8.0)	5	707
Minton	48 (9.6)	0 (0.0)	23 (4.6)	5	411
Clark	51 (10.2)	7 (1.4)	8 (1.6)	5	379
Roberts	67 (16.7)	5 (1.25)	61 (15.2)	4	535
Total	1,512	295	1,026	13	1,512

Note: Per term averages are in parentheses.

TABLE A2.   Number of Cases and Frequency with Which Quartet Justices Voted with Court's Majority Opinion during Quartet Period Years, 1941–53

	Jackson	Frankfurter	Black	Douglas
1941	113/128 (88.2%)	136/151 (90.0%)	126/146 (86.3%)	122/150 (81.3%)
1942	125/138 (90.5%)	130/148 (87.8%)	126/145 (86.9%)	125/147 (85.0%)
1943	105/125 (84.0%)	109/129 (84.4%)	106/127 (83.5%)	103/128 (80.4%)
1944	133/147 (90.4%)	132/154 (85.7%)	126/154 (81.2%)	103/128 (80.4%)
1945	—	106/133 (79.6%)	118/133 (88.7%)	112/134 (83.6%)
1946	116/135 (85.9%)	119/142 (83.8%)	113/139 (81.3%)	111/138 (80.4%)
1947	79/110 (71.8%)	82/110 (74.5%)	84/109 (77.1%)	79/110 (71.8%)
1948	79/110 (71.8%)	87/114 (76.3%)	91/114 (79.8%)	83/114 (72.8%)
1949	60/83 (72.2%)	55/84 (65.5%)	61/86 (70.9%)	12/17 (70.6%)
1950	71/89 (79.7%)	63/91 (69.2%)	57/90 (63.3%)	56/90 (62.2%)
1951	63/79 (79.7%)	58/74 (78.4%)	49/79 (62.0%)	53/80 (66.3%)
1952	75/92 (81.5%)	67/101 (66.3%)	65/101 (64.4%)	51/102 (50.0%)
1953	59/60 (98.3)	60/68 (88.2%)	45/66 (68.2%)	41/66 (62.1%)
Total	1,074/1,287 (83.4%)	1,203/1,498 (80.3%)	1,167/1,489 (78.4%)	1,078/1,426 (75.5%)

TABLE A3.   Number of Cases and Rates with Which, in Descending Order of Frequency, Individual Quartet Justices Voted with Majority Opinions of Various of Their Brethren, Excluding Byrnes, J., and Warren, C. J.

Jackson	Frankfurter	Black	Douglas
Stone 68/74 (91.8%)	Stone 88/96 (91.2%)	Murphy 106/111 (95.5%)	Murphy 99/112 (88.4%)
Roberts 53/61 (86.8%)	Roberts 60/66 (90.9%)	Rutledge 58/64 (90.6%)	Black 183/214 (85.5%)
Frankfurter 108/125 (86.4%)	Jackson 129/147 (87.7%)	Douglas 203/230 (88.3%)	Stone 81/96 (84.3%)
Reed 111/129 (86.0%)	Murphy 93/111 (83.8%)	Stone 84/106 (81.1%)	Vinson 53/69 (76.7%)
Vinson 59/71 (77.7%)	Black 176/228 (77.2%)	Roberts 45/66 (68.2%)	Rutledge 49/65 (75.4%)
Minton 45/55 (77.7%)	Vinson 59/77 (76.6%)	Reed 104/155 (67.1%)	Reed 101/150 (67.3%)
Black 147/181 (81.2%)	Burton 50/66 (75.7%)	Vinson 42/64 (65.6%)	Clark 21/31 (67.1%)
Murphy 71/88 (80.6%)	Rutledge 54/74 (72.9%)	Clark 32/49 (65.3%)	Roberts 40/64 (62.5%)
Clark 35/45 (77.7%)	Douglas 160/226 (70.8%)	Burton 41/63 (65.1%)	Jackson 82/135 (60.7%)
Burton 41/53 (77.3%)	Reed 109/155 (70.3%)	Jackson 90/145 (62.1%)	Frankfurter 68/113 (51.1%)
Douglas 138/189 (73.0%)	Clark 34/50 (68.0%)	Frankfurter 84/138 (60.9%)	Butler 29/57 (51.0%)
Rutledge 35/48 (72.9%)	Minton 30/46 (65.2%)	Minton 27/46 (58.7%)	Minton 17/36 (47.2%)
Total 911/1,119 (81.4%)	Total 1,046/1,342 (77.7%)	Total 916/1,237 (74.0%)	Total 942/1,142 (82.4%)

TABLE A4. Number of Cases and Rate with Which Jackson Voted with the Majority Opinions of Frankfurter, Black, and Douglas

	Frankfurter	Black	Douglas
1941	14/16	13/13	22/25
1942	7/7	19/22	15/21
1943	11/13	15/17	14/19
1944	15/16	16/19	15/17
1945	—	—	—
1946	11/12	23/28	23/27
1947	5/7	7/10	13/20
1948	6/13	15/19	10/19
1949	7/8	8/13	0/2
1950	8/8	7/12	7/12
1951	7/8	8/10	5/10
1952	10/10	8/10	8/11
1953	7/7	8/8	6/6
Total	108/125 (86.4%)	147/181 (81.2%)	138/189 (73.0%)

TABLE A5. Number of Cases and Rate with Which, in Descending Order of Frequency, Various Brethren, Excluding Byrnes, J. and Warren, C. J., Voted with the Majority Opinions of Quartet Justices

Jackson	Frankfurter	Black	Douglas
Minton 45/47 (95.7%)	Clark 38/39 (97.4%)	Clark 49/50 (98.0%)	Reed 214/229 (93.4%)
Vinson 78/84 (92.9%)	Stone 58/65 (89.2%)	Vinson 101/110 (91.8%)	Murphy 163/179 (91.1%)
Clark 39/44 (88.7%)	Jackson 108/125 (86.4%)	Murphy 151/167 (90.0%)	Vinson 95/105 (90.5%)
Frankfurter 129/148 (87.2%)	Burton 73/85 (85.9%)	Douglas 183/214 (85.5%)	Stone 105/117 (89.7%)
Stone 47/57 (82.5%)	Reed 117/141 (82.9%)	Reed 188/228 (82.4%)	Clark 35/39 (89.7%)
Reed 121/147 (82.3%)	Vinson 50/67 (74.6%)	Rutledge 129/137 (82.2%)	Rutledge 140/158 (88.6%)
Burton 73/90 (81.1%)	Rutledge 56/76 (73.7%)	Stone 84/104 (80.8%)	Black 203/230 (88.3%)
Roberts 42/52 (80.8%)	Minton 28/39 (71.8%)	Jackson 152/189 (80.4%)	Minton 39/45 (86.7%)
Murphy 74/100 (74.0%)	Roberts 37/52 (71.1%)	Minton 44/55 (80.0%)	Burton 122/142 (84.7%)
Rutledge 60/83 (72.3%)	Murphy 66/95 (69.5%)	Frankfurter 177/229 (77.3%)	Frankfurter 164/230 (71.3%)
Black 90/145 (62.0%)	Black 92/138 (66.6%)	Burton 115/151 (76.1%)	Jackson 129/186 (69.4%)
Douglas 82/135 (60.7%)	Douglas 68/133 (51.1%)	Roberts 44/70 (62.9%)	Roberts 51/78 (65.4%)
880/1,132 (77.8%)	791/1,055 (75.0%)	1,417/1,704 (83.1%)	1,460/1,738 (84.0%)

TABLE A6. Number of Cases and Rate with Which Frankfurter Voted with the Majority Opinions of Jackson, Black, and Douglas over Quartet Period, 1941–53

	Jackson	Black	Douglas
1941	11/12	15/17	23/26
1942	14/15	18/22	19/23
1943	16/17	10/17	14/19
1944	14/14	16/20	11/20
1945	—	31/32	20/27
1946	15/15	21/29	22/27
1947	14/17	15/18	14/22
1948	7/10	16/19	9/20
1949	12/12	6/13	0/3
1950	8/10	7/12	7/12
1951	7/8	7/10	6/8
1952	5/10	6/10	9/12
1953	6/7	8/9	6/7
Total	114/147 (77.6%)	176/228 (77.1%)	160/226 (70.8%)

TABLE A7. Number of Cases and Rate with Which Douglas Voted with Majority Opinions of Jackson, Frankfurter, and Black

	Jackson	Frankfurter	Black
1941	9/12	10/16	16/17
1942	10/15	5/9	22/23
1943	12/16	9/14	16/17
1944	9/12	11/16	19/19
1945	—	7/10	27/32
1946	11/14	6/12	25/28
1947	8/17	2/7	15/18
1948	5/10	6/14	16/19
1949	0/3	0/0	1/1
1950	6/10	3/8	10/12
1951	4/8	4/8	9/13
1952	3/10	4/11	4/10
1953	4/7	1/8	5/9
Total	81/134 (60.4%)	68/133 (51.1%)	184/214 (85.9%)

TABLE A8. Number of Cases and Rate with Which Black Voted with the Majority Opinions of Jackson, Frankfurter, and Douglas over Quartet Period, 1941–53

	Jackson	Frankfurter	Douglas
1941	10/12	11/16	26/26
1942	11/15	4/8	23/23
1943	13/15	10/14	18/19
1944	8/13	11/15	18/21
1945	—	6/10	24/27
1946	10/15	7/12	23/26
1947	7/17	2/7	19/22
1948	6/10	11/14	16/20
1949	9/13	5/8	4/4
1950	5/9	5/8	8/12
1951	5/9	4/8	7/11
1952	4/10	8/11	11/12
1953	4/7	0/7	6/7
Total	90/145 (62.1%)	84/138 (60.9%)	203/230 (88.3%)

TABLE A9. Number and Percentage of Unanimous Opinions of Each Justice and Court Generally, Relative to Total Number of Opinions Written, Quartet Period by Year

	Jackson	Frankfurter	Black	Douglas	Court
1941	6/10	2/15	11/17	16/27	75/151
1942	8/15	0/9	7/22	10/23	71/148
1943	3/17	1/4	7/17	3/19	34/129
1944	5/14	3/16	3/20	3/21	39/156
1945	—	2/10	14/32	9/28	34/135
1946	4/15	2/12	11/29	12/27	42/142
1947	1/17	0/7	4/18	6/22	20/110
1948	1/10	0/14	5/19	2/20	20/114
1949	5/13	2/8	3/13	0/4	20/87
1950	1/9	2/8	4/12	3/12	18/71
1951	1/9	0/8	2/11	2/11	8/82
1952	1/10	2/11	1/10	6/12	14/103
1953	1/7	0/8	0/9	5/7	19/68
Total	38/147 (25.8%)	16/140 (11.42%)	72/229 (31.4%)	77/223 (33.1%)	414/1,496 (27.7%)

NOTES

Preface

1. The following cases selectively incorporated criminal procedure rights: *Malloy v. Hogan,* 378 U.S. 1 (1964) (self-incrimination); *Benton v. Maryland,* 395 U.S. 784 (1969) (double jeopardy); *Crist v. Bretz,* 437 U.S. 28 (1978) (when jeopardy attaches); *Gideon v. Wainwright,* 372 U.S. 335 (1963) (right to counsel); *Pointer v. Texas,* 380 U.S. 400 (1965) (confrontation and cross-examination of adverse witnesses); *Klopfer v. North Carolina,* 386 U.S. 213 (1967) (speedy trial); *Washington v. Texas,* 38 U.S. 14 (1967) (compulsory process to obtain witnesses); and *Duncan v. Louisiana,* 391 U.S. 145 (1968) (jury trial).

2. For a similar assessment of judicial biography generally, see M. Boudin, *Members of the Warren Court in Judicial Biography: Commentary,* 70 N.Y.U. L. REV. 772, 777 (1995). Political scientists have a limited version of the personality approach that looks to the attitudes and values of the justices. See, for example, J. SEGAL & H. SPAETH, THE SUPREME COURT AND THE ATTITUDINAL MODEL (1993).

3. F. FRANKFURTER, THE COMMERCE CLAUSE 6 (1937).

4. F. Frankfurter, *The Impact of Charles Evans Hughes,* N.Y. TIMES, Nov. 18, 1951, at 1 (book review).

5. P. Stewart, *Jackson on Federal-State Relationships, in* MR. JUSTICE JACKSON: FOUR LECTURES IN HIS HONOR 63 (1969).

Chapter 1

1. 345 U.S. 972 (1953). For a behind-the-scenes account, see D. Hutchinson, *Unanimity and Desegregation: Decisionmaking in the Supreme Court, 1948–58,* 68 GEO. L.J. 1 (1979).

2. H. Friendly, *The Bill of Rights as a Code of Criminal Procedure,* 53 CAL. L. REV. 929, 934 (1965). For other, similar observations by noted scholars and com-

mentators, see A. Amar, *The Bill of Rights and the Fourteenth Amendment*, 101 YALE L.J. 1193, 1194 (1992).

3. Commentators have certainly written often about these justices, and while some of their books are exceedingly well done, and while each offers something, as a group they do not follow either the central story of the time, as played out in the personalities of the justices and the factions they formed, or the major ironies, both ideological and personal, that overlay the period. See J. SIMON, THE ANTAGONISTS: HUGO BLACK, FELIX FRANKFURTER AND CIVIL LIBERTIES IN MODERN AMERICA (1989); H. BALL & P. COOPER, OF POWER AND RIGHT: HUGO BLACK, WILLIAM O. DOUGLAS, AND AMERICA'S CONSTITUTIONAL REVOLUTION (1992); R. NEWMAN, HUGO BLACK (1994); BRUCE M. MURPHY, WILD BILL (2003); H. BALL, HUGO L. BLACK: COLD STEEL WARRIOR (1996); J. HOCKETT, NEW DEAL JUSTICE: THE CONSTITUTIONAL JURISPRUDENCE OF HUGO L. BLACK, FELIX FRANKFURTER, AND ROBERT H. JACKSON (1996); F. RUDKO, TRUMAN'S COURT: A STUDY IN JUDICIAL RESTRAINT (1988); M. UROFSKY, DIVISION AND DISCORD: THE SUPREME COURT UNDER STONE AND VINSON, 1941–53 (1997); M. UROFSKY, FELIX FRANKFURTER: JUDICIAL RESTRAINT AND INDIVIDUAL LIBERTIES (1991); G. WHITE, THE AMERICAN JUDICIAL TRADITION (exp. ed.) (1988). Also see Laura Krugman Ray, *Judicial Personality: Rhetoric and Emotion in Supreme Court Opinions,* 59 WASH. & LEE L. REV. 193 (2002).

4. Frankfurter to Rutledge, May 10, 1945, Rutledge Papers, Library of Congress.

5. Quoted in B. SCHWARTZ, SUPER CHIEF: EARL WARREN AND HIS SUPREME COURT 33 (1979).

6. See G. WHITE, THE AMERICAN JUDICIAL TRADITION 369–421 (exp. ed.) (1988).

7. 381 U.S. 479 (1965).

8. 316 U.S. 535 (1942).

9. 319 U.S. 624 (1943).

10. *United States v. Carolene Products,* 304 U.S. 92, 103 n.4 (1938) (Stone, J.)

11. 310 U.S. 586 (1940).

12. William O. Douglas Interviews, Mudd Library, Princeton University, 1961–63 at 51. The transcripts of these interviews are now on the internet, at http://libweb.princeton.edu/libraries/firestone/rbsc/finding_aids/douglas/index .html [hereinafter Douglas Interviews].

13. *Id.*

14. *West Virginia State Board of Education v. Barnette,* 319 U.S. 624, 646–47 (1943) (Frankfurter, J., dissenting).

15. *Id.* at 664.

16. *Id.* at 665.

17. J. Lash ed., FROM THE DIARIES OF FELIX FRANKFURTER 73 (1974).

18. 332 U.S. 46 (1947).

19. 211 U.S. 78 (1908).

20. *Adamson v. California,* 332 U.S. 46, 61–63 (1947) (Frankfurter, J., concurring). But see, A. Amar, *The Bill of Rights and the Fourteenth Amendment,* 101 YALE L.J. 1193 (1992).

21. *Adamson v. California,* 332 U.S. 46, 67–68 (1947) (Frankfurter, J., concurring).

22. *Id.* at 332 U.S. 46.

23. *Id.* at 332 U.S. 46, 67–68.

24. *Haley v. State of Ohio,* 332 U.S. 596, 603 (1948).

25. *Adamson v. California,* 332 U.S. 46, 68 (1947) (Frankfurter, J., concurring).

26. *Adamson* at 72, quoting *Ex parte Bain,* 121 U.S. 1, 12 (1887) ("It is never to be forgotten," Black quoted from *Ex parte Bain,* "that in the construction of the language of the Constitution . . . as indeed in all other instances where construction becomes necessary, we are to place ourselves as nearly as possible in the condition of the men who framed that instrument.").

Chapter 2

1. Though there is a biography of Jackson, the reader should first turn to the superior biographical sketches of Jackson in *Supreme Court Proceedings, In Memory of Robert Houghwout Jackson, in* R. Jacobs, MEMORIALS OF THE JUSTICES OF THE SUPREME COURT OF THE UNITED STATES 53–81 (1981), and *in* MR. JUSTICE JACKSON: FOUR LECTURES IN HIS HONOR (1969).

2. January 22, 1947, letter to Waldo Breeden, Robert Jackson Papers, Library of Congress [hereinafter RJLOC].

3. R. Jackson, *Training the Trial Lawyer: A Neglected Area of Legal Education,* 3 STAN. L. REV. 48, 50–51 (1950).

4. Robert Jackson Oral History, Columbia University Oral History Project, at 1365, as quoted in Philip Kurland, *Robert H. Jackson, in* 4 LEON FRIEDMAN & FRED ISRAEL, JUSTICES OF THE UNITED STATES SUPREME COURT (New York: Chelsea House, 1969), 2543, 2546 [hereinafter Kurland].

5. R. Jackson, *The County-Seat Lawyer,* 36 A.B.A. J. 497 (1950).

6. Kurland at 2545.

7. See, generally, P. IRONS, THE NEW DEAL LAWYERS (1982); and R. SHAMIR, MANAGING LEGAL UNCERTAINTY: ELITE LAWYERS IN THE NEW DEAL (1995).

8. F. Frankfurter, *Robert Jackson,* 68 HARV. L. REV. 937 (1955).

9. See, generally, W. Gardner, *Government Attorney,* 55 COLUM. L. REV. 438 (1955).

10. Freund Interview, October 18, 1982, University of Kentucky Stanley Reed Oral History Project, p. 37.

11. Senate Document 71 (1937).

12. Jackson to Rex Crosby, March 27, 1939 (RJLOC).

13. H. ICKES, THE SECRET DIARY OF HAROLD L. ICKES, vol. 2, p. 201 (1954) (December 12, 1937 entry).

14. TIME, VOL. 35, (Jan. 15, 1940) 11.

15. H. ICKES, THE SECRET DIARY OF HAROLD L. ICKES, vol. 2, p. 201 (1954) (December 12, 1937 entry).

16. *Id.* at 539 (January 1, 1939 entry).

17. H. ICKES, THE SECRET DIARY OF HAROLD L. ICKES, vol. 3, p. 55 (1954).

18. 75th Cong., First Session, on S. 1392, Pt. 1, pp. 37–64. See also S. Alton,

Loyal Lieutenant, Able Advocate: The Role of Robert H. Jackson in Franklin D. Roosevelt's Battle with the Supreme Court, 5 WM. & MARY BILL OF RTS. J. 527 (1997).

19. R. JACKSON, THE STRUGGLE FOR JUDICIAL SUPREMACY (1941); COH at 1365.

20. Kurland at 2541, 2555.

21. Paul Freund Papers, Harvard Law School Library.

22. Kurland at 2554.

23. R. JACKSON, THE STRUGGLE FOR JUDICIAL SUPREMACY 285 (1941).

24. Undated memorandum, Frankfurter Papers, Library of Congress [hereinafter FFLOC].

25. 314 U.S. 160 (1941).

26. We know through one of Jackson's friends that he was happy with what he had done. Harold Ickes reported in a late November entry that "Bob Jackson was in for lunch on Friday. I hadn't seen him for a long time and I was glad to have him since I thoroughly like him. He looked well and happy and I believe that he is more than content as a member of the Supreme Court. He had just written a separate opinion on the right of the State of California to exclude from the state people from other states seeking work." 310 U.S. 586 (1940). See H. ICKES, THE SECRET DIARY OF HAROLD ICKES, vol. 3, 656 (1954).

27. 319 U.S. 624 (1943).

28. 323 U.S. 214 (1944).

29. Much has been written about Jackson at Nuremberg. The most concise and illuminating account is Shawcross, *Robert H. Jackson's Contributions During the Nuremberg Trial, in* MR. JUSTICE JACKSON: FOUR LECTURES IN HIS HONOR 87 (1969).

30. 325 U.S. 897 (1945).

31. The best account of this episode is D. Hutchinson, *The Black-Jackson Feud,* 1988 SUP. CT. REV. 203 (1988).

32. As quoted in the NEW YORK TIMES, June 1, 1946, A3.

33. See table A1. In addition, 8 STAN. L. REV. 60, 60–71 (1955) lists and divides by subject all of Jackson's opinions.

34. R. JACKSON, FULL FAITH AND CREDIT, THE LAWYER'S CLAUSE OF THE CONSTITUTION (1945).

35. R. JACKSON, THE SUPREME COURT IN THE AMERICAN SYSTEM OF GOVERNMENT (1955).

36. R. JACKSON, THAT MAN: AN INSIDER'S PORTRAIT OF FRANKLIN D. ROOSEVELT (2003).

37. 8 STAN. L. REV. 60, 71–76 (1955) lists all of Jackson's published addresses, articles, and books.

38. R. Jackson, *Falstaff's Descendants in Pennsylvania Courts,* 101 U. PA. L. REV. 313 (1952).

39. 68 HARV. L. REV. 937 (1955); 55 COLUM. L. REV. 435 (1955); 8 STAN. L. REV. 1 (1955).

40. MR. JUSTICE JACKSON: FOUR ESSAYS IN HIS HONOR (1969).

41. R. JACKSON, DISPASSIONATE JUSTICE: A SYNTHESIS OF THE JUDICIAL OPINIONS OF ROBERT H. JACKSON, G. Schubert ed. (1969).

42. See table A2.

43. See table A3.

44. See table A4.

45. See table A5.

46. 317 U.S. 111 (1942).

47. R. JACKSON, FULL FAITH AND CREDIT, THE LAWYER'S CLAUSE OF THE CONSTITUTION (1945).

48. *Armour and Co. v. Wantock,* 323 U.S. 126, 130 (1944).

49. *United States v. Hess,* 317 U.S. 537, 557 (1943) (Jackson, J., dissenting)

50. *West Virginia State Bd. of Educ. v. Barnette,* 319 U.S. 624, 639 (1943).

51. In *Brinegar v. United States,* 338 U.S. 160, 180 (1949) (Jackson, J., dissenting), he opened his dissent in a Fourth Amendment case by writing that "when this Court recently has promulgated a philosophy that some rights derived from the Constitution are entitled to 'a preferred position,' I have not agreed. We cannot give some constitutional rights a preferred position without relegating others to a deferred position; we can establish no firsts without thereby establishing seconds. Indications are not wanting that Fourth Amendment freedoms are tacitly marked as secondary rights, to be relegated to a deferred position."

52. *Beauharnais v. Illinois,* 343 U.S. 250, 294 (1952) (Jackson, J., dissenting).

53. *Fay v. People of State of New York,* 332 U.S. 261, 295 (1947).

54. *Ashcraft v. Tennessee,* 322 U.S. 143, 174 (1944) (Jackson, J., dissenting).

55. *Watts v. Indiana,* 338 U.S. 49, 57 (1949) (Jackson, J., concurring).

56. 338 U.S. 49, 57 (1949) (Jackson, J., concurring).

57. *Brinegar v. United States,* 338 U.S. 160, 180–81 (1949) (Jackson, J., dissenting).

58. *Id.* at 183.

59. E. GERHART, AMERICA'S ADVOCATE (1958).

60. D. Hutchinson, *The Black-Jackson Feud,* 1988 SUP. CT. REV. 203, 224 (1988).

61. E. GERHART, LAWYER'S JUDGE (1961).

62. P. Kurland, *Judicial Biography: History, Myth, Literature, Fiction, Potpourri,* 70 N.Y.U. L. REV. 489, 497 (1995).

63. P. Kurland, *Robert H. Jackson, in* FRIEDMAN & ISRAEL, JUSTICES OF THE SUPREME COURT 2541 (1980).

64. D. CURRIE, THE CONSTITUTION IN THE SUPREME COURT: THE SECOND CENTURY, 1888–1986 278 (1990).

65. See K. Stark, *The Unfulfilled Tax Legacy of Robert H. Jackson,* 54 TAX L. REV. 171 (2000).

66. F. RODELL, NINE MEN 279 (1955).

67. *Id.*

68. G. WHITE, THE AMERICAN JUDICIAL TRADITION: PROFILES OF LEADING AMERICAN JUDGES 230–50 (exp. edition) (1988).

69. *Id.* at 231.

70. R. JACKSON, DISPASSIONATE JUSTICE: A SYNTHESIS OF THE JUDICIAL OPINIONS OF ROBERT H. JACKSON, G. Schubert ed. (1969), p. vii.

71. *Id.,* p. ix.

72. Jackson to Ernest Cawcroft, December 18, 1948 (RJLOC).

73. Jackson to Rutledge, May 27, 1947, quoted in S. FINE, FRANK MURPHY: THE WASHINGTON YEARS 247 (1980).

74. F. Rodell, *Justice Hugo Black,* AMERICAN MERCURY, August, 135, 145 (1944).

75. *Id.* at 137.

76. *Id.*

77. F. RODELL, NINE MEN (1955).

78. Irene Jackson to Frankfurter, July 19, 1955 (FFHLS).

79. Supreme Court Proceedings in Memory of Robert Houghwout Jackson, in Supreme Court Proceedings, In Memory of Robert Houghwout Jackson, *in* R. JACOBS, MEMORIALS OF THE JUSTICES OF THE SUPREME COURT OF THE UNITED STATES 15–16 (1981).

80. F. Frankfurter, *Robert Jackson,* 68 HARV. L. REV. 937, 939 (1955).

81. Jackson to Walter P. Armstrong, March 1, 1949 (RJLOC).

82. Jackson to Bernard Baruch, February 2, 1945 (RJLOC).

83. Quoted in C. Desmond, *The Role of the Country Lawyer, in* MR. JUSTICE JACKSON: FOUR LECTURES IN HIS HONOR at 14 (1969).

84. *Id.* at 19.

85. M. Urofsky ed., THE DOUGLAS LETTERS 120 (1987).

86. Jackson to Robert Benjamin, March 6, 1943, RJLOC.

87. Quoted in Remarks of John Lord O'Brian, Supreme Court Proceedings in Memory of Robert Houghwout Jackson, in Supreme Court Proceedings, In Memory of Robert Houghwout Jackson, *in* R. JACOBS, MEMORIALS OF THE JUSTICES OF THE SUPREME COURT OF THE UNITED STATES 74 (1981).

88. Quoted in E. GERHART, AMERICA'S ADVOCATE 122 (1958).

89. As quoted in D. Hutchinson, *The Black-Jackson Feud,* 1988 SUP. CT. REV. 203, 220 (1988).

90. Frankfurter to P. Kurland, November 26, 1962 (FFLOC).

91. Frankfurter to George Wharton Pepper, October 19, 1956, FFHLS.

92. Quoted in E. HIRSCH, THE ENIGMA OF FELIX FRANKFURTER 182 (1981).

93. *Id.* at 188.

94. Jackson to Frankfurter, June 19, 1946 (FFHLS).

95. H.B. Phillips to Frankfurter, July 10, 1955 (FFHLS).

96. F. Frankfurter, diary entry, January 30, 1943 (FFHLS).

97. Douglas Interviews at 216.

98. M. Howe ed., HOLMES-LASKI LETTERS 1034 (1953).

99. *West Virginia State Board of Education v. Barnette,* 319 U.S. 624 (1943).

100. *Id.* at 640–41.

101. Quoted in E. GERHART, AMERICA'S ADVOCATE 32 (1958).

102. E. London ed., THE WORLD OF LAW, vol. 2, THE LAW AS LITERATURE 467, 506 (1960).

103. Jackson to Norman Birkett, February 19, 1953 (RJLOC).

104. Jackson to John W. Davis, December 7, 1948 (RJLOC).

105. See table A1.

106. J. PALMER, THE VINSON COURT 142–48 (1990).

107. Letter from James Marsh to Eugene Gerhart, December 9, 1954, quoted in GERHART, LAWYER'S JUDGE 109 (1961).

108. Bennett Boskey Interview, March 18, 1981, University of Kentucky Stanley Reed Oral History Project, p. 11.

109. J. Lash ed., FROM THE DIARIES OF FELIX FRANKFURTER 209 (1974).

110. Frankfurter to Jackson, June 12, 1946 (FFLOC).

111. He writes, with sarcasm and self-pity, "[b]ut if I am to judge from the attitude of my contemporaries, the fight against this sort of thing is not worthwhile. Take the attitude of the [Washington] Post, for example. It demands that both Black and I resign and it must know that the only one it can possibly influence to resign would be me. The Post itself, along with the others, for weeks gave wide publicity to Black's threats to the President that he would resign, which states no grounds except dark hints. Neither the Post nor anyone else, so far as I can ascertain, took the slightest interest in finding out whether it was a mere petty and personal opposition or whether there was something serious in my record to warrant such a threat. Finally came the Fleeson article which plainly came from inside the Court. All these things, it appears, are quite acceptable and the only wrongdoing is to be candid and responsible in one's utterances. Well, we will see what effect it all has on future life on the Court." Jackson to Frankfurter, June 19, 1946 (FFHLS).

112. M. Lerner, *The Supreme Court Today,* HOLIDAY, Vol. 7 (1950), 73.

113. Douglas Interviews at 78–79.

114. *Id.*

115. Letter to author, March 30, 1997.

116. Jackson to Herman Oliphant, April 29, 1935, RJLOC.

117. Jackson to Henry Morgenthau, April 29, 1935, RJLOC.

118. Henry Morgenthau to Jackson, May 3, 1935, RJLOC.

119. See H. ICKES, THE SECRET DIARY OF HAROLD L. ICKES, II, 537–39; III, 51, 53–55 (1954).

120. December 10, 1912, letter from Jackson to Thomas J. Cummings, RJLOC.

121. H. ICKES, THE SECRET DIARY OF HAROLD L. ICKES, II, 593–94 (March 14, 1939 entry) (1954).

122. *Id.*

123. *Id.,* III, at 267.

124. *Id.* at 379.

125. Kurland at 2566.

126. *Id.*

127. See D. Hutchinson, *The Black-Jackson Feud* 203, 228, SUP. CT. REV. (1988).

128. Kurland at 2545.

129. *Id.* at 2562.

130. *Id.*

131. *Id.* at 2569.

132. *Id.*

133. As quoted in D. Hutchinson, *The Black-Jackson Feud,* 1988 SUP. CT. REV. 203, 222 (1988).

134. Kurland at 2565.

135. Jackson to Sidney Alderman, November 8, 1948 (RJLOC).

136. 329 U.S. 459 (1947)

137. December 1946 draft of Jackson opinion, Rutledge Papers, LOC.

138. Undated memorandum, Rutledge Papers, LOC.

139. Jackson to Dilliard, July 27, 1943 (RJLOC).

140. Jackson to Black, September 10, 1937 (RJLOC).

141. 338 U.S. 160 (1949) (Jackson, J., dissenting).

142. *West Virginia State Board of Education v. Barnette,* 319 U.S. 624 (1943).

143. Jackson to Norman Birkett, February 19, 1953 (RJLOC).

144. H.B. Phillips to Frankfurter, July 10, 1955 (FFHLS).

145. *Id.*

146. *Id.*

147. *Id.*

148. Prettyman to Frankfurter, October 10, 1955, FFLOC (emphasis in original).

149. Quoted in R. NEWMAN, HUGO BLACK 420 (1994).

150. *Id.*

151. Kurland at 2563.

152. 345 U.S. 972 (1953).

153. See D. Hutchinson, *Unanimity and Desegregation: Decisionmaking in the Supreme Court, 1948–58,* 68 GEO. L.J. 1 (1979); B. Schwartz, *Chief Justice Rehnquist, Justice Jackson, and the* Brown *Case,* 1988 SUP. CT. REV. 245 (1988).

154. B. Schwartz, *Chief Justice Rehnquist, Justice Jackson, and the* Brown *Case,* 1988 SUP. CT. REV. 245 (1988).

155. August 14, 1996, speech dedicating Memorial to Justice Robert Jackson, Jamestown, New York, as seen on C-SPAN.

Chapter 3

1. 371 U.S. x.

2. M. McManamon, *Felix Frankfurter: The Architect of "Our Federalism,"* 27 GA. L. REV. 697 (1993).

3. Frankfurter to Herbert Brownell, March 19, 1957, Frankfurter Papers, Library of Congress.

4. Justice Frankfurter, 148 NATION, Jan. 14, 1939, at 52–53.

5. A. MacLeish, Foreword at xxiii, in E.F. Pritchard and A. MacLeish eds., *Felix Frankfurter: Law and Politics* (1939).

6. NEW YORK TIMES, Jan. 6, 1939, at 20.

7. H. ICKES, THE SECRET DIARY OF HAROLD L. ICKES, vol. 2, at 533 (1954).

8. M. Freedman ed., ROOSEVELT AND FRANKFURTER: THEIR CORRESPON-DENCE, 1928–1945 (1967).

9. Their correspondence can be found in M. Urofsky & D. Levy eds. LETTERS OF LOUIS D. BRANDEIS (5 volumes) (1971); Menel & Compston eds., HOLMES AND FRANKFURTER: THEIR CORRESPONDENCE, 1912–1934 (1996).

10. G. White, *Holmes as Correspondent,* 43 VAND. L. REV. 1707, 1725 (1990).

11. Brandeis to Frankfurter, September 24, 1925, in Urofsky and Levy eds., 5 LETTERS OF LOUIS D. BRANDEIS 187 (1971).

12. NEW YORK TIMES Editorial, February 18, 1982, 22:1 *Judging Judges and History* (arrangement wrong because it violated ethical standards).

13. For Brandeis, VanDevanter is the least valuable member of the Court; Sanford is terribly tiresome, a dull bourgeois mind, who should never have risen above

a district judgeship; Taft is a "first-rate second-rate mind." He is an effective administrator, decisive mind, and cultivated man, the only one on the Court aside from Holmes; "Taft is the only other man with whom it is a pleasure to talk—you feel you talk with a cultivated man. He knows a lot, he *reads,* he has wide contacts"; Holmes is the best intellectual machine; Sutherland, a "mediocre Taft," is a far-western bourgeois and is, nonetheless, more cultured than Butler; Butler "has given no sign of anything except a thoroughly mediocre mind." Sanford "is nice—but no spark of greatness; thoroughly bourgeois." Marshall and Story outlived their usefulness, not because of waning intellectual powers but because of their failure to grow; Holmes should stay on the bench. He is still productive and his reputation will gain by staying on. M. Urofsky, *The Brandeis-Frankfurter Conversations,* SUP. CT. REV. 299, 313 (1985).

14. J. Lash ed., FROM THE DIARIES OF FELIX FRANKFURTER 175–76 (1974).

15. *Id.*

16. See D. Hutchinson, *Mr. Justice Frankfurter and the Business of the Supreme Court, 1949–1961,* 1980 SUP. CT. REV. 143 (1980).

17. *Graves v. People of State of New York,* 306 U.S. 466 (1939).

18. See table A1.

19. P. Elman, *The Solicitor General's Office: Justice Frankfurter and Civil Rights Litigation,* 100 HARV. L. REV. 817, 828, 843–44 (1987).

20. Douglas Interviews at 91.

21. A. Kaufman, *The Justice and His Law Clerks,* 223, 224–25, *in* Mendelson ed., FRANKFURTER: THE JUDGE (1964).

22. B. SCHWARTZ, SUPER CHIEF 61 (1979).

23. *Adamson v. California,* 332 U.S. 46 (1947) (Frankfurter, J., concurring).

24. See table A2.

25. *Id.*

26. *Id.*

27. See table A6.

28. See table A5.

29. 371 U.S. x. (1962).

30. *U.S. v. Lovett,* 328 U.S. 303, 320 (1946) (Frankfurter, J., concurring).

31. See P. Kurland ed., MR. JUSTICE FRANKFURTER AND THE CONSTITUTION 5–43 (1971).

32. *Id.* at 61–73.

33. 328 U.S. 549 (1946).

34. 369 U.S. 186 (1962).

35. See P. Kurland ed., MR. JUSTICE FRANKFURTER AND THE CONSTITUTION 39–46 (1971). According to at least one scholar, he ironically disregarded the principles of judicial restraint as they applied to him and aggressively worked to impose onto the Court his particular version of federalism, one that gave the states more leverage in their ongoing struggles with the federal government. He did this in various opinions by rewriting history in his treatment of ancillary jurisdiction and ignoring legislative intent as it related to the Anti-Injunction Act, which limited the ability of state courts to relitigate federal claims. See M. McManamon, *Felix Frankfurter: The Architect of "Our Federalism,"* 27 GA. L. REV. 697, 788 (1993).

36. *West Virginia State Board of Education v. Barnette,* 319 U.S. 624 (1943)

(Frankfurter, J., dissenting); *Kovacs v. Cooper,* 336 U.S. 77 (1949) (Frankfurter, J., concurring); *Haley v. State of Ohio,* 332 U.S. 596 (1948) Frankfurter, J., concurring); *Adamson v. California,* 332 U.S. 46 (1947) (Frankfurter, J., concurring); *Malinski v. People of State of New York,* 324 U.S. 401 (1945) (Frankfurter, J., concurring).

37. 304 U.S. 144, 152 n.4 (1938).

38. Frankfurter to Bickel, October 8, 1964, Frankfurter Papers, Harvard Law School [hereinafter FFHLS].

39. M. Ariens, *A Thrice-Told Tale, or Felix the Cat,* 107 HARV. L. REV. 620 (1994). For a refutation, see R. Friedman, *A Reaffirmation of the Authenticity of the Roberts Memorandum, or Felix the Nonforger,* 107 HARV. L. REV. 620 (1994).

40. E.F. Pritchard & A. MacLeish eds., FELIX FRANKFURTER: LAW AND POLITICS (1939); P. Elman ed., OF LAW AND MEN (1956).

41. H. Phillips ed., FELIX FRANKFURTER REMINISCES (1960).

42. J. Lash ed., FROM THE DIARIES OF FELIX FRANKFURTER (1974).

43. Frankfurter to Phillip Kurland, March 20, 1956 (FFLOC).

44. P. Kurland ed., OF LIFE AND LAW AND OTHER THINGS THAT MATTER (1965).

45. P. Kurland ed., MR. JUSTICE FRANKFURTER AND THE CONSTITUTION (1971).

46. A. Sacks, *Felix Frankfurter, in* L. Friedman & F. Israel eds., THE JUSTICES OF THE UNITED STATES SUPREME COURT 1216 (1980).

47. A. BICKEL, THE LEAST DANGEROUS BRANCH (1962).

48. P. Kurland, *Toward a Political Supreme Court,* 37 U. CHI. L. REV. 19 (1969); W. Mendelson, *Mr. Justice Frankfurter and the Process of Judicial Review,* 103 U. PA. L. REV. 295 (1954).

49. W. MENDELSON, JUSTICES BLACK AND FRANKFURTER: CONFLICT IN THE COURT (1961).

50. W. Mendelson ed., FRANKFURTER: A TRIBUTE (1964); and W. Mendelson ed., FRANKFURTER: THE JUDGE (1964).

51. H. Wechsler, *Toward Neutral Principles of Constitutional Law,* 73 HARV. L. REV. 1 (1959).

52. H. HART & A. SACKS, THE LEGAL PROCESS: BASIC PROBLEMS IN THE MAKING AND APPLICATION OF LAW (tent. ed. 1958).

53. A. Bickel and H. Wellington, *Legislative Purpose and the Judicial Process: The Lincoln Mills Case,* 71 HARV. L. REV. 1 (1957).

54. See L. KALMAN, THE STRANGE CAREER OF LEGAL LIBERALISM 260 (1996).

55. H. Hart, *The Supreme Court, 1958 Term, Foreword: The Time Chart of the Justices,* 73 HARV. L. REV. 84 (1959).

56. See M. Tushnet & T. Lynch, *The Project of the Harvard* Forewords, 11 CONST. COM. 463 (1994–95).

57. See *id.* at 493.

58. A. Lewis, *The Supreme Court and Its Critics,* 45 MINN. L. REV. 305, 324–25 (1961).

59. J. Lash ed., FROM THE DIARIES OF FELIX FRANKFURTER 142–44 (1974).

60. *Id.* 145–56.

61. *Id.* at 157–261.

62. *Id.* at 192; he took a stronger, more disingenuous line at nearly the same

time in a letter of June 5, 1943, to John Maguire, writing that he would not "dream of making any suggestion to the President" on a subject that was "even remotely connected with law or politics." (FFHLS).

63. J. Lash ed., FROM THE DIARIES OF FELIX FRANKFURTER 142 (1974).

64. *Id.* at 146.

65. *Id.* at 152.

66. *Id.* at 155.

67. *Id.* at 176.

68. *Id.* at 196.

69. *Id.* at 175.

70. *Id.* at 254.

71. *Id.*

72. *Id.* at 77.

73. NEW YORK TIMES BOOK REVIEW, p. 4, August 31, 1975.

74. J. Rauh, *Felix Frankfurter,* 173 NEW REPUBLIC 346 (October 11, 1975).

75. Frankfurter to Paul Freund, January 26, 1942 (FFLOC).

76. Frankfurter to C. Burlingham, March 18, 1957 (FFLOC) (describing Justice McReynolds's anti-Semitic behavior toward Justice Brandeis).

77. Frankfurter to C. Burlingham, June 12, 1952 (FFLOC).

78. *Id.,* May 15, 1952.

79. *Id.,* September 26, 1956.

80. Frankfurter to Alexander Bickel, December 28, 1956 (FFLOC).

81. Frankfurter to Philip Kurland, September 23, 1963 (FFLOC).

82. Frankfurter to Alexander Bickel, November 13, 1956 (FFLOC).

83. Frankfurter to Mark DeWolfe Howe, December 21, 1951 (FFLOC); Frankfurter to Alexander Bickel, March 25, 1957 (FFLOC).

84. Quoted in R. Steel, WALTER LIPPMANN AND THE AMERICAN CENTURY 220 n.20 (1980).

85. W. Douglas, GO EAST, YOUNG MAN 331–32 (1974).

86. Douglas Interviews at 90.

87. W. Shakespeare, *Julius Caesar,* I, ii, 192–210.

88. Hand Oral History Interview, Columbia University Oral History Project at 103–06.

89. A. Kaufman, *The Justice and His Law Clerks* 223, 227, *in* W. Mendelson ed., FRANKFURTER: THE JUDGE (1964).

90. Douglas Interviews at 282.

91. Quoted in B. Murphy, THE BRANDEIS/FRANKFURTER CONNECTION 191 (1982).

92. B. Canon, K. Greenfield, & J. Fleming, *Justice Frankfurter and Justice Reed: Friendship and Lobbying on the Court,* 78 JUDICATURE 224, 225 (1995).

93. Frankfurter to George Wharton Pepper, October 19, 1956 (FFLOC).

94. See chapter 2 at note 91.

95. See table A6.

96. The best example is *West Virginia State Board of Education v. Barnette,* 319 U.S. 624 (1943).

97. R. Jackson to Frankfurter, June 19, 1946 (FFHLS).

98. Frankfurter to Jackson, June 12, 1946 (FFLOC).

99. Douglas Interviews at 217.

100. Frankfurter to H. Black, September 30, 1950 (FFHLS).

101. Frankfurter to C. Burlingham, June 17, 1946 (FFLOC) ("I ain't saying nothing about the wisdom or propriety of what he did.").

102. Frankfurter, undated memorandum to P. Kurland (FFLOC).

103. Frankfurter to Douglas, November 25, 1942 (FFHLS).

104. Frankfurter to Charles Burlingham, February 14, 1958 (FFLOC).

105. *Wilkerson v. McCarthy,* 336 U.S. 53, 65 (1948) (Frankfurter, J., concurring).

106. *U.S. v. Monia,* 317 U.S. 424, 431 (1943) (Frankfurter, J., dissenting).

107. *Henslee v. Union Planters Nat'l Bank & Trust Co.,* 335 U.S. 595, 600 (1949) (Frankfurter, J., dissenting).

108. *McNabb v. U.S.,* 318 U.S. 332, 347 (1943) (Frankfurter, J.).

109. *Pearce v. Commissioner,* 315 U.S. 543, 558 (1942) (Frankfurter, J., dissenting).

110. *Haley v. Ohio,* 332 U.S. 586, 605 (1948) (Frankfurter, J., concurring).

111. *Malinski v. New York,* 324 U.S. 401, 414 (1945) (Frankfurter, J., concurring).

112. *United States v. L.A. Tucker Lines,* 344 U.S. 33, 39 (1952).

113. *Leland v. Oregon,* 343 U.S. 790, 803 (1952) (Frankfurter, J., dissenting).

114. *West Virginia State Board of Education v. Barnette,* 319 U.S. 624, 649 (1943) (Frankfurter, J., dissenting).

115. *Kovacs v. Cooper,* 336 U.S. 77 (1949) (Frankfurter, J., concurring).

116. *Id.* at 95.

117. *Id.* at 96–97.

118. *Adamson v. California,* 332 U.S. 46, 65 (1947) (Frankfurter, J., concurring).

119. *Wolf v. Colorado,* 338 U.S. 25 (1949).

120. *Id.* at 338 U.S. 25, 27 (1949).

121. Frankfurter to Black, October 31, 1939 (FFHLS).

122. New York Times 1932.

123. *Id.*

124. Douglas Interviews at 173.

125. *Id.* at 74.

126. *Id.* at 239–40.

127. *Id.* at 251–52.

128. E. Gressman, *Psycho-Enigmatizing Felix Frankfurter,* 80 Mich. L. Rev. 731, 738 (1982).

129. Douglas Interviews at 51.

130. Interview with Bayless Manning (1949 Reed law clerk), Stanley Reed Oral History Project, University of Kentucky Library, at 12.

131. Interview with F. Aley Allan (1949 Reed law clerk), Stanley Reed Oral History Project, University of Kentucky Library, at 8.

132. Frankfurter to W. Rutledge, February 8, 1947, Rutledge Papers, Library of Congress.

133. Frankfurter to Reed, April 5, 1948, Stanley Reed Papers, Library of Congress.

134. Frankfurter to Reed, December 2, 1941 (FFLOC).

135. *Id.*

136. Frankfurter to C. Burlingham, September 30, 1953 (FFLOC).

137. *Id.*, February 25, 1952.

138. Frankfurter to L. Hand, October 29, 1958 (FFLOC).

139. Frankfurter to L. Hand, June 15, 1953, quoted in A. Stone, *The Enigma of Felix Frankfurter* (book review), 95 HARV. L. REV. 346, 366 n.39 (1981).

140. Frankfurter to L. Hand, November 7, 1954, Learned Hand Papers, Harvard Law School.

141. *Id.*

142. *Id.*, November 5, 1954.

143. *Id.*

144. Quoted in J. SIMON, INDEPENDENT JOURNEY 217 n.21 (1980).

145. J. Lash ed., FROM THE DIARIES OF FELIX FRANKFURTER 230 (1974).

146. Frankfurter to L. Hand, June 30, 1957, quoted in G. WHITE, EARL WARREN 181 (1982).

147. Harold Ickes Diary, May 3, 1942, entry, Library of Congress.

148. H. PRITCHETT, THE ROOSEVELT COURT 132 (1948).

149. J. Frank, *The Supreme Court of the United States: 1949–50,* U. CHI. L. REV. 1, 46 (1950).

150. L. Jaffe, *The Judicial Universe of Mr. Justice Frankfurter,* 62 HARV. L. REV. 357, 358 (1949).

151. 369 U.S. 186 (1962).

152. In Memory of Honorable Felix Frankfurter, 86 S.Ct. 17, 23–24 (1965).

153. *Id.* at 30.

154. P. Freund, *Felix Frankfurter, in* DICTIONARY OF AMERICAN BIOGRAPHY, SUPPLEMENT 7, 260, 263 (1981).

155. P. Kurland ed., MR. JUSTICE FRANKFURTER AND THE CONSTITUTION 1 (1971).

156. *Id.* at viii.

157. J. Rauh, *Felix Frankfurter: Civil Libertarian,* HARV. C.R.-C.L. L. REV. 496, 505 (1976).

158. One commentator, H.N. HIRSCH in THE ENIGMA OF FELIX FRANKFURTER (1981), has looked to psychoanalysis to help explain Frankfurter's arrogance, Hirsch taking his cue from the psychoanalytical models of noted writers Erik Erikson and Karen Horney.

159. W. DOUGLAS, THE COURT YEARS 33–34 (1980).

160. The irony of Frankfurter's life and career, ROBERT BURT argues in his TWO JEWISH JUSTICES (1988), is that Frankfurter, who began his immigrant life in America as a quintessential outsider, especially as a Jew, was transformed, through his elite education and government and teaching positions, into the quintessential insider by the time he reached the Supreme Court.

161. Alan A. Stone, *The Enigma of Felix Frankfurter* (book review), 95 HARV. L. REV. 346, 352 (1981).

162. J. Lash ed., FROM THE DIARIES OF FELIX FRANKFURTER 176 (1974).

163. Frankfurter to T. Clark, January 17, 1958 (FFLOC) ("After all, opinions are written for judges and lawyers and perhaps a few others who can read.").

164. *Rochin v. California,* 342 U.S. 165, 172 (1952) (Frankfurter, J.).

165. 329 U.S. 459, 466 (1947).

Chapter 4

1. For a transcript of the interview, see 9 Sw. U. L. Rev. 937 (1977).

2. See D. Lee, *Senator Black's Investigation of the Airmail, 1933–34,* 53, Historian 423 (1991).

3. R. Newman, Hugo Black: A Biography 277 (1994).

4. A. Blaustein & R. Mersky eds., The First Hundred Justices 145 (1978).

5. R. Newman, Hugo Black 329 n.2 (1994).

6. M. Pusey, *The Roosevelt Supreme Court,* 58 American Mercury 596 (May 1944).

7. *Id.*

8. L. Jaffe, *The Supreme Court Today,* 174 Atlantic Monthly 76 (December 1944).

9. *Id.*

10. A. Schlesinger, *The Supreme Court: 1947,* 35 Fortune 73 (1947) (January 1947).

11. *Id.*

12. See, for example, *U.S. v. Dennis,* 332 U.S. 46 (1947).

13. *Davis v. Department of Labor,* 317 U.S. 249 (1942).

14. H. Black, *The Bill of Rights,* 35 N.Y.U. L. Rev. 865 (1960).

15. W. Douglas, *The Bill of Rights Is Not Enough,* 38 N.Y.U. L. Rev. 207 (1963).

16. *Id.* (italics in original)

17. 381 U.S. 479 (1965).

18. M. Klarman, Book Review, 12 L. & Hist. Rev. 399, 401 (1994).

19. 332 U.S. 46 (1947).

20. 342 U.S. 165 (1952).

21. *Id.* at 177 (footnote omitted).

22. Elizabeth Black to Mary Rodell, March 12, 1966, Fred Rodell Papers, Haverford College.

23. *Griswold v. Connecticut,* 381 U.S. 479, 508 (1965) (Black, J., dissenting).

24. *Id.* at 510.

25. See table A2.

26. See table A3.

27. See table A8.

28. 372 U.S. 335 (1963).

29. See W. Domnarski, In the Opinion of the Court 80 (1996).

30. See, for example, *Von Molke v. Gillies,* 332 U.S. 708 (1948), and *Klapprott v. U.S.,* 336 U.S. 942 (1949).

31. H. Black Jr., My Father: A Remembrance 135 (1975).

32. *Milk Wagon Drivers Union v. Meadowmoor Dairies.* 312 U.S. 287, 302 (1941) (Black, J., dissenting).

33. *Chambers v. Florida ,* 309 U.S. 227, 240 (1940).

34. *Bridges v. California,* 314 U.S. 252, 260 (1941).

35. *Mercoid Corp. v. Mid-Continent Investment Co.,* 320 U.S. 661, 673 (1944) (Black, J., concurring) (criticizing Frankfurter dissent).

36. J. Frank, Mr. Justice Black: The Man and His Opinions (1949).

37. C. Williams, Hugo L. Black: A Study in the Judicial Process (1950).

38. H. BALL, THE VISION AND THE DREAM OF JUSTICE HUGO L. BLACK (1975).

39. G. DUNNE, HUGO BLACK AND THE JUDICIAL REVOLUTION (1977).

40. Quoted in B. Schwartz, *Hugo L. Black, in* THE WARREN COURT: A RETROSPECTIVE 202 (1996).

41. J. MAGEE, MR. JUSTICE BLACK: ABSOLUTIST ON THE COURT (1980).

42. R. NEWMAN, HUGO BLACK (1994).

43. H. Black, *Reminiscences,* 18 ALA. L. REV. 1 (1965); H. BLACK & E. BLACK, MR. JUSTICE AND MRS. BLACK (1986).

44. Black to Rodell, March 3, 1961, Fred Rodell Papers, Haverford College.

45. H. BLACK JR., MY FATHER (1975).

46. H. BLACK & E. BLACK, MR. JUSTICE AND MRS. BLACK 170 (1986).

47. *Id.* at 99.

48. See, generally, D. MEADOR, MR. JUSTICE BLACK AND HIS BOOKS (1974).

49. H. BLACK JR., MY FATHER 138 (1975).

50. Examples would include *Johnson v. Eisentrager,* 339 U.S. 763, 798 n.4 (1950) (Black, J., dissenting) (Tacitus); *Barenblatt v. U.S.,* 360 U.S. 109, 153–54 (1959) (Black, J., dissenting) (Plutarch); *Martin v. Strutgers,* 319 U.S. 141, 143 n.3 (1943) (Jefferson); *Joint Anti-Fascist Refugee Committee v. McGrath,* 341 U.S. 123, 146–49 (1951) (Black, J., concurring) (Macaulay); *Engel v. Vitale,* 370 U.S. 421, 433 n.18 (1962) (PILGRIM'S PROGRESS); and *In re Summers,* 325 U.S. 561, 575 n.1 (1945) (Bible).

51. *U.S. v. Louisiana,* 394 U.S. 11, 79 n.4 (1969) (Black, J., dissenting).

52. C. WILLIAMS, HUGO L. BLACK: A STUDY IN THE JUDICIAL PROCESS 83 (1950).

53. R. NEWMAN, HUGO BLACK 274 (1994).

54. *Id.* at 275.

55. Letter to author from Daniel Meador, November 13, 1996.

56. J. Frank, *Hugo L. Black, in* THE JUSTICES OF THE U.S. SUPREME COURT, L. Friedman and F. Israel eds. 1175–76 (1975).

57. E-mail responses to author April and May 1999 from eleven former Black law clerks.

58. D. MEADOR, MR. JUSTICE BLACK AND HIS BOOKS 17 (1974).

59. Douglas Interviews at 137.

60. *Id.* at 137–38.

61. W. DOUGLAS, THE COURT YEARS 20 (1980).

62. *Arizona v. California,* 373 U.S. 546, 628 (1963) (Douglas, J., dissenting).

63. H. BLACK & E. BLACK, MR. JUSTICE AND MRS. BLACK 156 (1986).

64. Douglas Interviews at 63.

65. *Id.* at 76.

66. Quoted in R. NEWMAN, HUGO BLACK 519 (1994).

67. H. Black, *Mr. Justice Frankfurter,* 78 HARV. L. REV. 1521 (1965).

68. R. NEWMAN, HUGO BLACK 546 (1994).

69. *Id.* at 549.

70. *Id.* at 485.

71. Douglas Interviews at 212.

72. April 4, 1994, Interview, Ed Cray Papers, UCLA Special Collections, Box 54.

73. J. Lash ed., FROM THE DIARIES OF FELIX FRANKFURTER 174 (1974).

74. *Id.* at 209.
75. *Id.* at 226–27.
76. Quoted in H. BALL, HUGO BLACK 257 n.91 (1996).
77. M. Kelman, *The Forked Path of Dissent,* SUP. CT. REV. 227, 251–53 (1985).
78. Quoted in R. NEWMAN, HUGO BLACK 319 (1994).
79. M. Tushnet, *Members of the Warren Court in Judicial Biography: Themes in Warren Court Biographies,* 70 N.Y.U. L. REV. 748, 752 (1995); B. Schwartz, *Supreme Court Superstars: The Ten Greatest Justices,* 31 TULSA L.J. 93 (1995).
80. Quoted in R. NEWMAN, HUGO BLACK 570 (1994).
81. As described in R. NEWMAN, HUGO BLACK 595 (1994).
82. *Id.*
83. G. SCHUBERT, THE CONSTITUTIONAL POLITY 127 (1970).
84. R. NEWMAN, HUGO BLACK 594 (1994).
85. D. CURRIE, THE CONSTITUTION IN THE SUPREME COURT: THE SECOND CENTURY, 1888–1986 455–56 (1990); D. Currie, *The New Deal Court in the 1940s: Its Constitutional Legacy,* 1997 J. SUP. CT. HIST. 87, 94–95.
86. G. WHITE, THE AMERICAN JUDICIAL TRADITION 334 (1988 exp. ed.); G. White, *The Renaissance of Judicial Biography,* 23 REV. AM. HIST. 719 (1995).
87. 369 U.S. 186 (1962).
88. J. Magee, *Mr. Justice Black: Absolutist on the Court* (1980).
89. *Duncan v. Louisiana,* 391 U.S. 145, 162 (1968) (Black, J., concurring). Black went through his arguments for the full incorporation and also offered a rebuttal of Professor Fairman's 1949 law review article and its legislative history analysis.
90. See, for example, Black's majority opinion in *Gideon v. Wainwright,* 372 U.S. 335 (1963).
91. *Wolf v. Colorado,* 338 U.S. 25 (1949).
92. *Mapp v. Ohio,* 367 U.S. 643, 661 (1961) (Black, J., concurring).
93. *Id.* at 661–62.
94. Quoted in J. Frank, *The Shelf Life of Hugo L. Black,* 1997 WIS. L. REV. 1, 4 (1997).
95. J. Frank, *The Shelf Life of Hugo L. Black,* 1997 WIS. L. REV. 1 (1997).
96. An audio recording of the address is now available on the internet at Northwestern Law School's Oyez Project, at www.oyez.nwu.edu.
97. *Id.*
98. *Duncan v. Louisiana,* 391 U.S. 145, 162 (1968) (Black, concurring).

Chapter 5

1. A. BLAUSTIN & R. MERSKY, THE FIRST HUNDRED YEARS 145 (1978).
2. 381 U.S. 479 (1965).
3. 410 U.S. 113 (1973).
4. 316 U.S. 535 (1942).
5. *Doe v. Bolton,* 410 U.S. 179 (1973).
6. Douglas Interviews at 36–37.
7. *Id.* at 37.
8. See table A2.

9. See table A3.

10. See table A4.

11. *Id.*

12. See table A9.

13. See table A5.

14. *Id.*

15. See table A6.

16. 354 U.S. 476, 512–13, 514 (1957) (Douglas, dissenting).

17. *Superior Films, Inc. v. Department of Education,* 346 U.S. 587, 589 (1954) (Douglas, J., concurring).

18. 316 U.S. 535, 541 (1942).

19. 274 U.S. 200, 208 (1927).

20. Douglas Interviews at 160.

21. See, for example, *Boddie v. Connecticut,* 401 U.S. 371 (1971).

22. *Rochin v. California,* 342 U.S. 165, 179 (1952) (Douglas, concurring).

23. W. Douglas, *The Supreme Court and Its Case Load,* 45 CORNELL L.Q. 401 (1960).

24. Y. Rogat, *Mr. Justice Pangloss,* NEW YORK REVIEW OF BOOKS, October 22, 1964, at 5.

25. *Id.*

26. *Id.* at 6 n.1.

27. J. SIMON, INDEPENDENT JOURNEY (1980).

28. See table A1.

29. See table A2.

30. M. Urofsky, *Getting the Job Done, in* HE SHALL NOT PASS THIS WAY AGAIN, Wasby ed., 34 (1990).

31. *Id.*

32. Letter to author, October 21, 1998.

33. J. PALMER, THE VINSON COURT (1990).

34. L.A. Powe, *The First Amendment and the Protection of Rights, in* HE SHALL NOT PASS THIS WAY AGAIN, Wasby ed., 69, 133 (1990).

35. Douglas Interviews at 54.

36. Richard Benka, *Justice Douglas, in* REMEMBRANCE OF WILLIAM O. DOUGLAS BY HIS FRIENDS AND ASSOCIATES: IN CELEBRATION OF THE FIFTIETH ANNIVERSARY OF HIS APPOINTMENT AS ASSOCIATE JUSTICE OF THE SUPREME COURT OF THE UNITED STATES 12 (1989). When Fred Rodell interviewed him in 1965 for a book on the Supreme Court, Douglas told the story of writing both opinions and said that the majority opinion appeared under Justice Whittaker's name. Fred Rodell Papers, Haverford College.

37. S. Duke, *Douglas and the Criminal Law, in* HE SHALL NOT PASS THIS WAY AGAIN, Wasby ed. 133 (1990).

38. Quoted in D. Glancy, *Douglas's Right of Privacy, in* HE SHALL NOT PASS THIS WAY AGAIN, Wasby ed. 166 (1990).

39. Walter F. Murphy, Introduction to William O. Douglas Oral History, http://libweb.princeton.edu/libraries/firestone/rbsc/finding_aids/douglas/douglas-intro.html, at 4.

40. *PUC v. Pollak,* 343 U.S. 451, 469 (1952).

41. *Wilkerson v. McCarthy,* 336 U.S. 53, 68 (1949) (Douglas, J., concurring).

42. *Fishgold v. Sullivan Drydock and Repair Corp.,* 328 U.S. 275, 285 (1946).

43. *Murdock v. Pennsylvania,* 319 U.S. 105, 112 (1943).

44. *Barsky v. Board of Regents,* 347 U.S. 442, 473 (1954) (Douglas, J., dissenting).

45. *Youngstown Sheet & Tube Co. v. Sawyer,* 343 U.S. 579, 629 (1952) (Douglas, J., concurring).

46. *Robinson v. California,* 370 U.S. 660, 676 (1962) (Douglas, J., concurring).

47. *Terry v. Ohio,* 392 U.S. 1, 39 (1968) (Douglas, J., dissenting).

48. *Donnelly v. DeChristoforo,* 416 U.S. 637, 648–49 (1974) (Douglas, J., dissenting).

49. *Furman v. Georgia,* 408 U.S. 238, 253 (1972) (Douglas, J., concurring).

50. *Colten v. Kentucky,* 407 U.S. 104, 122 (1972) (Douglas, J., dissenting).

51. M. Urofsky, *William O. Douglas and His Law Clerks,* 3 W. LEGAL HIST. 1 (1990); W. Cohen & C. Constantinou eds., REMEMBRANCE OF WILLIAM O. DOUGLAS BY HIS FRIENDS AND ASSOCIATES (1989).

52. Douglas Interviews at 78–79.

53. *Id.* at 17.

54. *Id.* at 97.

55. *Id.* at 145.

56. See chapter 4.

57. Douglas Interviews at 58.

58. *Id.* at 51.

59. THE DOUGLAS LETTERS, M. Urofsky ed., 90 (1987).

60. Douglas Interviews at 174.

61. DOUGLAS LETTERS, M. Urofsky ed., 85 (1987).

62. Richard Chambers, *Remembrance, in* REMEMBRANCE OF WILLIAM O. DOUGLAS BY HIS FRIENDS AND ASSOCIATES 14 (1989).

63. DOUGLAS LETTERS, M. Urofsky ed., 240 (1987).

64. F. Rodell, *Goodbye To Law Reviews,* 22 VA. L. REV. 38 (1936).

65. Douglas to Rodell, June 7, 1946 (Fred Rodell Papers, Haverford College).

66. *Id.,* January 20, 1944.

67. *Id.,* October 25, 1943.

68. *Id.,* May 4, 1947.

69. *Id.,* November 5, 1945.

70. *Id.,* June 25, 1953.

71. *Id.,* May 14, 1947.

72. *Id.,* May 23, 1949.

73. *Id.*

74. *Id.,* May 14, 1949.

75. *Id.,* May 22, 1949 (emphasis in original).

76. F. RODELL, NINE MEN (1955).

77. V. COUNTRYMAN, DOUGLAS OF THE SUPREME COURT: A SELECTION OF HIS OPINIONS (1959); V. COUNTRYMAN, THE JUDICIAL RECORD OF WILLIAM O. DOUGLAS (1974); V. COUNTRYMAN, THE DOUGLAS OPINIONS (1977); V. Countryman, *The Constitution and Job Discrimination,* 39 WASH. L. REV. 74 (1964).

78. W. Cohen, *Justice Douglas and the* Rosenberg *Case: Setting the Record Straight,* 70 CORNELL L. REV. 211 (1985). In large part Cohen's article responded to Parrish, *Cold War Justice: The Supreme Court and the Rosenbergs,* 82 AM. HIST. REV. 805 (1977).

79. J. Frank, *The Supreme Court of the United States: 1949–50,* U. CHI. L. REV. 1, 46 (1950).

80. J. Frank & Vern Countryman, *William O. Douglas, in* THE JUSTICES OF THE U.S. SUPREME COURT, L. Friedman & F. Israel eds. 1220–46 (1975).

81. *Id.* at 1245.

82. The details of this paragraph come from Walter Murphy's letter to the author, dated June 8, 1996. More details on how the interviews were conducted can be found in Professor Murphy's introduction to the Douglas Interviews. See http://libweb.princeton.edu/libraries/firestone/rbsc/finding_aids/douglas/douglas-intro.html.

83. Douglas Interviews at 85.

84. *Id.* at 174–75.

85. W. DOUGLAS, THE COURT YEARS 8 (1980).

86. Douglas Interviews at 138.

87. *Id.* at 26–27.

88. *Id.* at 187.

89. *Id.*

90. *Id.* at 249–51.

91. *Id.*

92. *Id.*

93. *Id.*

94. Douglas to Rodell, May 5, 1949 (Fred Rodell Papers, Haverford College).

95. *Id.,* October 27, 1949.

96. Douglas Interviews at 369.

97. *Id.*

98. *Id.* at 74.

99. *Id.*

100. *Id.* at 138.

101. Douglas to Rodell, June 7, 1946 (Fred Rodell Papers, Haverford College).

102. L.A. Powe, *The First Amendment and the Protection of Rights, in* HE SHALL NOT PASS THIS WAY AGAIN 69, Wasby ed. (1990).

103. See M. McManamon, *Felix Frankfurter: The Architect of "Our Federalism,"* 27 GA. L. REV. 697 (1993).

104. Douglas, friends report, had long been a teller of tall stories about himself, so much so that his colleagues would sometimes kid him about it. As Chief Justice Burger explained the matter, "Bill had another form of 'expressive fun' in presenting with a straight face—what was likely a fantasizing of some early experience. Once, I think it was John Harlan who said to Bill, 'You've told that story so often, you're beginning to believe it.' Bill just grinned." W. Burger, *Remembrance, in* REMEMBRANCE OF WILLIAM O. DOUGLAS BY HIS FRIENDS AND ASSOCIATES 18 (1989).

105. J. Simon, *William O. Douglas, in* THE WARREN COURT: A RETROSPECTIVE, B. Schwartz ed. 211, 218–19 (1996).

106. B. WOLFMAN, J. SILVER, & M. SILVER, DISSENT WITHOUT OPINION: THE BEHAVIOR OF JUSTICE WILLIAM O. DOUGLAS IN FEDERAL TAX CASES (1975).

107. F. Rodell to W. Douglas, August 16, 1968, Fred Rodell Papers, Haverford College.

108. 384 U.S. 11 (1966).

109. 385 U.S. 589 (1967).

110. D. CURRIE, THE CONSTITUTION IN THE SUPREME COURT: THE SECOND CENTURY, 1888–1986 456 (1990).

111. Letter to author, September 27, 1996.

Chapter 6

1. *Brown v. Allen,* 344 U.S. 443, 540 (1953) (Jackson, J., concurring).

2. M. KAMMEN, A MACHINE THAT WOULD GO OF ITSELF 357–81 (1986).

BIBLIOGRAPHY

Alton, S. Loyal Lieutenant, Able Advocate: The Role of Robert H. Jackson in Franklin D. Roosevelt's Battle with the Supreme Court. 5 WM. & MARY BILL OF RTS. J. 527. 1997.

Amar, A. The Bill of Rights and the Fourteenth Amendment. 101 YALE L.J. 1193. 1992.

———. *The Constitution and Criminal Procedure*. 1997.

Ariens, M. A Thrice-Told Tale, or Felix the Cat. 107 HARV. L. REV. 620. 1994.

Aynes, R. Charles Fairman, Felix Frankfurter, and the Fourteenth Amendment. 70 CHI.-KENT L. REV. 1995.

Ball, H. *Hugo L. Black: Cold Steel Warrior*. 1996.

———. *The Vision and the Dream of Justice: Hugo L. Black*. 1975.

Ball, H., & P. Cooper. *Of Power and Right: Hugo Black, William O. Douglas, and America's Constitutional Revolution*. 1992.

Barber, S. *The Constitution of Judicial Power*. 1993.

Barnum, D. *The Supreme Court and American Democracy*. 1993.

Benka, R. Justice Douglas. In *Remembrance of William O. Douglas by His Friends and Associates*. 1989.

Bickel, A. *The Least Dangerous Branch*. 1962.

Bickel, A., & H. Wellington. Legislative Purpose and the Judicial Process: The *Lincoln Mills* Case. 71 HARV. L. REV. 1. 1957.

Black, H., and E. Black. *Mr. Justice and Mrs. Black: The Memoirs of Hugo L. Black and Elizabeth Black*. 1986.

Black, H. The Bill of Rights. 35 N.Y.U. L. REV. 865. 1960.

———. Mr. Justice Frankfurter. 78 HARV. L. REV. 1521. 1965.

———. Reminiscences. 18 ALA. L. REV. 1965.

Black, H., Jr. *My Father: A Remembrance*. 1975.

Blaustein, A., & R. Mersky, eds. *The First Hundred Justices*. 1978.

Boudin, M. Members of the Warren Court in Judicial Biography: Commentary. 70 N.Y.U. L. REV. 772. 1995.

Burger, W. Remembrance. In *Remembrance of William O. Douglas by His Friends and Associates.* 1989.

Burt, R. *Two Jewish Justices.* 1988.

Burton, H. Harold Burton Papers. Library of Congress.

Canon, B., K. Greenfield, & J. Fleming. Justice Frankfurter and Justice Reed: Friendship and Lobbying on the Court. 78 JUDICATURE 224. 1995.

Chambers, R. Remembrance. In *Remembrance of William O. Douglas by His Friends and Associates.* 1989.

Cohen, W. Justice Douglas and the *Rosenberg* Case: Setting the Record Straight. 70 CORNELL L. REV. 211. 1985.

Cohen W., & C. Constantinou, eds. *Remembrance of William O. Douglas by His Friends and Associates.* 1989.

Cooper, P. *Battles on the Bench.* 1995.

Countryman, V. The Constitution and Job Discrimination. 39 WASH. L. REV. 74. 1964.

———. *Douglas of the Supreme Court: A Selection of His Opinions.* 1959.

———. *The Douglas Opinions.* 1977.

———. *The Judicial Record of William O. Douglas.* 1974.

Currie, D. *The Constitution in the Supreme Court: The Second Century, 1888–1986.* 1990.

———. The New Deal Court in the 1940s: Its Constitutional Legacy. 1997 J. SUP. CT. HIST. 87. 1997.

Davis, R. *Decisions and Images: The Supreme Court and the Press.* 1994.

Dean, G. Remarks. In Supreme Court Proceedings, In Memory of Robert Houghwout Jackson. In R. Jacobs, *Memorials of the Justices of the Supreme Court of the United States.* 1981.

Desmond, C. The Role of the Country Lawyer. In *Mr. Justice Jackson: Four Lectures in His Honor.* 1969.

Domnarski, W. *In the Opinion of the Court.* 1996.

Dorsen, N., ed. *The Evolving Constitution: Essays on the Bill of Rights and the U.S. Supreme Court.* 1989.

Douglas, W. The Bill of Rights Is Not Enough. 38 N.Y.U. L. REV. 207. 1963.

———. *The Court Years.* 1980.

———. *Go East, Young Man.* 1974.

———. The Supreme Court and Its Case Load. 45 CORNELL L.Q. 401. 1960.

———. William O. Douglas Papers. Library of Congress.

Duke, S. Douglas and the Criminal Law. In *He Shall Not Pass This Way Again,* S. Wasby, ed. 1990.

Dunne, G. *Hugo Black and the Judicial Revolution.* 1977.

Elman, P. The Solicitor General's Office: Justice Frankfurter and Civil Rights Litigation. 100 HARV. L. REV. 817. 1987.

———, ed. *Of Law and Men.* 1956.

Epstein, L., H. Spaeth, T. Walker, & J. Segal. *The Supreme Court Compendium.* 1994.

Fine, S. *Frank Murphy: The Washington Years.* 1980.

Frank, J. Hugo L. Black. In *The Justices of the U.S. Supreme Court,* L. Friedman and F. Israel, eds., 1175. 1975.

———. *Mr. Justice Black: The Man and His Opinions.* 1949.

———. The Shelf Life of Hugo Black. 1997 Wis. L. Rev. 1. 1997.

———. The Supreme Court of the United States: 1949–50. U. Chi. L. Rev. 1. 1950.

Frank, J., & V. Countryman. William O. Douglas. In *The Justices of the U.S. Supreme Court,* L. Friedman & F. Israel, eds., 1220. 1975.

Frankfurter, F. *The Commerce Clause.* 1937.

———. The Impact of Charles Evans Hughes. N.Y. Times, Nov. 18, 1951, at 1. Book review.

———. Felix Frankfurter Papers. Library of Congress.

———. Felix Frankfurter Papers. Harvard Law School Library.

———. Robert Jackson. 68 Harv. L. Rev. 937. 1955.

Frankfurter, F., & J. Landis. *The Business of the Supreme Court.* 1927.

Freedman, M., ed. *Roosevelt and Frankfurter: Their Correspondence, 1928–1945.* 1967.

Freund, P. Felix Frankfurter. In *Dictionary of American Biography, Supplement 7,* 260. 1981.

———. Paul Freund Papers. Harvard Law School Library.

Friedman, R. A Reaffirmation of the Authenticity of the Roberts Memorandum, or Felix the Nonforger. 107 Harv. L. Rev. 620. 1994.

Friendly, H. The Bill of Rights as a Code of Criminal Procedure. 53 Cal. L. Rev. 929. 1965.

Gardner, W. Goverment Attorney. 55 Colum. L. Rev. 438. 1955.

Gerhart, E. *America's Advocate.* 1958.

———. *Lawyer's Judge.* 1961.

Glancy, D. Douglas's Right of Privacy. In *He Shall Not Pass This Way Again,* Wasby, ed. 1990.

Goldstein, J. *The Intelligible Constitution: The Supreme Court's Obligation to Maintain the Constitution as Something We The People Can Understand.* 1992.

Gressman, E. Psycho-Enigmatizing Felix Frankfurter. 80 Mich. L. Rev. 731. 1982.

Hart, H. The Supreme Court, 1958 Term, Foreword: The Time Chart of the Justices. 73 Harv. L. Rev. 84. 1959.

Hindman, E. *Rights v. Responsibilities: The Supreme Court and the Media.* 1997.

Hirsch, E. *The Enigma of Felix Frankfurter.* 1981.

Hockett, J. *New Deal Justice: The Constitutional Jurisprudence of Hugo L. Black, Felix Frankfurter, and Robert H. Jackson.* 1996.

Horwitz, M. *The Warren Court and the Pursuit of Justice.* 1998.

Howard, J. *The Shifting Wind: The Supreme Court and Civil Rights from Deconstruction to Brown.* 1999.

Howe, M., ed. *Holmes-Laski Letters.* 1953.

Hutchinson, D. The Black-Jackson Feud. 1988 Sup. Ct. Rev. 203. 1988.

———. *The Man Who Once Was Whizzer White: A Portrait of Justice Byron R. White.* 1998.

———. Mr. Justice Frankfurter and the Business of the Supreme Court, 1949–1961. 1980 Sup. Ct. Rev. 143. 1980.

———. Unanimity and Desegregation: Decisionmaking in the Supreme Court, 1948–58, 68 Geo. L.J. 1. 1979.

Ickes, H. *The Secret Diary of Harold L. Ickes.* Vols. 2 and 3. 1954.

Irons, P. *The New Deal Lawyers.* 1982.

Jackson, R. The County-Seat Lawyer. 36 A.B.A. J. 497. 1950.

———. *Dispassionate Justice: A Synthesis of the Judicial Opinions of Robert H. Jackson,* G. Schubert, ed. 1969.

———. Falstaff's Descendants in Pennsylvania Courts. 101 U. Pa. L. Rev. 313. 1952.

———. *Full Faith and Credit, The Lawyer's Clause of the Constitution.* 1945.

———. Robert Jackson Oral History. Columbia University Oral History Project.

———. Robert Jackson Papers. Library of Congress.

———. *The Struggle for Judicial Supremacy.* 1941.

———. *The Supreme Court in the American System of Government.* 1955.

———. *That Man: An Insider's Portrait of Franklin F. Roosevelt,* J.Q. Barrett, ed. 2003.

———. Training the Trial Lawyer: A Neglected Area of Legal Education. 3 Stan. L. Rev. 48. 1950.

Jacobs, R. *Memorials of the Justices of the Supreme Court of the United States.* 1981.

Jaffe, L. The Judicial Universe of Mr. Justice Frankfurter. 62 Harv. L. Rev. 357. 1949.

———. The Supreme Court Today. 174 Atlantic Monthly 76. December 1944.

Kahn, R. *The Supreme Court and Constitutional Theory, 1953–93.* 1994.

Kalman, L. *Abe Fortas: A Biography.* 1990.

———. *The Strange Career of Legal Liberalism.* 1996.

Kammen, M. *A Machine That Would Go of Itself.* 1986.

Kaufman, A. The Justice and His Law Clerks. In Mendelson, ed., *Frankfurter: The Judge* 223. 1964.

Kelman, M. The Forked Path of Dissent. 1985 Sup. Ct. Rev. 227.

Klarman, M. Book Review. 12 L. & Hist. Rev. 399. 1994.

———. An Interpretive History of Modern Equal Protection. 90 Mich. L. Rev. 213. 1991.

Kurland, P. Earl Warren, the "Warren Court," and the Warren Myth. 67 Mich. L. Rev. 1968.

———. Judicial Biography: History, Myth, Literature, Fiction, Potpourri. 70 N.Y.U. L. Rev. 489. 1995.

———. Robert H. Jackson. In 4 L. Friedman & F. Israel, *The Justices of the United States Supreme Court* 2541. 1969.

———. Toward a Political Supreme Court. 37 U. Chi. L. Rev. 19. 1969.

———, ed. *Mr. Justice Frankfurter and the Constitution.* 1971.

———. *Of Life and Law and Other Things That Matter.* 1965.

Landes, W., L. Lessig, & M. Solimine. Judicial Influence: A Citation Analysis of Federal Court of Appeals Judges. 27 J. Legal Stud. 271. 1998.

Lash, J., ed. *From the Diaries of Felix Frankfurter.* 1974.

Lee, D. Senator Black's Investigation of the Airmail, 1933–34. 53 Historian 423. 1991.

Lerner, M. The Supreme Court Today. *Holiday.* Vol. 7, 73. 1950.

Leuchtenburg, W. *The Supreme Court Reborn: The Constitutional Revolution in the Age of Roosevelt.* 1995.

Lewis, A. *Gideon's Trumpet.* 1964.

———. The Supreme Court and Its Critics. 45 MINN. L. REV. 305. 1961.

Lewis, F. *The Context of Judicial Activism: The Endurance of the Warren Court Legacy in a Conservative Age.* 1999.

London, E., ed. *The World of Law.* Vol. II, *The Law as Literature.* 1960.

Magee, J. *Mr. Justice Black: Absolutist on the Court.* 1980.

Mason, A. *Harlan Fiske Stone: Pillar of the Law.* 1956.

McManamon, M. Felix Frankfurter: The Architect of "Our Federalism." 27 GA. L. REV. 697. 1993.

Meador, D. *Mr. Justice Black and His Books.* 1974.

Mendelson, W. *Justices Black and Frankfurter: Conflict in the Court.* 1961.

———. Mr. Justice Frankfurter and the Process of Judicial Review. 103 U. PA. L. REV. 295. 1954.

———, ed. *Frankfurter: A Tribute.* 1964.

———. *Frankfurter: The Judge.* 1964.

Menel, R., & C. Compston, eds. *Holmes and Frankfurter: Their Correspondence, 1912–1934.* 1996.

Mr. Justice Jackson: Four Lectures in His Honor. 1969.

Murphy, B. *The Brandeis/Frankfurter Connection.* 1982.

———. *Fortas: The Rise and Ruin of a Supreme Court Justice.* 1988.

———. *Wild Bill.* 2003.

NEW YORK TIMES. Editorial. February 18, 1982.

NEW YORK TIMES BOOK REVIEW. August 31, 1975.

Newman, R. *Hugo Black: A Biography.* 1994.

O'Brien, D. *Storm Center: The Supreme Court in American Politics.* 4th ed. 1996.

O'Brien, J. Supreme Court Proceedings in Memory of Robert Houghwout Jackson. In R. Jacobs, ed., *Memorials of the Justices of the Supreme Court of the United States.* 1981.

Palmer, J. *The Vinson Court.* 1990.

Parrish, M. Cold War Justice: The Supreme Court and the Rosenbergs. 82 AM. HIST. REV. 805. 1977.

Phillips, H., ed. *Felix Frankfurter Reminisces.* 1960.

Posner, R. Judicial Biography. 70 N.Y.U. L. REV. 502. 1995.

Powe, L.A. The First Amendment and the Protection of Rights. In *He Shall Not Pass This Way Again* 69, S. Wasby, ed. 1990.

———. *The Warren Court and American Politics.* 2000.

Pritchard, E., & A. MacLeish, eds. *Felix Frankfurter: Law and Politics.* 1939.

Pritchett, H. *Civil Liberties and the Vinson Court.* 1954.

———. *The Roosevelt Court.* 1948.

Proceedings of the Supreme Court in Memory of Honorable Felix Frankfurter. 86 S.Ct. 17. 1965.

Pusey, M. The Roosevelt Supreme Court. 58 AMERICAN MERCURY 596. May 1944.

Rauh, J. Felix Frankfurter. 173, NEW REPUBLIC 346 October 11, 1975.

———. Felix Frankfurter: Civil Libertarian. HARV. C.R.—C.L. L. REV. 496. 1976.

Ray, L. K. Judicial Personality: Rhetoric and Emotion in Supreme Court Opinions. 59 WASH. & LEE L. REV. 193. 2002.

Reed, S. Oral History Project, University of Kentucky.

Rogat, Y. Mr. Justice Pangloss. NEW YORK REVIEW OF BOOKS, October 22, at 5. 1964.

Rodell, F. Fred Rodell Papers. Haverford College.

———. Goodbye to Law Reviews. 22 VA. L. REV. 38. 1936.

———. Justice Hugo Black. AMERICAN MERCURY, 135. August 1944.

———. *Nine Men.* 1955.

Rudko, F. *Truman's Court: A Study in Judicial Restraint.* 1988.

Sacks, A. Felix Frankfurter. In L. Friedman & F. Israel, eds., *The Justices of the United States Supreme Court* 1216. 1980.

Schlesinger, A. The Supreme Court: 1947. 35 FORTUNE 73. January 1947.

Schubert, G. *The Constitutional Polity.* 1970.

Schwartz, B. Chief Justice Rehnquist, Justice Jackson, and the *Brown* Case. 1988 SUP. CT. REV. 245. 1988.

———. *How the Supreme Court Decides Cases.* 1996.

———. Hugo L. Black. In Schwartz, B., ed., *The Warren Court: A Retrospective* 202. 1996.

———. *Super Chief: Earl Warren and His Supreme Court.* 1979.

———. Supreme Court Superstars: The Ten Greatest Justices. 31 TULSA L.J. 93. 1995.

Segal, J., & H. Spaeth. *The Supreme Court and the Attitudinal Model.* 1993.

Shakespeare, W. *Julius Caesar.* 1599.

Shamir, R. *Managing Legal Uncertainty: Elite Lawyers in the New Deal.* 1995.

Simon, J. *The Antagonists: Hugo Black, Felix Frankfurter, and Civil Liberties in Modern America.* 1989.

———. *Independent Journey.* 1980.

Slotnick, E. *Television News and the Supreme Court.* 1998.

Spaeth, H. *Studies in U.S. Supreme Court Behavior.* 1990.

Stark, K. The Unfulfilled Tax Legacy of Robert H. Jackson. 54 TAX L. REV. 171. 2000.

Steel, R. *Walter Lippmann and the American Century.* 1980.

Stewart, P. Jackson on Federal-State Relationships. In *Mr. Justice Jackson: Four Lectures in His Honor* 63. 1969.

Stone, A. *The Enigma of Felix Frankfurter.* Book review. 95 HARV. L. REV. 346. 1981.

Sunstein, C. *One Case at a Time: Judicial Minimalism on the Supreme Court.* 1999.

TIME.Vol. 35, 11. Jan. 15, 1940.

Tushnet, M. Members of the Warren Court in Judicial Biography: Themes in Warren Court Biographies. 70 N.Y.U. L. REV. 748. 1995.

Tushnet, M., & T. Lynch. The Project of the Harvard *Forewords.* 11 CONST. COM. 463. 1994–95.

Urofsky, M. The Brandeis-Frankfurter Conversations. 1985 SUP. CT. REV.

———. *Division and Discord: The Supreme Court under Stone and Vinson, 1941–53.* 1997.

———. *The Douglas Letters.* 1987.

———. *Felix Frankfurter: Judicial Restraint and Individual Liberties.* 1991.

———. Getting the Job Done. In *He Shall Not Pass This Way Again* 34, S. Wasby, ed. 1990.

———. William O. Douglas and His Law Clerks. 3 W. LEGAL HIST. 1. 1990.

————. William O. Douglas as a Common Law Judge. 41 DUKE L.J. 133. 1991.

Urofsky, M., & D. Levy, eds. *Letters of Louis D. Brandeis.* 5 volumes. 1971.

Wechsler, H. Toward Neutral Principles of Constitutional Law. 73 HARV. L. REV. 1. 1959.

White, G. *The American Judicial Tradition.* Exp. ed. 1988.

————. Biographies of Titans. 70 N.Y.U. L. REV. 576. 1995.

————. *Earl Warren: A Public Life.* 1982.

————. Holmes as Correspondent. 43 VAND. L. REV. 1707. 1990.

————. The Renaissance of Judicial Biography. Book review. 23 REV. AM. HIST. 716. 1995.

Williams, C. *Hugo L. Black: A Study in the Judicial Process.* 1950.

Wolfman, B., J. Silver, & M. Silver. *Dissent Without Opinion: The Behavior of Justice William O. Douglas in Federal Tax Cases.* 1975.

INDEX